AND AWAY ...

AND AWAY ...

BOB MORTIMER

GALLERY BOOKS UK

First published in Great Britain by Gallery Books,
an imprint of Simon & Schuster UK Ltd, 2021
Copyright © Bob Mortimer, 2021

1 3 5 7 9 10 8 6 4 2

Simon & Schuster UK Ltd
1st Floor
222 Gray's Inn Road
London WC1X 8HB

www.simonandschuster.co.uk
www.simonandschuster.com.au
www.simonandschuster.co.in

Simon & Schuster Australia, Sydney
Simon & Schuster India, New Delhi

A CIP catalogue record for this book is available from the British Library

Hardback ISBN: 978-1-3985-0529-2
Trade Paperback ISBN: 978-1-3985-0802-6
eBook ISBN: 978-1-3985-0530-8

Typeset in Bembo by M Rules
Printed in the UK by CPI Group (UK) Ltd, Croydon, CR0 4YY

For Eunice Mary Mortimer
1922–2004

CONTENTS

PART TWO

PART THREE

PART FOUR

PART FIVE

AND AWAY ...

PREFACE

Welcome to my book. It contains all the stories from my life that came to mind during its writing. Some of these memories are clearer than others. Where there are gaps in my remembering I have tried to fill them in as best as I can using my knowledge of myself and the people involved. My guess is that around 90 per cent of the content is true and reliable. In a couple of the chapters I have left it to the reader to decide which stories are the truth and which are lies. The book contains very little opinion or advice, which I hope you will agree is a good thing. There is one piece of advice, though, that I feel is worth stating before you commence:

Always enter your shoes before wearing them.

PART ONE

In which I tell the tale of my early life and adventures, framed within the intriguing story of a brush with mortality and laziness.

1

OCTOBER 2015

In every dream home a heartache
And every step I take
Takes me further from heaven

Roxy Music, 1971

I am fifty-six years old. My life is trundling along like a podgy golden retreiver being dragged along the pavement by an indifferent owner. I wake up in my bed to the distant sound of a building site and the *click click drip* of the central heating system.

I sleep on a thick memory-foam mattress so there is always a certain stickiness to my risings. The undersheet clings to my back as I sit up, then floats back to its base as if giving out a sigh of relief. My knees click along with the radiators as I make my way to the bathroom.

I look in the mirror and see before me a face like a puddle of spaghetti hoops; bloated, creased and tired. I'm always tired.

No amount of sleep can shift the massive ball of pure weariness that has lodged itself to the rear of my eyes.

I get very breathless at any exertion. I put it down to my age and the years of smoking. I have tried to quit in the past but have never been able to manage more than five hours without a cigarette. Maybe next year.

I am about to embark on a month-long tour of the UK with my comedy partner Jim Moir, whom you may know as Mr Vic Reeves. It's an anniversary tour marking thirty years since we first stepped on stage together. There will be energetic, sometimes aquatic, singing, athletic and handsome dancing, and tight little bundles of concentrated slapstick. I need to get myself into some sort of recognisable shape, but the tour starts in three weeks.

I decide to do some staircase exercise nonsense. You know – up and down at a discernible pace and stepping on and off the bottom step at various approximate speeds. But before that I whimbrel into the kitchen and cook myself a fullish English breakfast. Beans near, and not on, toast, a fried egg, three rashers of back bacon, fried mushrooms and tomatoes. I wash it all down with a mug of tea containing five sugars and then suck hard on a wonderful post-baked-bean cigarette. That's better.

Then to the stairs. I hate exercise. I curse the inventor of exercise and all his disciples. I turn my back towards shops that sell exercise equipment. I send moonlight shivers to each and every jogger that has forced me to walk through their sweaty pavement haze. Exercise is my nemesis. I would rather clean a 747 jumbo jet using a mouse's eyepatch than exercise.

I run up the two flights and back down again. I repeat times ten. I get clammy and my mind turns towards the dreary. I can't do it. It's just too unpleasant a way to spend even two minutes of your life. Out of breath, I slump onto my sofa with another cup of tea (and another five sugars) and draw heavily on my second cigarette of the day.

That's when I feel it: a sharp but not really significant pain just behind the lower sweep of my left ribcage. It's gone almost as soon as it came. No big deal. I finish my cigarette, get up from the sofa – and there it is again.

My immediate thought is that it is what my mum would have called 'a cold on your chest'.

'Have a mug of Bovril, sit with your coat on and sweat it out,' she would say (with a fag in her mouth). But with my tour coming up, I think it best to phone the GP and get an appointment. I book in to see him later that day.

My doctor is a lovely, caring man called Bob Bowes. I always enjoy going to see him, not least because in the corner of his consultation room he has the lowest sink I have ever seen. I reckon it stands about two and a half feet off the ground. I've asked him if it is specifically for children. He says not. I've asked him if the person who fitted it was particularly small and fixed its height according to his requirements. He says not. I've asked him if its height gives it a specific medical use or advantage. He says not. I've asked him if it is made of lead and sinking into the ground. He says not. I've asked him if he's ever considered employing a sink raiser to sort it. He says not. I sense he is never going to tell me. I suppose it's his sink, and if he's happy with it then that's all I really need to know. I've learned to mind my own business when it comes to preferred sink heights.

I tell him about the little pain behind my rib and he listens to my chest with his stethoscope. He doesn't like whatever it is he's hearing and says that I need my heart checked. It's a bit of a shock, but the pain is so minimal that I'm not really worried. However, with the tour imminent, he arranges for me to see a cardiologist a couple of days later.

The following night I take the train up to London with my partner Lisa to see the band Squeeze at the Royal Albert Hall. We meet up with Matt Berry and my long-time TV-producer guru, Lisa Clark. I sit next to Matt for the show. I have always adored Squeeze and will always adore Matt. He's funny, polite, unassuming, a musical and comedic frontrunner. When he laughs, his face beams with pure joy. He's got a great big beard and a great big heart.

A lovely night is had by all. Matt loves a bit of gossip and is quite ruthless in his assessments of other players in the comedy world. (Matt, the wonderful Reece Shearsmith and I occasionally meet up for drinks in London. They are strictly 'gossip only' evenings, our favourite topic always being which of our contemporaries are currently sitting around the dining table at 'The Lucky Club'.)

The next day I visit the cardiologist, where electrical wires are attached to my chest while I run at my fullest, most athletic pelt on a running machine for eight long minutes. This procedure is known as the treadmill stress test. Its purpose is to assess how well your circulatory system and heart are performing when you put it under some pressure.

The test is easy. The worst part is the removal of the wires that are attached using sticky little pads. I have a middling to gross amount of chest hair and suffer terribly from anticipatory pain fret. I don't think all nurses enjoy this torturing, but I suspect a few do.

The results of my test are printed out and are laid on the cardiologist's table when I enter his office (no sink). He explains to me that the test is very much a screening exercise and not a diagnostic tool but that nevertheless it does indicate a possible narrowing of the arteries surrounding my heart. Probable worst-case scenario is that I might have to have a few stents inserted into the more seriously blocked pipes to open them up and allow the blood to flow freely. I'm told it's an outpatient procedure and you can go back to work after a couple of days.

'Will I still be able to go on tour with Jim?' I ask.

'Yes, absolutely.' He explains that the next step is for me to have an angiogram at the local hospital. This involves having a catheter inserted into an artery in my wrist or groin. (I choose the wrist.) A special dye will be passed through the catheter and X-ray images taken of my arteries as the dye explores all the avenues and alleyways surrounding my heart. It's all about discovering how strong the blood flow is and whether there is any narrowing. If there are any dangerous blockages then stents will be inserted during the angiogram. I arrange to have the procedure in a couple of days' time.

I'm not worried. After all, my good friend Paul Whitehouse has had a couple of stents inserted and he's still as magnificent as he ever was.

I quite like hospitals. They have such a purposeful vibe. In the past I've had jobs in the civil service and local government and hated the general malaise that permeated those institutions, due, I suspect, to the lack of a real sense of purpose or direction. The ever-present nagging feeling that you are achieving absolutely nothing. Whereas a hospital is a full-on, in-your-face, achievement factory.

The room where the angiogram is administered is like the cockpit of a 1980s movie spaceship. A lot of serious-looking kit and a lot of silent medical personnel attending to their roles with precision and quiet calm. For the first time, I am scared.

I can feel the catheter as it travels up my arm and into my chest. The dye it releases feels cold and alien as it flushes through my arteries. The sharp, cold squirreling around my chest is taking much longer than I expected. I can sense that the surgeon is not happy with what he is seeing, and I feel the mood change in the room. The procedure is halted for a while and out of the corner of my eye I can see the surgeon in the adjacent control room. I think he is speaking to someone on the phone. I sense the beginnings of dread and panic in my ample stomach.

He returns and tells me he is going to try a procedure to help the catheter penetrate my pipes. I know not what he did or what tools were employed, but I am suddenly hit with a massive bolt of electricity in my chest. It raises me up off the slab. Then it hits me again. I have never experienced such pain in my life. It feels like a tiny hippo has snuck into my heart and is having the largest yawn it can muster while trying to escape using an ice pick.

I'm silently begging for him to stop, but he delivers three or four more hippo bolts. And then it is over. It would seem that the procedure has either been completed or abandoned. I'm wheeled out and my gurney is placed under a large set of open-tread stairs. A wandering inpatient recognises me and comes over to say hello.

He thinks that I will be fine because I have been on the telly.

Then the surgeon arrives in my little understairs den and I can immediately tell from his face that it is not good news. He sombrely explains that the blockages in my arteries are too advanced and in such awkward places that they cannot be stented. I will have to undergo open-heart surgery and have a number of my arteries bypassed. He will try to find a bed for me as soon as possible.

'Will I have to cancel my tour?'

'Yes, definitely.'

Strange that my work should be the first thing on my mind. That will change very soon indeed.

I am wheeled back to my reception room where my wife has been waiting. I give her the thumbs down motion and, like a watery fig, tears form in my eyes. I telephone Jim from my gurney and explain what's happened and that the tour will have to be cancelled. Jim seems a bit shell-shocked, not because of the aborted tour but that, out of the blue, I should be so ill. I apologise profusely.

I have subsequently, of course, found out that heart surgery is not that big a deal at all. Though complicated and requiring incredible skill, the procedure is bordering on the routine these days. Perhaps it's because of my age that the fear is so intense. When I was young, open-heart surgery was in its infancy and was viewed more as life-*extending* than life-saving. To my generation, the mention of open-heart surgery has the whiff of death about it.

I arrive home and my body feels different. I am suddenly aware of every single beat of my heart, every little muscle movement in my chest and every little jump and rumble from my stomach. I can feel and hear my heartbeat in my ears, in my brain and in my imagination.

The consultant had explained that some of my arteries were as much as 95–98 per cent blocked. How long would it take for that last 2 per cent to close up? Should I remain completely still? Will I be spending the rest of my life stood staring out of my window watching parcels being delivered to neighbours? Will I be making a special occasion out of bin day, when the street action is at its most vibrant? What should my heart rate be? How do I stop my heart from racing with fear of what lies ahead? Am I going to die?

I phone the consultant and tell him I can't cope. He's heard it all before and gives me a prescription for Valium to see me through to the operation. He doesn't accuse me of being as pathetic as an abandoned dishcloth, but I can kind of tell that's what he's thinking. I am strangely reassured.

After the angiogram, my world became tiny. All it contained was my home, my partner Lisa and thoughts of my two sons, Harry and Tom.

I thought nothing about work or the world outside my four walls. I went into the kitchen to make a cup of tea. My mind started to focus on all the little trinkets and frou-frou that usually went unnoticed and unthanked in my kitchen. My favourite mug; my favourite egg cup; the teaspoon with the long bent handle; the tea towel we bought on holiday; the mat that my cats slept on; the picture of me and Lisa in Paris when we first met. All of them made me feel incredibly sad, and I burst into tears.

I hadn't felt this vulnerable for a long, long time. Not since 1970, when I was eleven years old.

2

1959–1970

Shyness is nice and shyness can stop you
From doing all the things in life you'd like to

The Smiths, 1987

I was born on my mum's bed in a 1950s semi-detached house near the centre of Middlesbrough in the North East of England. It was a truly magical place to grow up. There was a playing field over the fence that you were free to use as your own, and another one just across the road where we would make shitty shotty weapons by attaching some dog dirt to the end of a bendy stick. Just beyond this field was a small drainage beck surrounded by bushes and overgrowth, ideal for making dens or for tying a rope to a tree to make a tarzy to swing over the dirty water. My only problem was that I didn't really have anyone to share this wonderland with.

I was the youngest of four brothers: Jonathan, nine years older than me; Richard, seven years; followed by Sam, three years;

and me. I was the irritating runt, constantly trying and failing to get the attention of my brothers. Very early on I realised that I was fighting a losing battle and took the easier route of keeping out of people's way and observing home life rather than participating in it.

My brothers were funny, gregarious and outgoing. I simply didn't believe that I could compete with them or successfully tag along with their antics. Why would they want me to? I had little to add or contribute. It became less painful not to try.

I have very few memories of my early years, mainly just dull little moments from an ordinary life.

I remember being around four or five years old, on a family day out in Saltburn-by-the-Sea. I somehow found myself separated from the others and started wandering through some sort of municipal park with freshly cut grass and numerous paths from which to choose. The further I walked the more panic set in. I began to gently sob as I walked aimlessly, trying to catch sight of my family.

A man approached me and asked if I was OK. I must have told him I'd lost my mum and dad. He lifted me on his shoulders and we strolled around until I spotted my family. Boy was I pleased to see them. They were elated to have found me, too, and I think it was the first time I had really felt important.

I remember in my infant school, aged around seven, standing in the playground surrounded by other children. I had pulled down my trousers and was displaying my underpants to a little crowd that had gathered around me. I think the underpants had some cartoon motif on them like Deputy Dawg or Dick Dastardly. I was working hard to be a player, a character,

13

someone to take a shine to. A teacher dispersed the kids and I was left stood with my trousers around my ankles like some sort of junior pervert.

A couple of days later a letter arrived at my home informing my parents of what had occurred. I was marched upstairs to my bedroom and told to lay on my bed as my father administered several blows to my bony arse with his leather belt. So much for trying to place myself at the centre of attention. Better to be on the outside looking in, I decided.

One strange day when I was about six or seven my mother took me to the home of a boy who lived about 100 yards further along the road. I now realise that the intention of this visit was to 'find a friend for Robert'. I was ushered into a room with this potential saviour, where I think he was playing with some Meccano or such like.

He looked up at me from the carpet. His head was huge. He was literally one-third head. I remember thinking, *You need to boot this head and destroy it or it will devour you and use your bones as modelling supports.*

And then he spoke.

'Mum says I have to play with you but I don't want to. You can play with that Lego if you want.'

I sat down by a cardboard box full of bits of Lego and half-finished Meccano models and started to add bits to one of the incomplete models. All was quiet and I thought that maybe I could get through this encounter in one piece. Then suddenly The Head ran towards me, grabbed the model from my hands and ran his massive cranium out of the room in tears, complaining to his mum that I had ruined his toy. We left shortly after,

The Head staring at me from the doorstep as we left. I don't remember seeing him again but would always shiver a little when I had to walk past The Head's lair on my way into town.

One time I had a terrible pain in my stomach and so Mum took me to the doctor. He was called Dr Longbottom and he was as blind as a bat. I don't think he could actually make out the shape of a human, but he could always sense their presence. I was told to take my trousers off and lie on his examination table. He squeezed my stomach a bit and asked me where it hurt. Then he put on some medical gloves and felt around my bottom crack until he located the hole. Once there, he inserted his middle finger right up and I let out a fart that can only be described as lengthy and important.

'There she blows,' stated Dr Longbottom. 'Better an empty house than an unruly tenant.' My mum laughed out loud, which is something I rarely remember her doing. I still use the doctor's phrase to this day if the circumstances are suitably riotous. Funny thing to recall, but there you go.

Halfway up the stairs in our house was a window with a ledge you could sit on. From this vantage point I could see right up the road into the distance. There was a playing field, and then after about 200 yards the semi-detached houses commenced again on either side of the road. There was a small gap in the fence to the field on the right that we kids used to access the field, and one day, while sitting on the window ledge on the half landing, I saw a young lad about my age crouch down to get through the gap, just as two older lads arrived and pushed him out of the way. The little lad immediately adopted a classic Queensbury rules stance and faced up to the bigger boys and started peppering them with stylish but very weak jabs and punches. The big lads seemed unsure what to do. *Go on, little un,* I was thinking. *Knock them out!* Suddenly one of the older guys lunged at him, grabbed him round the waist and pile-drived him onto the concrete pavement headfirst. The little lad lay perfectly still on the floor. One of the big 'uns gave him a kick and then they ran off into the field. *Please get up, please get up,* I chanted to myself, but he didn't. I put my school shoes on and ran out of the house and up the road to the gap in the fence. The young lad was nowhere to be seen. All that remained of the incident was a few drops of bright-red blood on the floor. I think, in my juvenile mind, I presumed he was dead. The sight of him being smashed into the cold hard pavement stayed present in my mind for many months. Eventually I mentioned the incident to one of my older brothers and they reassured me that the young boy would be OK.

My most vivid memory of these early childhood days, how-ever, is a sunny day in January 1967, when I returned home mid-afternoon to the sight of a police car parked outside my house. As I entered the front door I was quickly ushered out by a neighbour and told to go and play football in the field over the back garden fence. My brother Sam was already there kicking a ball against a brick wall.

Something was wrong. Neighbours were in and out of the house, and we got an occasional glimpse of a policeman through the kitchen window. I saw my mum just outside the back door and she seemed to be crying.

Eventually we were called into the house for our tea. The atmosphere was strange but everything seemed relatively normal. Later, when my mum was drying me with a towel after my bath, I asked where Dad was and when he would be coming home.

'Daddy was in a car crash and he won't be coming home. He's in heaven now but he will always be looking after us,' she replied.

'So will I ever see him again?'

Mum shook her head and I could see tears forming in her eyes. I had never seen her cry before and something about seeing it for the first time made me realise she was definitely telling the truth. I ran into my bedroom and cried myself to sleep.

My dad, Charles Stockton Mortimer, was a salesman for Fox's biscuits at this time, and I have very few memories of him.

I know he liked cars, because he forked out for a green Ford Zephyr convertible with cream leather bench seats front and back. It was a pretty flash vehicle at the time, and I have fleeting memories of him allowing us to sit on the top of the rear seats as he drove around Middlesbrough with the Zephyr's top down.

I know that he liked to wear lederhosen – those grey leathery suede shorts that have a bib attached and straps that go over your shoulders to keep them up. My elder brothers have often told me of their embarrassment when they were seen out with him on a lederhosen day. I think, *Good for you, Pops*. I love that sort of shit.

I am aware that he was quite strict, but have no feelings of fear or foreboding associated with him. On Saturday afternoons I used to watch the wrestling on ITV's *World of Sport* with him. He would allow me to practice moves on him and pretend to submit if I managed to clamber on top of him.

He would take us for days out to the seaside or for ice creams in the villages on the North York Moors, and he liked to sing around the house. He smoked Players Senior Service, which was undoubtedly the king of the non-tipped fag scene, and he used Brylcreem, which gave him a cheeky outlook. He had a lovely brown checked Jaeger suit, and he always wore brown shoes. I like men who wear brown shoes. It hints at a confidence not born of the shoe but by the person whose foot is inside it.

On one occasion one of my elder brothers (I've always suspected Rick, though he always denies it) wrote in lipstick on the back of the toilet door, in large letters, 'RICHARD IS A C**T'.

My dad gathered Sam and me into the hallway outside the toilet door and demanded to know which one of us had written it. We both denied it, because of course Rick was the author. Dad then proceeded to bang our heads together to get one of us to admit it. It hurt like hell but neither of us broke. Dad later apologised and life moved on. I think quite a tight bond was forged that day between me and Sam.

One Christmas morning when I was around six years old, I was the first to wake up and sneaked downstairs to the living room to see if Santa had been. Jonathan and Richard would hang their stockings either side of the mantelpiece, Sam's would be hanging from the top of the TV, and mine was on the chair facing the TV.

When I got in the room I immediately saw a tiny drum kit in front of the TV. It was just a toy one, probably from Woolworths, but it looked magnificent. Sam must have played a blinder behaviour-wise this past year. My main present was a plastic rifle (again from Woolworths). It was a decent piece of loot, but it paled significantly in comparison to that drum kit.

Then a thought crossed my evil childish mind. I was the first one to wake up, so no one else actually knew what gifts Santa had intended for which boy. If I swapped the drum kit for the rifle, nobody would ever know. I quickly did it, and then sneaked back up to my bedroom. As soon as I heard my brothers get up, I followed them downstairs. It worked. I was now the lad in the house who owned a drum kit.

Dad eventually came downstairs and of course must have immediately realised what I'd done. I hope it made him smile. He explained to me that, actually, he had bumped into Santa when he'd got up in the night and Santa had asked him to help put the presents out. He remembered Santa had *specifically* said that the drum kit was for Sam, and that Dad must have made a mistake.

To be honest, I remembered being incredibly relieved. I knew I had done a bad thing but it seemed I had got away with it and wouldn't be punished. As it turned out, the drum kit was a piece of shit and the 'bass drum' split in two after just a morning's bashing with the 'drum pedal'. My rifle, however, could actually fire authentic-looking grey plastic bullets that you could aim at the little toy soldiers that came in my stocking. I was now the lad in the house who had a future in military operations.

My dad was thirty-eight years old when he died. He was driving his green Hillman Super Minx on the A19 just outside Thirsk when he ploughed into an articulated lorry while overtaking another car. The coroner concluded that he had been blinded by the very low early-morning sun. The steering wheel crushed Dad's ribcage to smithereens, and he died more or less instantly.

So that's it. Those are my memories of my dad. Not much at all really. But I suspect the loss of him was the single most defining moment of my life.

While I was writing this book, my brother Rick sent me a little package of my school reports and exercise books that my mum had kept. One contained my English essays from 1967. I wrote this little story just two weeks after my dad died.

18th January 1967
One day when I woke up it had been snowing so when I had finished my breakfast I went out and built a snowman. When I came in again I heard my mummy saying that she wanted the big tree in the garden cutting down. All that night I was thinking about what mummy had said. The next morning I looked outside and the big tree had gone. It made me very sad.

My abiding memory of the months after his death is that my day-to-day life didn't change much. Same bed, same house, same school, same clothes, same routines. However, I now had a real purpose in life: an overpowering and ever-present need to protect my mum at all costs. I didn't want her to be sad. I didn't want her to be lonely. I didn't want her to feel underappreciated, or her life to be a burden. I didn't want her to leave like Dad had.

From then on, looking after her became my job. I would cook with her, clean the house with her, take the washing to the launderette with her, go shopping with her, do the gardening with her, watch the TV with her, and most of all I would try to cause her no bother or upset. I would get out of bed as soon as I was called and go to bed as soon as I was told. I would dry the dishes and plates with a tea towel as she stood next to me at the sink washing them.

I became Mummy's Little Helper.

My mum, who had never smoked before, started smoking the day of her husband's death. She later explained to my brother Sam that his pack of cigarettes had felt like her last connection to him. She somehow felt a closeness to him by smoking just as he had. Then, of course, addiction took over and she became something of a chain smoker.

On reflection, I think I similarly took a shine to another mood-altering substance after Dad died: by the time I was about ten years old, I was taking sixteen sugars in my tea and coffee. It seems such an odd habit to get hooked on, but hooked is definitely the word. The ever-so-slightly amusing aspect of this sugar addiction was that if I ever put seventeen sugars in by mistake (it was easy to lose count), it was far too sweet for me and I would throw it down the sink.

I started smoking when I was eleven or twelve years old. At first I would just nick the odd fag from my mum's packet, but soon enough it would become my main expenditure. You could buy cigarettes individually from the newsagents at this time, and I remember it was half a pence for a couple of No. 6 filter. A tiny but very pleasant cigarette.

My mum, Eunice Mary Mortimer, was born in 1922 in Consett, Northumberland. She was a small, thin, extremely elegant lady with strawberry blonde hair. Our humble house, just a five-minute walk from the centre of Middlesbrough, was a great expression of her personality. This is how I remember the downstairs when I finally left home in 1977:

From the front door you entered into a hallway carpeted with a zigzag-patterned carpet of brown, orange and white stripes. Hanging from the hallway ceiling was a huge, bright-orange, plastic geometric lampshade. The hallway and staircase were covered in a wallpaper with massive, jungle-like fern leaves. The stair carpet was orange and thick underfoot.

The kitchen floor was orange and white square lino tiles. It had orange Hygena QA fitted cabinets with white countertops. All the plates, cups and saucers were orange melamine from Habitat. The knives and forks had orange handles. The walls of the kitchen were covered in three-dimensional stainless steel tiles (which were a bastard to clean). There was an orange roller blind on the window facing the playing field and orange curtains on the window looking out to the back garden.

The gas cooker was a Parkinson Cowan 2000. I remember it fondly because it had the eye-level grill. I miss eye-level grills. I love to stare at my bacon or fish fingers as they cook. Modern cookers have taken this simple pleasure away from us.

The living room walls were covered in a wallpaper patterned with 3D-effect yellow and silver cubes. The carpet was mid-brown (a bit like the chocolate brown you would see on an Austin Allegro), and in front of the Gas Miser Fire was a large, shag-pile orange rug. My mum's chair was orange and the curtains were orange. There were two tall cylindrical table lamps with large, orange fibreglass lampshades. And the TV was – you've guessed it – orange.

Yeah, Mum was 'the orange lady'. Our house was identified

by our neighbours as 'the house with orange curtains'. A few years later this changed when Mum had the whole of the outside of the house painted. It then became known as 'the pink house'.

(I paid a visit to my mum's old house for the *Gone Fishing* Christmas Special while writing this book, and stood on the very spot in the playing field where I saw my mum crying at the back door on the day that Dad died. The house still has its pink exterior, but it is all blistered and neglected. The back garden is chest-high with weeds and brambles. It was the garden that made me most sad. I imagined my mum beavering away with her arthritic hands and tired legs trying desperately to keep up appearances, her black-and-white cat Billy by her side as she tended to the flowers and the shrubs all set out to her design. She was very proud of her garden and it would have broken her heart to see it in this state. You can't take it with you, and sadly you can't always leave things in safe hands.)

I only know scant details of my mum's life before I arrived in the world. She was an only child, and was brought up by her grandparents, as her dad was a railway engineer and largely worked in Africa and South America. After her schooling, she went to the Athol Crescent Cookery School in Edinburgh. She worked for the Polish and American Red Cross in Cambridgeshire during the war, and afterwards she was employed by the Ministry of Food to travel the country teaching people how to make the best of rationed ingredients.

After marrying my dad, I know they managed a hotel in Epping Forest called The Bell Inn, and then a hotel in Hull. My dad managed front of house and Mum was the chef. I presume neither of these ventures worked out, though, as come the 1960s

Mum was teaching home economics in Middlesbrough and Dad was flogging biscuits around the north of England. My dad's parents died when I was just a baby. His father ran a bus company in Stockton-on-Tees. By all accounts he was an unpleasant character. My parents had to elope because he wouldn't give them permission to marry. Mum was seven years older than Dad and his father didn't like that.

My mum's father was around until I was nine years old, but I have very few memories of him other than the fact that he had massive hands, like all grandads do. I was always told that my mum's mother returned from Africa suffering from the after-effects of a tropical disease (apparently caught from a parrot) and that had led to the onset of Alzheimer's. Ever since, I remember, she was an 'inmate' at St Luke's Mental Asylum in Middlesbrough. Mum never took us to visit her. I do recall her spending one Christmas Day with us, however, and I caught her sneaking out of the front door. When she saw me she gave me five pounds and told me to keep quiet about her escape. I did as I was told and not long afterwards she was returned to our house by a policeman who explained he had found her on the street trying to hand out money to strangers. I felt guilty, but was kind of glad that I had kept quiet.

I wish I knew more, but I never asked. If your parents are still alive, do make sure you talk to them about their lives. You will regret it if you don't.

So there I am in the Swinging Sixties, a young boy beavering away to keep Mum happy and largely avoiding the company of others. Basically, and in a nutshell, I had turned out to be a shy boy. Shyness is so frustrating, a proper omnipresent curse.

You have things to say but you can't or dare not say them. You watch on as others chat and laugh and you yearn to be part of those moments.

The one thing that made me happy, the one thing at which I excelled, was football. I was good. I honestly had a real talent. I attended Green Lane Junior School, whose first team was made up of eleven-year-olds in their final year. Such were my skills that I played for the school team from when I was just nine years old. I hated the pre-match kickabouts and banter and the journeys to opposing schools in the minibus. I wasn't part of the 'gang', but I was never picked on. Presumably because of my undeniable, jaw-dropping, breathtaking, in-your-face footballing skills.

As soon as the matches kicked off, I was in heaven. Teammates clapped me and hugged me. I was someone worth knowing on that pitch, and my feet did the talking that my mouth was unable to do.

I suppose because these matches were my happiest of times, I can still remember nearly all the names of my teammates from that Green Lane football team even though none of them could have been described as close friends.

There was Tom Holdsworthy, Gary Cheeseman,[1] Nigel McManus, Keith Brine, Ian Belton, Alan Crombie, Steve Byetheway, Paul Tootil, Geoff Craggs and Neil Grannycombe,

---

[1] Gary 'Cheesy' Cheeseman came back into my life many years later when I was appearing on the TV show *Would I Lie to You?* I was telling some tale from my childhood when I mentioned his name and remarked that Gary had a huge head and was therefore known as 'The Sniper's Dream'. Interestingly, the headmaster of Green Lane School, Mr Portugal, walked with a limp and was known as 'The Sniper's Nightmare'.

but sadly, of all these lads, the only one that evokes any particular memory is Geoff.

It was one afternoon in the school playground. We used to play a game where each boy from the year had to run from one end of the exterior brick wall of the assembly hall to the other. While running, other pupils would kick footballs at you as hard as they could from about ten yards away. If you got hit, you had to go back in the runners' queue. If you avoided being hit, then you joined the ranks of the kickers.

Geoff was a slight boy whose parents insisted on him having a 1950s side-parted hairstyle. He had an unusual face. There was a lump on the top of his cheekbone, about the size of a large marble, which earned him the nickname 'Eyeball'. If The Head had had one of these lumps it really would have felt like the end of times. Anyway, he went for his death dash and got hit full on the side of his face with a leather football. He went down like a slinky off the mantelpiece. A few of us went to his aid, and when I picked him up onto his feet I noticed a tiny spot of what looked like Primula cheese in the centre of his face lump. He wiped it away and another piece of cheese emerged in the centre of the lump. Now, I was a spotty kid, and well used to squeezing pus from bumps all over my body. I told him that the lump needed squeezing and relief would be certain. He begged me not to, saying that his mum had told him he must never touch it. But something told me I was right, so I went in with my forefingers and achieved classic spot-squeezing grip on either side of the lump.

As I increased the pressure, lo and behold, a constant stream of pus started to erupt from the lump. It wasn't quite liquid;

more like the consistency of butter. Onlookers screamed as this stream of pus actually formed and fell in one, unbroken pipe from his cheek to the floor. I reckon it was about four feet long. I'd hazard a guess that it might be the longest unbroken pus rope ever to have been produced by a human. Before long, his lump had disappeared. It was a playground miracle and I was the hero. Geoff lost his nickname Eyeball only for it to be replaced with 'Pussy' Craggs. Swings and roundabouts.

Away from home, football gave me a purpose, an identity and happiness. I would play football before school, at lunchtime, at play time, and would practise in the playing field next to my house as soon as I got home – sometimes with my brother Sam, sometimes on my own. After tea it was time to practise again until Mum called me in from over the garden fence. I got really good. As far as my young mind was concerned, I was going to be a professional footballer. There was no one at my school as good as me, so I reckoned it would be an easy ride into Middlesbrough Football Club's first team.

One memory from these times that is indelibly burned onto my mind-grooves occurred in November 1969. I was eagerly anticipating bonfire night, and in those days my brother Sam and I would make a Guy out of old clothes stuffed with newspaper with a painted balloon on top for a face. We would sit it on our front garden wall and ask passers-by, 'Penny for the guy, penny for the guy'. We always did well enough to buy a decent-sized box of 'Standard' brand fireworks from the local newsagents.

A couple of days before bonfire night, I was alone in the house and decided to open the box of fireworks and drool over the contents and their descriptions: Air Bomb; Golden Rain; Fireball; Spitfire; Mine of Serpents; Super Sonic Boom; Shooting Star. While looking at the description on a packet of sparklers, I noticed that it contained the warning 'Not Suitable For Indoor Use'. For some reason that I've never been able to properly explain, I managed to convince myself that this really meant they *were* suitable for indoor use, but that you would just need to be careful. I knew what sparklers did and they seemed pretty benign. The little sparkles land on your hand and they don't burn or hurt you. Basically I thought the warning was on there because people *do* use them indoors but the firework makers don't want to take responsibility, so I took a match off the mantelpiece and lit one. Needless to say, it was a big mistake.

A cascade of sparks fell down into the open box of fireworks and the contents started to fizzle and ignite. Panicking, I grabbed hold of the box and ran through with it into the kitchen. I threw the box down then watched in horror as a Mine of Serpents exploded across the floor. Golden Rain cascaded over the linoleum. A Shooting Star flew at the window and bounced around the frame like a trapped fly looking for escape. I was helpless and just stood there, watching aghast and terrified from the hallway. Eventually all was quiet and the show was over.

The kitchen was left with huge scorch marks on the orange and white lino floor, on the cupboard fronts, on the surfaces and on the window frames. My heart was pounding. If Mum found the kitchen in this state, I would be murdered. I set to work to try to clean up the mess using a bucket of water and Brillo pads. Some of the scorching could be removed, but there were areas where the lino, wood and plastics had actually burnt. I knew

I was fighting a losing battle, but I thought the better I could make it look, the less trouble I would get into. I scrubbed and I scrubbed and I scrubbed. After a while I suddenly became aware of strange noises coming from the living room.

When I walked back in, I was met with a wall of flames. I had obviously left or dropped a firework in there, as the whole room was now ablaze. 1960s nylon and foam soft furnishings are only slightly more fire retardant than petrol. I ran outside to my next-door neighbours, two elderly spinsters called Mrs Haze and Mrs Best. I banged furiously on their door and eventually they answered.

'My house is on fire! My house is on fire!'

'You know what, we thought it was. Would you like us to phone the fire brigade, then?'

The firemen arrived shortly afterwards, by which time dense black smoke was gushing out of the front door and the windows, where the glass had smashed open. They pumped gallons of water everywhere and put out the fire. A policeman arrived and asked me what had happened. I told him that I had accidentally set off a sparkler by getting it too near the fire. I could tell he didn't believe a word. I began to think I was off to jail.

Mostly because of smoke and water damage, the house was a write-off. I remember my mum arriving home and getting out of a car opposite our house. She was clearly looking for me. When she spotted me, she ran over and gave me a massive motherly hug. I was OK and that's all that seemed to matter to her. I was so relieved. Maybe I wouldn't have to go to jail after all. I have often reflected that if all I had done was scorch the kitchen, I would have been in the worst trouble of my life.

Somehow, by actually burning the whole house down, I felt a little bit of a hero, and not an angry word was said to me.

Because the family was basically homeless now, my brother Sam and I were sent off to live with my Auntie Jessie in Redcar. She was a lovely lady and the youngest of my dad's six older sisters. I was struck by what a happy atmosphere there was in the house. Jessie was chatty, fun and outgoing, not at all like my mum, who was always very demure and reserved. On a couple of occasions Jessie's husband, Stan, took us to his workplace at the gelatine factory. Basically, at one end of the factory, lorry loads of animal bones were dumped. Then they passed though various cleaning, crushing and cooking machines until tubs of the finished product rolled out of the back gates. The smell of the factory was very challenging, like opening up a hot-water bottle that has been filled with pork residue and horse sweat. You never got used to it. *Thank God I'm going to be a footballer*, I thought to myself.

By 1970, I am more or less certain that Santa doesn't exist anymore, but a little tiny near-exhausted bit of belief remains. I go downstairs on Christmas Day and there on the chair opposite the TV is my stocking and a little pile of presents. My 'big' present looks decent. A large box wrapped neatly in bright-red Christmas paper. Exciting. I rip the paper off in a frenzy and find ... a Pifco steam blackhead removal and face sauna unit. It was basically the bottom half of an electric kettle with the heating element beneath a perforated metal plate. On top of that you put a wide plastic funnel, which you put your face in and steamed the living shit out of it. It was a modern version of putting a towel over your head above a bowl of hot, steaming water.

The idea was that it opened your pores so that you could then really go to town on your blackheads. I can't recall if it worked. All I can remember is sitting on my bed staring at the thing and then out of the window where other children were playing with their new bicycles or footballs or roller skates. It also stole from me that last drip of belief in Santa. Only a mum could have thought this a quality gift for a ten-year-old.

One hot summer's day a few months later, it was just me and Mum at home. She was in the downstairs toilet at the bottom of the stairs, and I heard her fall and shout out. Then there was silence. I stood outside the toilet door and called to her, 'Mum? Mum, are you OK? Mum, what's the matter?'

There was no reply. Just silence. The pit of my stomach revolved like a mill wheel cutting through chip oil and I wandered around the downstairs of the house sobbing and terrified. I was certain in my little mind that Mum was dead, and I thought I was going to have to leave my lovely house forever.

'Goodbye, kitchen.'

'Goodbye, table.'

'Goodbye, living room.'

'Goodbye, Mum's chair.'

3

October 2015

He took her hand
They took the floor
She was his all time favourite dancer

Orange Juice, 1982

And now here I am, forty-five years later, having just been told that I require open-heart surgery, wandering around my own kitchen with similar feelings of dread and fear. Mum wasn't dead, of course. She must have fainted or something that day, as when she emerged from the toilet she assured me nothing was untoward. My extreme panic must have been born from a real and painful insecurity.

Here in my kitchen I'm not actually saying goodbye to my egg cup, favourite mug and tea towel; I'm just suddenly desperately appreciative of how important the simple, mundane, ordinary things of life are to me and how much I would miss them if death took them away from me. I'm not feeling insecure anymore, just very scared.

I live with my partner, Lisa. We have been together for some twenty-five years. We have two sons, Harry and Tom, aged eighteen and sixteen. Lisa and I met in the Grove pub in Camberwell back in the '90s. We are a tight unit. She is tall, elegant and beautiful. The love of my life. Stood there in my kitchen with the smell of bleach rising from the sink, I am suddenly overcome by the desire to ask her to marry me. It's something that Lisa and I have never really talked about before. There just didn't seem to be any need to rubber-stamp our relationship. Now, however, it feels very important to me indeed.

Lisa came into the kitchen and I blurted out, 'We should get married.' I think she laughed. 'No, I'm serious,' I continued, 'if we're not married and I don't make it through the operation then there could be all sorts of problems. I don't even have a will.' We hug and the deal is done.

The next day I find a local solicitor on the internet and arrange to make a will. On returning home from the solicitor's, he phones to tell me that he has spoken to the local registry office and that they can see me that afternoon. He says I should ask if I can obtain a special licence that would allow me to get married before my operation in four days' time. Usually twenty-eight days' notice is required before the ceremony can take place. He advises that I should contact my consultant, Dr Lawson, and ask him to provide me with a letter to take to the registry office explaining that there is a reasonable chance that I will not survive the twenty-eight-day notice period.

Later that day, Lisa and I attend our appointment at the registry office, which is just a couple of hundred yards from our home. We are interviewed separately and have to tell the history of our relationship and confirm that we want to marry of our own free will. I explain the urgency of our application and hand over the letter from Dr Lawson. When we get home, the lady from the registry office telephones to tell me that the application has been sent off to London for the Chief Registrar's office to consider. If it is granted, she has a slot at 9.30 available on Monday morning when we can be married – the day I will be admitted to hospital for the operation. Today is Friday.

She calls us the next day to say that the special licence has been granted. I shiver to think what that letter from Dr Lawson actually said and what effect it would have had on me if I had read it. (Lisa still has a copy but I have never opened it.)

Monday arrives and we are seated in the ceremonial marriage room at the registry office. The only people in attendance are me and Lisa, our sons, Harry and Tom, and Lisa's lifelong friend Roma. In the pictures of that day, Lisa looks beautiful. I look like death warmed up. Like a fingerprint on an abandoned mirror. When it comes to saying the vows, I am crying like a baby who's just tasted cold Bovril for the first time, but these are tears of happiness. My little family all here together to witness me and Lisa declare our love and commitment to each other.

After the ceremony, we walked down to the high street from the registry and went for our wedding breakfast in a local café. I knew that after the operation I would be on a strict, no-saturated-fat diet, so the boys and I indulged in what I presumed would be, whatever the outcome, my final full English breakfast. It was hard to enjoy, knowing what lay ahead later that day, but it still has to be one of the happiest mornings of my life. I have no idea how worried my boys were. They seemed a bit quiet, though they knew the science and the stats were greatly in my favour. If they were worried, it was most likely because of my pathetic demeanour and appearance.

That afternoon Lisa drove me up to the hospital, where I was admitted and processed. I had a lovely room with a view of the River Thames. Lisa checked into a nearby hotel so that she could be on call if needed, and early that evening my surgeon, Chris Young, came to see me. He explained the procedure and its risks but assured me that he had only lost one patient in thirty-odd years of doing the operation. The nurses had found out that we had got married that morning and very kindly bought us a cake. Being a melodramatic little sap, I did wonder if this cake would be my final meal. If so, I could have done a lot worse.

Lisa left for her hotel around 7 p.m. I cried; she smiled. Tomorrow was a Big Day. I have had a few of those in my life.

4

SEPTEMBER 1971: A FRIEND AT LAST

I, well I don't know when I'll be content
But I do know I need a brand-new friend

Lloyd Cole, 1985

It's September 1971 and my first day at big school. For some administrative reason or other I am sent to a secondary school where none of my primary classmates are going. I have no doubt it will be a horror house of total strangers and the chances of me managing to make a friend are zero. Still, each year had its own football team, and hopefully I would be chosen to play.

My first lesson was English. I took a seat right at the front by the teacher's table. As the classroom filled up, no one came to sit next to me. Perhaps I would get lucky, I thought, and the seat would remain vacant. No such luck. Suddenly, a huge lanky boy with a mop of curly hair plonked his arse on the chair next to mine.

'Is this the English class?' he asked me in his deep, flat Teesside accent.

'No, this class is for Germans only,' I replied. He laughed.

'What's your name?'

'Rob. What's your name?'

'Keith, but people call me Cagsy.'

I had spoken to a stranger. I had made a stranger laugh. I was sitting next to a stranger and it felt OK. The teacher hadn't yet arrived so we continue to chat. He asks me where I live and unexpectedly I start to lie and invent a home and a life far from the truth. I am desperate to impress. I tell him that I live in a big manor house in the countryside at Great Ayton. That I have a swimming pool and an athletics track. There is a river at the bottom of the garden, I explain, where I catch fish and paddle in my canoe. I even draw him a map of the 'estate'. I need to make this boy like me, I think. He just might be my way out of this lonely life I have built for myself.

We sit together for the rest of that morning's classes. We have similar interests – football, music – and, above all, a shared sense of humour. I don't know if I've enjoyed laughing so much in my life. At lunchtime, however, he disappears, and I am left alone. There is a game of football being played on the field after lunch and I can see Cagsy playing. I don't have the balls to go over and join in. The lads he is playing with are from his previous school, which means he already has a gang of friends. I doubt he will have any need for me, I think. My only hope of good times would once again be playing football.

After a few weeks, I am chosen to play for my year's football team. I arrive in the changing room pre-match with that familiar feeling of dread at having to mix with strangers. I find a bench and hook as far away from the centre of things as possible, get changed as quick as I can, go out onto the pitch and start kicking a ball about. I am soon joined by the terrifying presence of Nobby Smith, who had the reputation of being the hardest lad this side of Middlesbrough. He was a good foot taller than me and built like a crocodile with horse's legs. There is nowhere to hide out here on the pitch, and so we start to pass the ball back and forth. I'm nervous, and one of my passes goes well wide of him and off into the distance, towards the school gates.

'Go and get it,' he commands, and I scurry off after the ball like a whippet with its arse on fire.

After the practice session, I am the first out of the communal shower and am drying myself when Nobby pops his head out and calls to me, 'Get over here, have a look at this.' I instantly obey. There is a skinny lad in the showers. 'Do that thing,' says Nobby. 'Do that thing with your knob.' The lad is clearly happy to oblige. His stomach muscles twitch for a moment and then, slowly, like a worm backing into a hosepipe, his penis retracts into his body, leaving what can only be described as a belly button where his penis should be. It's a superb party piece and I laugh along with everyone else in the cubicle. Then our PE teacher, Ray 'Piggy' Piggersgill, enters.

'What's going on?' he demands.

Silence.

'What's going on?!' he repeats.

'Nothing, sir,' mumble a few boys.

'What's all the noise about?'

Silence.

'I said, what is all the noise about?'

'Nothing, sir,' another mumble from the boys.

Piggy can clearly tell from his years of intimidation that I look the most likely to crack.

PIGGY: You, boy, answer me. What's going on?

ME: Nothing, sir.

PIGGY: Last chance, boy. Tell me what's going on!

ME: Thompson retracted his penis, sir.

Everybody broke into laughter.

Piggersgill immediately grabbed me, slapped my arse for being cheeky and issued a detention. But it was well worth it: I felt the tiniest hint of a bond growing with the rest of the team.

Some weeks passed and my classroom-only friendship with Cagsy continued. I eventually had to admit that I actually only lived about half a mile from the school, not on an estate. I can't remember how I explained my lie. I've asked Cagsy and he can't remember either, so I have to presume he forgave me. We both loved music, and we would spend many hours talking about our favourite bands. In those days, owning an LP was a very precious thing. Cagsy's prize possession was his copy of *Abraxas* by Carlos Santana; mine was *Free Live* by my favourite band, Free.

Because I was the youngest of four brothers, I had access to quite a decent library of music in my home – maybe thirty or so albums. My friendship with Cagsy had remained strictly classroom-based, but then, somehow, one day I plucked up the courage to ask him if he would like to come round to my house one evening and listen to some music. He said he would.

The evening arrived and at 7 o'clock there was a knock on my front door. I opened it, and there, to my shock and horror, was not just Cagsy, but a gang of his mates from his previous school: Harry Harriman, Pete 'Pazza' Palmer, Steve 'Stava' Allen and, most dauntingly of all, Nobby Smith. This was the first time I had seen anyone from my school out of their uniform, and they were all dressed identically: dark-blue Crombie coats, checked button-down Ben Sherman shirts, two-tone blue and green Levi Sta-Prest slacks, and chunky, thick-soled black brogue shoes. They all had their hair teased forward into unruly fringes. They were Suedeheads. It felt like some hillbilly section of the FBI had come calling for me.

At this time I was still wearing clothes chosen by my mum or hand-me-downs from my brothers. As I recall, my chosen style was flared Wrangler jeans (with an extra 'V' section of denim sewn into the flare by mum to give added width), a patterned shirt with a large rounded collar and a crew-neck jumper. On my feet I wore my school shoes. They were all that I had.

Cags immediately said he had bumped into his mates on the way round and wondered if I fancied coming out to hang around the chippy on Acklam Road. I wanted to say no but thankfully I said yes. We walked up my road and I was immediately struck by the noise these lads' shoes made as they strode along. When I asked what the noise was they all sat themselves on a wall and proudly displayed the soles. Every inch of available leather had been covered with small metal segs, 'Blakey's Shoe Protectors', which meant that when they walked it sounded like a small army of heavy soldiers was approaching. This was the sound of the Suedehead gang, and I found it quite exhilarating.

In the following weeks I changed my hairstyle and begged my mum for a Crombie, a Ben Sherman shirt, Levi slacks and some brogues from Clarks. She was happy to oblige. Out of context, these were some of the most parent-friendly clothes I could have requested. My brother Johnny was a rocker, decked out in his badge-adorned leather jacket, wild hair, oily jeans and biker boots. Rick was a Mod, with his massive parka coat and clown shoes, and Sam was in a hippie phase: Afghan coat, loons and Budgie jacket. And here was I asking for some sensible, rather smart clothing. Little did she know that it was technically 'gang' apparel.

So, yeah, the day I met Cagsy was a 'Big Day'. I was now part of a gang, and I belonged to someone other than my mum. I had reinvented myself as a Suedehead and had a life beyond my home. The following years were some of the happiest of my life, and Cagsy and I are still best friends to this day.

5

OCTOBER 2015

Now that I've found peace at last,
Tell me, Jesus, will it last?

The Blue Nile, 1996

I am woken up early as I am first up for the operation. My upper body is shaved by a nurse and I have a shower using special anti-bacterial gunge for soap. My vitals are checked and then Chris Young pops into the room and tells me he feels in good nick today and that I shouldn't worry.

'See you at tea time,' he says.

'Not if I see you first,' I reply, then instantly think, *What a shit thing to say.*

Imagine if that was the last thing you ever said on this earth? It still rankles me to this day – you know, like some shit comments often do.

(Another shit comment that I have never been able to wash from my embarrassment files happened when I met Sinéad

O'Connor sometime in the early '90s. I had been to the filming of a comedy entertainment show in central London in which Sinéad had appeared. All the boys I was with were in quiet disbelief about how beautiful she was in the flesh. After the show, Jim, Jools Holland and I kind of queued up to chat to her as she stood at the bar. When my turn came, I fell to pieces in the face of her radiance and blurted out, 'Hi, Sinéad, do you have a local shop near to where you live?' She politely answered 'Yes' and then turned away. It still hurts to think of it.)

So I'm cleaned and shaved and ready to be opened up. I'm put on a gurney and transported to the operating theatre. That's the last thing I remember.

I've spoken to Chris since the operation and he gave me an idiot's guide to what he actually did to me. Firstly, a 2ft incision was made in my left leg from my knee to my ankle. An artery was removed for use as the bypass routing material. Then, using an electric saw, my sternum bone was cut down the middle. A huge clamp was then placed either side of the sternum to open up the chest cavity. I was then placed on a ventilator and my lungs deflated to aid access to my heart. The heart is then pulled out of the chest and rests above the cavity, where it is injected with potassium, which shuts it down completely. It would be impossible to operate on a bouncing heart, after all, so a machine does its job in the meantime. Another artery is then removed from my chest for use as plumbing. The three worst areas of artery blockage are bypassed using the arteries harvested from my leg and chest, joined by micro-stitching. Chris told me that each surgeon has their own unique sewing pattern, so that if a patient returns for more surgery you can instantly tell which surgeon previously fixed his pipes.

Another injection turns the heart back on, then it's put back in its preferred location. The lungs are re-inflated, metal staples are used to fix the sternum back into one piece, and the incision is stitched closed. My heart was 'dead' for thirty-two minutes in total. That's quick work. Chris should enter *The Great British Sewing Bee*.

The next thing I actually remember is waking up in the spaceship that is the modern-day intensive care unit. There's a TV in my room and it is showing the football match between Manchester United and Middlesbrough in the League Cup. I have been supporting The Boro for some fifty years. Can this be real? Yes, I think it is. I can consciously remember that this game was scheduled to be played tonight, which means I have survived. I am alive.

Soon after this I become aware of how difficult I'm finding it to breathe, and how painful my whole chest area feels. A nurse appears, a wonderful, quiet and gentle man from Bulgaria. He informs me that if the pain becomes too much then I can press this little button to administer a dose of morphine. I press it hard, like it was the doorbell to a pie-and-mash party. My breathing continues to worsen. It feels like there is no space for air in my lungs. I begin to panic, then I feel a blockage in my windpipe. I cannot breathe. My chest spasms and sputters, and a lump of jelly moves up my throat and into my mouth. It slides off my tongue and drops onto my light-blue hospital gown. It looks like a huge, black garden slug. My throat is clear again and I suck in some air as greedily as a captured trout.

44

I ask the nurse what is happening, my instant thought being that a part of my lung has disintegrated.

'It's tar from years of smoking that loosened when they re-inflated your lungs,' he explains.

'Is this normal?' I ask.

'Yes. Just try your best to bring it up. Don't worry, you are going to be OK.' I didn't believe him. I breathe in hard, but again don't seem to be able to get air into my lungs. I glance up at the TV. The match has gone to penalties. Grant Leadbitter, the Middlesbrough captain, strides up to the penalty spot and slots it home. Ten thousand Boro away fans go ape and the Boro players are in a heap of ecstasy. It should be one of the happiest moments of my football-supporting life, but I don't give a shit. They are in heaven and I fear I might soon be joining them.

My windpipe blocks up again. I can't breathe and I can't shift it. I look at the nurse with blind panic in my eyes. I cannot get any air into my lungs. It feels like I am drowning and then everything goes dark. I begin to float upwards through a long, cylindrical tunnel of beautifully trimmed yew hedge. At the end of the tunnel above me is a wonderful blue sky. I can't wait to get there. I feel an intense euphoria. I'm passing on through to a wonderful place. Peace at last.

6

MIDDLESBROUGH 1972–1977: WOULD I LIE TO YOU?

I lied to you, I've cheated too
So what friend can I be?

Squeeze, 1991

Between the ages of thirteen and sixteen, I spent most nights of the week prowling the local streets of Middlesbrough in my Crombie coat and oxblood-red Doc Martens boots. Our gang headquarters was a parade of shops on Acklam Road, which had an off-licence and a fish-and-chip shop. The off-licence would sell cider (but not beer or spirits) to anyone who looked over about fourteen. All the gang apart from Cagsy smoked, but we rarely bought cider as we were surviving on pocket money only. A hot bag of chips with 'scraps' was the usual climax to our evening. ('Scraps' are the tiny bits of batter that fall off the fish when it is placed into the fryer. They are one of life's supreme pleasures but I have never seen them served anywhere but the North East.) The core gang members were as follows:

Keith 'Cagsy' Bridgewood. My best friend and saviour. 6ft 2ins, slim, featuring a wavy Suedehead hairstyle with curling fringe tips. Deep monotone Teesside accent. Excellent runner. Useless at spitting, smoking and whistling. Able to do that trick where you can make your iris disappear into the roof of your eye socket. Quiet but deeply funny boy. Cries when he laughs.

Steve 'Stava' Allen. 5ft 10ins, skinny with a slightly side-parted and frizzy Suedehead. A skilled-mimic-and-sarcasm parcel. Excellent footballer and stone-thrower. Knew how to wear a trouser and display a cheeky cuff or collar. Probably the most 'mouthy' and confident of the group. Able to spit through the gap in his two front teeth, giving him great distance and accuracy.

Peter 'Harry' Harriman. 6ft and eighteen stone. Jet-black straight hair worn in a centre parting with rear feathering – not a mullet, but with a whiff of that design. Often preferred a black Harrington jacket with tartan lining to a Crombie. Would literally do anything for a caper. His dad rented out fruit machines to pubs and clubs and Harry would often have spare change on him to finance our potato-, tobacco- and cider-fuelled evenings. Superb ball-to-eye coordination. Could eat a hot dog in one enormous swallow. Held his cigarettes between the very tips of his middle and index fingers.

Mickey Bellas. 5ft 8ins, medium build, ginger-haired with brown Sellotaped NHS glasses. Nutcase and occasional fighter. Continuously cracked his knuckles and adjusted his specs when in conversation, otherwise very much a hands-in-pockets man. Held his cigarettes between thumb and forefinger and objected to anyone else using his technique. (I held mine deep in the well between my forefinger and middle finger so that my whole mouth was covered when I took a drag. It looked good but led to severe tobacco tarnish of the palm.) Was able to honk like a goose and would use this noise as his greeting and his farewell.

I bumped into Mickey many years ago pushing a pram with a kid in it around Middlesbrough. He gave me a near perfect example of North East humour. It went something like this:

'Alright, Mickey. How's it going?'

'*Honk honk*. Alright, mate. Not too bad.'

'Is that your kid?'

'Yeah, he's deaf and has permanent diarrhoea.'

'Sorry to hear that, can't be easy.'

'Nah, don't be daft, I'm just looking after it for a bloke down the bookies. Who the fuck would want kids? Anyway, best get going, nice seeing you. *Honk honk*.'

Peter 'Pazza' Palmer. Tall, dark and handsome. The pretty boy. Sharp as a pin. Not as vocal as the rest of us but definitely gave the gang a touch of class. Probably the most skilled and enthusiastic drinker. Smoked Consulate menthol cigarettes between his index and little finger. Least sporty of us all and the only one of us that would turn towards the belligerent in drink.

Trevor 'Nobby' Smith. A 6ft 2in brick building. Textbook rear-to-front Suedehead haircut. First to develop acne and first to achieve genuine sideburns rather than bumble fluff. Had the heaviest, noisiest brogues. Superb footballer (centre half). Reputedly the best fighter this side of Middlesbrough for his age, though, in truth, I never actually saw Nobby raise a fist in anger.

So, they were the core gang members, and what follows is a selection of the horsefoolery that we got up to during my teenage years. I've put in a couple of 'lies' – see if you can guess which ones they are. In some ways, it's a homage to teen life before the mobile phone and internet kidnapped it. This is what used to be called 'mucking about', 'fannying around' or 'having a daft laugh'. Teenagers still do it now, but we used to do it every day. They were some of the happiest times of my life, and I often ache for these times of innocence and unbridled joy shared with friends whose sole objective was laughter.

Space Fruit

The Lakes estate was an area of 1950s housing beyond the playing field opposite my house on the way to our base at the Acklam shops. It was our evening playground. Every night we would wander its streets looking for antics and tom- foolery. Occasionally we got lucky and could play a game of Space Fruit.

Getting lucky meant seeing the fully loaded flatbed fruit- and-veg truck parked outside a house on Ullswater Avenue. The produce was covered and tied down under a green canvas tarpaulin. It was, however, easy to loosen a rope or two and reach inside to steal some fruit and veg. It was always a bit of a lucky dip depending on how the fruit had been packed, though you could usually get some oranges, grapefruits and apples – maybe even a melon or a cauliflower. Anyway, you just grabbed whatever you could and scarpered over the road to the playing field with your booty.

'I challenge you with the heft of a grapefruit,' one of us would say.

'I will receive that grapefruit heft,' another of us would reply.

The challenger would then throw the fruit as high into the air as he could and the challengee would try to guess its trajectory and stand stock still on the point at which he thought it would land plum on his head.

If the fruit landed full on the top of the challengee's head, the whole gang would scream 'SPACE FRUIT' and we would run around frantically in celebration as if we had just detonated every single firework in a fireworks warehouse.

Of course, the real joy of the game was the jeopardy of taking a melon or a large King Edward to the skull. The point of a honeydew melon is not something to take lightly or without some kind of impact insurance.

(This childish game would rear its head again later in life, when we used its basic principles for an endgame in the BBC comedy panel show *Shooting Stars*. We would select the captain of the winning team to stand on a box centre stage and then drop increasingly heavy fruits on their head. They either took the heft of all the fruits and emerged victorious or bottled out. On one occasion we attached the comedian David Walliams to a wire and threw him at the contestant under the description of 'the largest fruit in the world'. I think this might have been David's first television appearance.)

Snow Patrol

One winter evening, Middlesbrough was enjoying a deep covering of snow and my mum had agreed that I could have a party in our garage with some mates. I think I would have been about sixteen years old.

I swept the concrete garage floor and plugged in the family stereo. So, we had concrete and music, but no booze. Harry Harriman, however, had a plan. The local rugby club stored its beer barrels behind the club house in an area protected only by a five- or six-foot wooden fence. The rugby club was only half a mile away, and if we were able to lift a barrel over the fence, we could roll it back to my house. The majority of the journey would be across a playing field, so the chances of being spotted were low.

So, Cags, Harry and I made our way to the rugby club and climbed over the fence. We found a full barrel by utilising our knowledge of weights, i.e. heavy equals full. We lifted it to the top of the fence, where Harry, standing on an empty barrel on the other side, was able to grab it and ease it down onto the ground. It was an aluminium barrel with wide rims at the top and bottom.

We rolled it along a few small roads and then onto the playing field, straight up my drive and into the garage. There was a sense of success and accompanying exhilaration, though with a background feeling of dread.

The barrel had some sort of valve fixing at the top through which the beer was presumably meant to flow, but we couldn't work out how to penetrate this valve and access the beer inside.

We started to hit it with a hammer. This didn't shift anything, however, so we placed a large chisel at the edge of the valve and started to whack it. Suddenly it was breached and a continuous jet of beer started to fire out of the valve. And it wouldn't stop. There was beer on the ceiling, on the windows and, sadly, on the concrete floor. We opened the garage doors so that we could direct the beer plume outside, and as we did so were greeted by four burly adult males. They were from the rugby club.

'That's our beer, you little bastards,' said one of them.

'No, it's not,' said Harry. 'It's my dad's barrel.'

'Look, son, we followed the lines it made in the snow as you rolled it all the way from the back of the club up your front drive.'

Every crime scene reveals a clue or two, it's true, but we had left a whopper: a perfect set of beer-barrel imprints in the snow for the entirety of its guilty journey.

Mum came to see what was happening and offered to pay for the barrel, which the men accepted. We were then left in the front garden to watch the beer dissipate all over the drive until there was not even a drop inside.

The Witch's House

I assume every neighbourhood has the neglected house with an overgrown garden that the local children label 'The Witch's House'. Mine was on the corner of Green Lane and Kingston Avenue, and I had passed it every school day since I was five years old. It was a large Edwardian house with a low front wall, and shrubs and trees that more or less hid the house itself from view. It had no driveway for cars, just a green wooden gate with blistered and fading paint. On the gate in white emulsion were the words 'No Thank You'. Nobody, and I mean *nobody*, had ever seen a living person leave or enter that house, but when darkness drew in, the lights inside the house would come on and occasionally classical music could be heard being played on a piano from inside.

One night, when we were around fourteen years old, Cagsy and I decided to investigate. It was dark, but the street lights provided enough light to see ourselves through the overgrowth and to another solid wooden gate that led to the rear of the house. We tried the latch but it wouldn't shift. Cagsy gave me a leg up and I was the first into the back garden. The latch on the rear of the gate was bent but I was able to force it up and let Cagsy in. There was a light on in the furthest ground-floor window, so we slowly made our way past the dustbins and the kitchen window and arrived outside the lit room. I slowly craned my neck past the frame to peer inside. It was an extraordinary sight: there, right in the middle of the room, was a tiny Shetland pony seemingly watching the TV that was in the opposite corner of the room. I motioned for Cags to take a look. He took the briefest glance at the pony then immediately declared, 'Shit, let's get out of here.' We turned to make our escape, at which moment the light went on in the kitchen and we froze against the back wall. Then, horror of horrors, the back door opened and a head poked out and sniffed the air.

'I know you're there,' spoke the head, and then it turned and stared straight at us. 'There you are, now get out of here or I'll phone the police.'

It was an old lady. She had a full head of grey hair and the biggest, woolliest bright-red jumper you've ever seen. Its arms went well beyond her hands and it went down to her knees, beneath which she was bare-legged and slippered. My heart was racing but I managed to say, 'Sorry to have disturbed you, it's just that we heard you had a little horse in the house and we just wanted to see it. We both love horses.'

'You're one of the Mortimer boys, aren't you?' she said.

'Yes, very much so. Really, really sorry to have disturbed you. We'll get out right away,' I blurted.

'Would you like to come in and see him? He's very friendly.'

It didn't feel like we could refuse, having just expressed our deep love for horses.

'Yes, please!' I said. 'That's very kind of you.'

She then beckoned us with her hand and we followed her into her lair. The place smelt of horse and paraffin with a side portion of beef stew, and it was hot – very hot. We followed her down a short hallway, then into the room that housed the horse.

'There he is,' she gestured. 'His name is Max. He's very sweet. You can give him a stroke if you want.'

We both bent down and started to make a fuss of Max, and the old lady left the room.

'What should we do?' whispered Cags.

'Well, we can't stay here much longer, this horse fucking stinks!' I replied.

The old lady returned to the room holding a broken toilet seat. 'Would you take this for me? I'll give you some money to get rid of it.'

'Yes, of course!' I replied. 'No need to give us any money though.'

'No, that wouldn't be right, you must be paid,' she said, holding out some coins for me to take. I tried to refuse but she insisted, and so I took it from her and we both thanked her profusely. As we left through the back gate with the toilet seat in hand, we could hear her banging at the latch to make sure it couldn't be opened.

I never saw the lady again, but would always gaze at the house whenever I passed it and wonder if Max was still there watching his TV. Some years later, on a visit to Middlesbrough, I noticed that the house had been knocked down and replaced with a block of flats. The neighbourhood had lost its witch's house, and it made me sad.

Transit Tale

In the early to mid-'70s, Cags, Harry and I used to go to Middlesbrough FC away matches in a battered old transit van with my brother Sam and some of his mates. There was no seating in the back and we would roll around the floor as the daft van made its way over Valley and Dale. I remember that we had a large plastic funnel that we would poke through a hole in the back door and use as a mobile toilet.

In those days, football hooliganism was nearing its peak. Attending an away match was risky business and the last twenty minutes of the match would be ruined by the frightening prospect of getting back to your transport without receiving a kicking. In many ways, it was the non-hooligans such as ourselves that were in most danger. The hardcore fighters would generally be escorted en masse to the railway station or their coaches by the police. Little groups like our own had to furtively and silently scramble though the back streets, trying as best we could to blend in with the home support.

On this occasion, as I walked with my brother through anonymous side streets, we were approached by some Leeds fans who asked us if we knew the time. They wanted to hear us speak so they could tell whether we were from Leeds or Teesside. As soon as Sam spoke, one Leeds fan announced that he had located some Boro fans. Sam and I instantly ran off as fast as we could. A couple of hundred yards up the hill I turned around to see him crouched on the road being kicked and punched by a group of about ten Leeds fans. My instincts kicked in and I ran back to try to help him. When I was about twenty feet from the melee a young boy, probably only seven or eight years old, stepped out in front of me and smashed an old-fashioned bottle of Coca-Cola into the side of my face. I stumbled and fell to the ground, the cut above and to the side of my eye bleeding profusely. I got up and carried on to try to help Sam just as one of the Leeds fans kicked him in the head so hard that his eye socket fractured. I suddenly realised that I was well outnumbered and that a similar fate probably awaited me. At that moment, a car screeched to a halt between myself and Sam and the driver told us to get in the car. He whisked us away to safety. Sam spent the next few days in hospital. I told the rest of the gang that I had been hit by an animal hooligan but the truth of course was that I had been brought down by a child.

Shoe Waterfall

Myself, Cags and Harry used to spend a lot of time in Middlesbrough town centre looking for ways to entertain ourselves. One of our favourites was a simple candid camera-style set-up that we called Shoe Waterfall. In those days, shoe shops such as Dolcis, Shoefayre and Freeman, Hardy and Willis would display a selection of their shoes on freestanding racks along the shopfront and lining the entrance. We would take a bobbin of fishing line with us and tie one end of it to the top corner of one of these racks. Then we would stand a few feet away and wait for someone to come along and pick up a shoe from the rack to which the line was tied. As soon as they did, we would yank on the line, causing the whole rack to fall over onto the pavement. The embarrassed shopper would immediately feel obliged to gather up the fallen shoes and put the rack back in order. Sometimes we would help them in the task and receive their thanks as good Samaritans. A cascade of 1970s shoes was a beautiful thing indeed.

Theft and Shrubbery

This was a game/antic we usually played at the very end of the evening before we made our separate ways home. We would select a house that had its lights on and had direct access from the front to the rear gardens. It was best if the house was centrally located in a long run of semi-detached properties. The Lakes estate was perfect for this. We would use extreme stealth to move from the front of the house to the very rear of the back garden without troubling the occupants. We would then line up and slowly, very slowly, make our way towards the rear living room window chanting the words: 'We do beg your pardon but we are in your garden,' in the style of hypnotized monks. The chant would increase in volume the nearer we got to the window.

'We do beg your pardon but we are in your garden.'

'We do beg your pardon but we are in your garden.'

'WE DO BEG YOUR PARDON BUT WE ARE IN YOUR GARDEN.'

At some point, usually sooner than we wished, the occupants would hear us and pull back their curtains to see what was going on. This was our cue to run away in various directions to make our escape. Going back the way we came in was always the most risky option, as the homeowner would often come out of the front door to investigate. The preferred route was to go fence-jumping across the neighbouring back gardens and then escape via a front drive further up the road. It was a thrilling game and perhaps one of the earliest examples of the adrenalin sports that are all the rage these days.

Make-Up Club

The school I attended from the age of twelve, where I met Cags and the rest of the gang, was called King's Manor. It was not particularly academic and, as I remember, most pupils left at age sixteen to get an apprenticeship in some trade or other. I didn't make any great effort in lessons and put my energy mainly into playing football, smoking and larking about. I have no memory whatsoever of doing homework. I guess I drew an oxbow lake or two and maybe did a bar graph or a drawing of a Bunsen burner at some point. I don't think parents got involved with their children's schoolwork in those days. I must have done enough to avoid my lack of application being noticed.

I do however remember the larking about very well. One of our favourite games was called 'make-up club'. This involved selecting a victim from our group behind their back. Once selected, they would be grabbed and held in the cloakroom area. We would then borrow a girl's make-up bag and do a full lipstick, eye shadow and blusher makeover on their face. The victim would then be taken to the hallway outside the staff room and, while the others all watched on the stairwell, they would knock on the door. When the door was opened, they had to say something like: 'Sorry, sir, I just wondered if any of the staff had any make-up remover pads?' Or: 'Hello, sir, I just wanted to say I'm made up about the new Wednesday afternoon options!' Or: 'Sir, some of the young lads are getting really lippy in the dining hall.' Or: 'Sir, I was thinking of doing a foundation course and wondered if you have any leaflets?'

Depending on the member of staff that answered the door, you might just be told to piss off, get a detention or, worst of all, be sent to the headmaster's office to be caned. On one occasion that was my fate, and I made the long walk to the headmaster's office, which was located in an older building at the front of the school. Once inside, I made straight for the toilets to wash off the make-up with hard white soap and water. Try as I might, I was still left with residue around my eyes and mouth, which made it look like I had two black eyes and had been eating a bowl of raw liver.

I knocked on the headmaster's secretary's door and entered.

'Oh my God,' the secretary blurted. 'What's happened to you! Are you OK?'

'Yes, miss, I was just messing about putting some make-up on . . .'

At this moment the headmaster entered the room and told me to follow him into his office. It had a pretentiously large mahogany desk and its walls were adorned with oil paintings of old ships. There were also a number of glass-fronted display cabinets that held old sporting and academic trophies. The head-master's name was Mr Hugill. He was a short, sweaty barrel of a man with a red face and a fat neck that bulged above his tight-collared starched white shirt. He had black hair Brylcreemed into a tight, flat side parting, and he always wore a pin-striped three-piece suit with his cufflinks on display and a hankie in his pocket. He was old-school – a dying breed enjoying the last years of corporal punishment and dictatorship over his little kingdom.

'What is it this time, Mortimer?'

'Sir, I put some . . .'

'What is the matter with your face? Have you been fighting?'

'No, sir, it's make-up.'

'Make-up? Why would you have make-up on your face?'

'I just borrowed it from one of the girls.'

'I didn't ask you how you got it. I asked you why you have it on your face.'

'I thought it would be funny, sir.'

'And is it? Is it funny?'

'No, sir.'

'Did you want to look like a clown? Because that's what you look like!'

'No, sir.'

'Clowns are funny, aren't they, Mortimer?'

'Yes, sir.'

'But you're not funny, are you?'

'No, sir.'

'Why are you here?'

'Because I went to the staff room wearing the make-up, sir.'

'Why did you do that? Did you think it would be funny?'

'No, sir, I just wanted to ask if they had any wipes to get it off.'

'Don't lie to me, boy. It's some sort of game or challenge, isn't it?'

'No, sir.'

'You and your friends think it's funny, don't you?'

'No, sir.'

'Do you think it's funny that you are going to be caned?'

'No, sir.'

'Put your hand out, palm upwards.'

Hugill rose up from behind his desk and took his cane out of the umbrella stand in the corner of the room. It was about three feet long and made of one of the darker woods. It looked handmade, like a miniature gnarly walking stick – solid, not whippy. He positioned my hand to a height of his liking and raised the cane in the air above his head. This was always the worst moment: anticipating the pain and trying desperately to convince yourself not to move your hand away before impact. If you did that, then you would get an extra smack. I grimaced and looked away. *Here it comes . . .*

61

But it didn't. What did come was the sound of glass smashing behind me. The cane had slipped out of Hugill's sweaty palm on its way down and smashed one of the display cabinets.

'Now look what you've made me do!' Hugill roared. 'Get out! GET OUT!'

Needless to say, I found this very funny.

Old Man Christmas

Every Saturday and most days during school holidays Cagsy and I would walk into Middlesbrough town centre to see what fun could be had and to rifle through the LPs and posters at the record shops.

One of our favourite activities was to go into clothes shops and try on the biggest items of clothing we could find in the shop. It's what might be called a reveal joke for the benefit of the person waiting outside the changing room. Believe me, a young man with a Herbert's haircut emerging from behind a curtain wearing a suit that is ten sizes too big for him is quite a moment to relish.

The lighting department in Binn's department store was also great for a reveal moment. Not many people seem to realise that a decent-sized lampshade placed upside down on your head makes for an unusual and characterful hat. You could also combine the reveal with a pair of extra-large or ladies gloves to add a bit of a leathery flavour.

One Christmas Eve, Cags and I were in a pub in the Cleveland Centre shopping mall having a festive pint. We were underage at the time, but the pubs seemed to turn a blind eye to that sort of thing on Christmas Eve. Sat next to us was a little skinny old fella with a few wisps of white hair. Beside him on the bench seat was a half-full Tesco's plastic carrier bag. He must have been in his seventies and was wearing a white shirt and tie under a worn and much lived-in woollen overcoat. He was on his own drinking a pint and just gazing upon his surroundings. As Cags and I chatted, he got up to leave, but on taking his first step fell to the ground, spilling the contents of his carrier bag on the floor. It contained a tin of Goblin-brand beef pudding, a tin of peas, a packet of instant mash and a box of Milk Tray chocolates.

We bent down to help him and saw that the paper-thin skin of his cheek was bleeding after an impact with the table. He kept apologising but seemed very unsure of what had happened or who we were. He told us that he wanted to go home, but when we offered to walk him or get him on the bus he refused our help and wandered slowly out of the pub. We both felt that we couldn't leave him to his own fate. The roads and pavements were covered in slush and ice, so we decided to follow him from a discreet distance just so we could make sure he was OK. He made his way out of the mall across to the grassy town square in front of the municipal library where, exhausted or confused, he took a seat on a damp wooden bench and bowed his head.

We approached him and asked him if he was OK. 'I just want to go home,' he replied. He told us he lived in Borough Road, which was just a couple of hundred yards away, and finally he agreed to let us walk there with him. It was slow progress and it was awful to see the blood occasionally drip from his chin. Soon we arrived outside a large Victorian house that had been converted into individual flats or bedsits. At the doorway he fumbled around in his coat pockets for his keys but couldn't find them. Cags knocked on the door and rang a few of the doorbells but there was no response. We wondered if he had dropped his keys in the pub or left them on the table. Cags ran back to check while I stayed to keep the old man company.

'Have you got family coming for Christmas?' I asked.

'No, I don't think so.'

'Will you be having a Christmas dinner?'

'Yes, I've got a meat pie and some other bits and pieces.'

'Shouldn't you be having a turkey?'

'We never have turkey. My wife doesn't like it.'

'So is your wife at home?'

'No, I don't think so.'

Cags returned and sure enough he had found the man's keys underneath the seat in the pub. We got him through the front door and he turned to us with the box of Milk Tray in his hands. 'Here, you can have these, lads. I've not really got anyone else to give them to.'

We tried to refuse but he insisted and when we took them he gave a little smile. He promised to clean up his cheek and put a plaster on it. We waved him goodbye and walked away.

I think about Mr Goblin Meat Pie every Christmas Eve and it still makes me sad.

Chicken Shit

From the age of fourteen I always tried to get a summer job to give me some extra money to spend on records, Airfix kits, football magazines and new clothes. Spud-picking was always available but was absolutely backbreaking and badly paid, so this particular summer I tried my luck with a job at the Chubby Chicken frozen chicken factory near Stokesley.

So, one morning I arrived at the factory early, around 7 a.m. It was a hot summer's day and I was just wearing some old jeans and an old Middlesbrough Football Club replica shirt.

All the summer students were asked to gather in the yard until the foreman came out and allocated the individual jobs. When he got there, he sent the first group of lads to take the chickens out of the cages when they arrived on the lorries. They were then placed upside down secured by their feet onto a sort of eye-level conveyer belt that trundled them into the factory.

The next group of lads were taken into the factory, where they stood either side of a conveyer belt and used a gun-like machine to inject water into the chickens' thighs and breasts.

The third group of lads were sent off to the packing station, where they would put the frozen chickens in boxes, tape them up and load them into the fridges or the refrigerated lorries that arrived every hour or so.

Only two of us remained. The other lad was given a broom and told to sweep the yard and the loading bays. Then the foreman turned to me.

'Right, only you left, son. Come with me, I've got a special job for you,' he said. He handed me a blue boiler suit and a pair of huge rubber boots that went over your shoes, and I followed him into the factory. The first room I encountered was like something out of a *Saw* movie. Along one wall at table height was a long, stainless steel trough that disappeared through the far wall into the next section of the factory, and it was flowing with a river of bright-red blood.

The chickens would arrive in this room suspended on the conveyor belt they had been trussed to outside. Seated in front of the trough was one solitary lady. As each chicken approached her, she would pull its neck downwards and slit it wide open with a razor, allowing the blood to start spurting into the trough. The thing that struck me more than anything is that this lady was doing this in complete isolation. It was just her, the vibrant red blood, the shining steel trough and the final cries of the chickens. What must her dreams have been like?

I was then taken up some metal stairs to the first floor and along a corridor to the far end of the building. We went into a large room that was completely empty apart from one of those big commercial wheelie bins with a lid that you find around the back of the shops. The room had brick walls and a shiny concrete floor, and there was one door at the end of it marked Fire Escape. The foreman then revealed the nature of my 'special' job.

In the ceiling at one end of the room was a large hole about the size of a dustbin lid, directly above the wheelie bin. At the other end of the room was another dustbin-sized hole, but this time it was cut into the floor.

'You are stood on top of what is basically an oven,' the fore-man explained. 'From time to time all the chicken bits that can't be eaten will come out of that hole in the ceiling and drop into the bin. When it's full, you wheel it over and open the panel on the side to spill out the contents and then fork them into the oven hole.

He handed me a garden fork and then walked away, only stopping at the door to shout, 'Sunderland till I die!', before disappearing down the corridor, laughing as he went. Sunderland Football Club are the local rivals to Middlesbrough, whose jersey I was wearing.

I had made a terrible mistake in my choice of clothing.

I stood in the empty room, getting hotter and hotter, for an hour or so, and nothing happened. Then the atmosphere in the room began to change. Invisible vapours were coming from the oven hole that smelt like a mixture of fish food and kebab meat that's been pissed on by a dog. And then I heard it – quite distant at first: a low, growling rumble coming towards me from above. It sounded like a huge serpent with the moo of a cow making its way through the pipes to seek me out and destroy me. The first substance to arrive at the hole in the ceiling was a cylindrical mass of wet feathers, so dense they kept their form and shape as sections of it broke off and landed in the wheelie bin.

As soon as the wheelie bin was three-quarters full, I dragged it over to the hole in the floor and opened the door panel on the side. The feathers had formed into one uncooperative lump in the shape of the bin. I had to dig into it with my fork and loosen small lumps of it before I could pull them by hand out of the bin.

Meanwhile, at the other end of the room, the wet feathers are continuing to drop from the ceiling and a small mountain of them is forming. I decide that the wheelie bin is not the best tool for this job. I walk over to the feather mountain and begin manipulating the whole lot towards the oven hole. By the time I have stuffed them down the hole into the oven, a new feather mountain has already formed.

The room is getting hotter and more humid. And the smells are changing. The dog is now shitting on the kebab meat right next to a burning pyre of chimps' fingers.

I began to push the new boulder of feathers and am halfway across the room when the rumbling stops and the feather cascade ceases. Sweet relief, I just need to get this lot into the oven and I'm done till the next batch. Then a new noise comes from the pipes above the room – louder, more urgent, a bit like bricks in a concrete mixer or heavily booted mice invading a downpipe.

SPLAT!

This was not a cascade; this was an avalanche, and it kept coming and coming ... hundreds and hundreds of complete chicken heads, chicken feet and various pieces of unidentifiable ligaments, cartilage and tubings. Soon they were spreading and forming a small lake of misery. Every time I thrust my fork into the mass to move it towards the oven hole, my fork would emerge with a head or a foot attached to its prongs. The slop kept coming and coming, and the smell started to burn and scratch at my brain and my lungs. It was now about halfway up my rubber wellies and I was making slow progress in teasing it into the hole. The natural slope of the floor was not in my favour, either.

And then, yet another noise from above as the avalanche of heads and feet stopped – like a washing machine or dishwasher on a rinse cycle. As before, it got louder the nearer it came and then ...

SPLASH!

A waterfall of blood, faeces, leakages and residues rushed down from the ceiling and onto the mass of heads and feet. This was a torrent, and soon it was over the rim of my wellies. The smell was unbearable. I felt like I was breathing and eating the air at the same time. My stomach began to wretch and I puked into the quagmire of chicken death. I could bear it no more and ran over to the fire escape door and unbolted it. Beyond it was a metal escape ladder that I clambered down, into an empty field at the back of the factory. I didn't want to explain myself to the foreman, or anyone else for that matter, so I just removed the boiler suit and boots and ran out of the compound via the nearest hedge.

A few days later, I received four hours' pay for that morning of horror. As I remember it was about £3, which of course nowadays would be about the price of a cheap frozen chicken.

The Band

Harry Harriman, Cagsy and I decided to form a punk band in the long hot summer of 1976. We were all seventeen years old. My eldest brothers both played bass guitar for local bands, and there was a lovely semi-acoustic Hofner in our house that I would often strum upon when my brothers were out. So that was me on the bass and vocals. Cagsy agreed to be drummer despite having no drums and Harry declared himself the guitarist despite having no guitar.

Harry's dad agreed to fork out for a guitar and amp for him, so we all went to Hamiltons music shop in the town centre to help chose his axe and amplifier. All three of us were immediately drawn to a see-through Perspex flying-V-shaped guitar. Its makers had no pedigree and it was of dubious quality, but it was SEE-THROUGH! Just imagine being able to stare at Harry's huge gut via the prism of cheap Japanese Perspex. It was an easy choice. For our amp, we bought a unit that promised the most volume for the least outlay. As I recall, it was a bruised and battered second-hand 100-watt Marshall stack – a brutal unit that could certainly rattle the pipes of a two-bed bungalow or vibrate the decking outside a Wimpy executive four-bed detached house.

All we needed was a set of drums, and in our local newspaper, the *Evening Gazette*, we saw a small ad offering a set of drums for £8. Cags and I arranged to go and see them. They were owned by a slim, shifty-looking middle-aged bloke living in a terraced two-up two-down house in central Middlesbrough. He answered the door in his donkey jacket and never took it off. He smoked a roll-up cigarette that he was able to keep attached to his lip as he spoke. I can't remember his name, so let's call him Alfie Tobacco.

'Alright, mate, we're here about the drum kit.'

'Oh aye, drum kit is it. Come in, it's in the front room.'

We walked through into this front room, which was empty apart from a TV, an easy chair, a large cardboard box and a glass tank with a big snake in it.

'Sorry about the heat in here, it's for the snake. It needs heat or it canea gan.'

'No worries, have you got the kit to look at?'

'Oh you want to see it, d'ya?'

'Yeah, that would work well for us.'

'It's in the box. You'll have to unpack it yerselves. My fingers are fucked. I got our lass to pack it up and she's up the social.'

Cags bent down and began to unpack the various pieces from the box. It held a bass drum, a tom-tom, a snare drum and a hi-hat, along with various metal rods, clamps and pedals. Having no knowledge of drum kits or drumming, Cags just picked bits up, stared at them for a few moments, then returned them to the box. He then turned to the bloke and said, 'Does it work?'

'Aye, if ya bang at it hard enough. Do you want to see me snake?'

'Yeah, why not? Is it slithery?'

'Aye, all snakes are slithery because of the way they move, but he's not slippery if that's what ya mean. Here, let me fetch him.'

Alfie lifted the lid off the plastic tank and pulled out a large fat yellow snake, some sort of python I think. He placed it over his shoulder like a yoke. The snake's head poked out horizontally and licked the air. We had to hope that it didn't bear any sort of grudge against non-drummers.

'What's he called?'

'Filbert. You know, like the old-fashioned nut. Give him a stroke.'

'Do you mind if I put the kit together and check it all fits?' asked Cags.

'There's no need to do that, son, it's all there. I had a final bang about on it yesterday and it worked perfect. Here, have a touch on Filbert.'

Alfie took a few steps over to Cags and encouraged the snake to investigate him. The snake slowly lifted its head upwards so that it was staring directly at Cagsy's chin.

'Go on, give him a stroke. He likes having a fuss.'

Cagsy stretched out his hand and gave Filbert a little rub along its chest. Filbert didn't like it and started to emit a low rumbling noise from his throat. Cags withdrew his hand sharply and then Filbert raised his head even higher and opened his mouth wide to hiss directly into Cagsy's face.

'Don't worry about Filbert. He's just in a bad mood. Do you want the kit then or not?'

Cags was desperate to get away. 'Yeah I'll take it, seems a nice kit,' he blurted. He quickly took the £8 from his pocket and we scarpered out of there as quickly as we could.

The next day we held our first band practice in the garage of Harry's house. As Cags assembled his drum kit, it became immediately apparent that it was a small kit for the larger child. At 6ft 2ins, it hardly came above Cagsy's knees. I guess we had been 'Filberted'. Still, like Alfie had said, it made a decent noise if you banged at it hard enough, and our new amplifier certainly made a racket.

The first job, of course, was to choose a name for the band. The ones I can remember being suggested were:

Haversack

11 Heads

Spew

Nutty Shite

In the end, though, we settled on the name Dog Dirt. We must have thought it sounded rebellious and provocative. The first song we wrote reflected this faux attitude and was called

'Suits Me Fine'. It was awful. I can still remember the lyrics, and my embarrassment is not over yet.

> *I don't want to go to school*
> *Cos it just isn't cool*
> *I'll break every rule*
> *Because I'm nobody's fool*
>
> *And*
> *It suits me suits me suits me fine*
> *Yes*
> *It suits me suits me suits me fine*
>
> *I don't want to comply*
> *And I'll tell you why*
> *I'll save doing what I'm told*
> *Till when I'm sick and old*
>
> *And*
> *It suits me suits me suits me fine*
> *Yes*
> *It suits me suits me suits me fine*
>
> *Don't ask me to stand in line*
> *You'll be wasting your time*
> *You drink lemon and lime*
> *I drink whiskey and wine*
>
> *And*

It suits me suits me suits me fine
Yes
It suits me suits me suits me fine

The song was about ninety seconds long and instead of a middle eight had a short, children's-drum-kit solo. We practised at Harry's house for a few weeks until we had a set list of four songs: 'Suits Me Fine'; 'I'm Going to Mars (Where They Have No Cars)'; 'All People Are Fat'; and 'Alright Now' (cover version).

Our first gig was at a youth club held in a small church hall on Green Lane. In preparation for the night, I had bought myself some skinny-leg black corduroy trousers. These were not easy to source in Middlesbrough, as the shops were full of work and military wear, loon trousers (28ins minimum bottom leg hem), various versions of flared jeans and the ubiquitous 'A' line slacks. I eventually found what I needed in the womens-wear section of C&A. I was a skinny boy back then. I adorned my black barathea school jacket with safety pins and badges and tied a load of my mum's belts around my ankles. To top it all off, I spiked my hair up to a good height using a sugar-and-water solution.

There were other bands playing that night and we were first up on stage. This was to be my first ever public appearance and the first words I ever uttered to an audience.

'Good evening. We are Dog Dirt!' And then we tore into the opening of 'Suits Me Fine'. I can still remember the strange feeling of exhilaration in my stomach and my chest. I could hardly bark out the pathetic lyrics through the huge grin that literally took over my face. And then it came to the drum solo. Crash, bang fricking wallop went Cags, and then disaster: the bass drum pedal supplied by Alfie Tobacco buckled under the pressure and collapsed. Cags was unable to bluff a solo on his little tom-tom drum and, lacking the experience to ride this moment, we stopped playing, apologised and left the stage. So that was Dog Dirt indeed.

I don't recall us ever performing live again. We'd got up on stage and given it a go. We had no talent, but we'd had a laugh, and at least I get to say I was in a punk band back in the day.

Among all this arsefoolery, I continued to play football both for my school team and for Middlesbrough Boys Under 16s. I wasn't the best player in the team, but I wasn't far off. Middlesbrough Football Club usually signed up about three or four players from the boys' team on Youth Training Scheme contracts, so I reckoned I had a sniff. After the final training session of the season, the squad was told to stay behind and one by one we were summoned into the coach's hut to find out our fate. I was about the eighth to be called in.

'Have you enjoyed the season, Robert?'

'Yes, sir.'

'You don't seem to mix very well with the other lads. Is there some sort of problem?'

'No, sir.'

It's true what he was saying. Throughout the three years with the team I doubt I had said more than a couple of words to my teammates. They were all from other schools and my shyness forbade me from speech. I would just turn up, get my kit on, practise, play and then leave as quickly and as quietly as I could. Even with my new-found gang of friends, those practices and matches were a dreadful reminder of how ill-equipped I still was for the real world.

'You're a good little player, son, but we don't think you've got what it takes, so I'm sorry, the club won't be signing you on.'

'Thank you, sir.'

'I hope you'll continue to play, and always remember that you play football for the fun of it and for the companionship. Good luck.'

Well, he was right in one respect. I had enjoyed the football, but I hadn't made a single friend.

So, my dream was shattered in just one short minute. I walked slowly from the sports ground, passing the mental asylum where my granny was being cared for. I stopped outside its gates and stared at the huge Victorian brick edifice with its fancy clock tower and manicured front lawns. 'I didn't make it, Granny,' I whispered under my breath. The building just stared back at me, impenetrable, ominous and chilling ... just like how my future felt at that moment.

7

OCTOBER 2015

Everybody's a dreamer
And everybody's a star
And everybody's in showbiz
It doesn't matter who you are

The Kinks, 1972

We are back in my bed in the intensive care unit of the hospital. It's the morning after I took my floating journey up the yew-lined tunnel towards my peaceful destiny. I open my eyes and my son Harry comes into focus, and then beside me my wife, Lisa. I'm not dead. A charge of elation courses through my body. I say hello and then drift back off to sleep.

Later that day I am woken by a nurse and find myself seated upright in a chair in the intensive care unit. Lisa is there. We both cried and I ate a jelly. As happens with me most days of my life, I was absolutely craving a pork pie. It was an intense craving that can only be sated by the touch of hard, watery pastry against my lips. I knew deep down that my pie-eating days were coming to end, as they are not really compatible with a heart-healthy diet, but at this moment, in my vulnerable state, I was the new Baby King and could demand whatever I wanted. The nurse said that the main priority was to get my bowels moving, and that if a pork pie was what I fancied, then a pork pie is what I shall have. Lisa went and fetched me the pie and a custard trifle (she knows me well). I devoured the pie, poured the trifle down my throat, and fell asleep.

The following day I was moved to a single room. I was still attached to quite an array of medical machinery but I was now wide awake and fully conscious. The downside of this was that I was also now much more aware of the pain in my chest and my left leg where they had taken an artery for grafting. The incision into my breastbone had been stuck back together with metal staples, and any small movement in any direction would make the unhealed bone creak and pop. Laughing or coughing became a frightening experience. Sneezing was like taking a sniper's bullet dead-centre of your chest. Unfortunately, due to the state of my lungs, it was very important that I forced myself to cough regularly to bring up the remaining tar and nonsense that had become dislodged. I had a special towel that had been rolled up into a cylinder and taped into shape. Whenever I coughed, I would press the towel into my chest in an attempt to take some of the pressure off the staples.

I seemed to be recovering well though, and it slowly dawned upon on me that I had been given a second chance in life – or at least a shove to a new beginning.

Lisa stayed in a nearby hotel and visited me twice every day.

There was a Marks & Spencer near the hospital, so she would regularly pop out and get me something I fancied. I had lots of processed meats – corned beef, tongue, more pork pie – and lots of cream cakes. I was also approved to have visitors. I was still on a drip for parts of the day and I had a number of tubes coming out of my lower neck. I thought it would be good for people to see me like this so they might think me a brave and fearless hero.

Now, I should say that, at this point in my life, I didn't have many friends. I still saw my old mate Cags from time to time, usually to go to see Middlesbrough football team play. And about twice a year I might arrange to see Matt Berry and Reece Shearsmith for a boozy gossip club night in London.

Reece is the most pleasant, unpretentious and hilarious company you could ever wish for. He specialises in a faux grumpiness that could be unsettling to an observer, and he is beyond question the best improviser in the business. The first time I worked with him was in 2003 on the comedy drama *Catterick*, written by me and Jim. On the first day of shooting he was playing a thief that had to pretend to be a used-car salesman because I interrupted him while he was in the middle of robbing the showroom. To keep his cover intact, he had to take me on a test drive of a vehicle, and we needed to improvise a little bit of chit-chat before we set off.

'You ever driven an automatic before?' he asked.

'No,' I said. 'But I've heard of them.'

'Oh, well as long as you've heard about them, we're alright, aren't we? If you've heard of them, then we're all sitting pretty, aren't we?'

79

It was said with such disgust and dismissiveness that I buckled up with laughter. It took five or six takes for me to complete the scene without corpsing. He knows he can crack me up at the drop of a hat when we are acting together and I can usually see the mischievous look in his eye when he has decided to corpse me off.

Matt Berry is another wholly unpretentious gem of a man who giggles like a big cuddly baby when amused. He has a total but loving contempt for me and everything I have ever done, and is another one that has no fear of winging it when we work together. The first time I met Matt was in 2005, when we were filming a sketch I had written for the TV show *Monkey Trousers*. In the sketch I played an antiques expert who had a slot on a morning TV show presented by Matt. I met him just outside the studio door and we both agreed that the sketch was pretty weak. I asked him if he had any ideas about how we could liven it up. 'Well,' he said, 'I can burp on demand,' and then proceeded to reel off a sequence of differently pitched burps. 'That's it,' I said. 'Let's swap roles and you can be a miserable antiques expert who burps after every other sentence.' Matt agreed and we basically just winged the little sketch, as neither of us had learned the other's lines. We filmed three of these sketches that morning and both ourselves and all the crew were reduced to tears of laughter for hour after hour. (I believe there is an out-take tape of that morning, which I highly recommend you hunt down.)

And of course there was Jim. We would write together nearly every day in the kitchen at my house. He would arrive at about ten in the morning and we would work through to around two or three o'clock depending on how our creative juices were flowing. It never felt like work and we had been hard at it for the past twenty-five years. So, basically, I spent my days with Jim and my evenings with Lisa watching the telly. I love watching the telly with a beer, cheese and a bar of chocolate.

Sadly, this behaviour would have to stop after my discharge. The dietician at the hospital had instructed me that I was only allowed to eat a matchbox-sized piece of cheese every week, and chocolate only at Christmas and Easter. Thankfully she didn't mention the booze.

It was a right pick-me-up to have visitors. Jim came in, a bit worse for wear from a Halloween party at Jonathan Ross's house the night before. I hadn't spoken to him since our telephone call when I told him about my operation and we cancelled the tour. He was very emotional and gave me a hug as we both shed a tear. Jim isn't much of one for flaunting his emotions, but this was quite an epic moment. I think it made us both realise just how intertwined and reliant upon each other we were and also shone an awful little light on the fact that one day in the future we wouldn't have each other to play with. Later that week, Jim painted a lovely picture of me laid in my bed with all the tubes and pipes coming from my neck and arms. He painted a big colourful vibrant heart on my chest and had me giving the thumbs-up sign. Like me, I think he was hoping for the best for the two of us in the coming years.

Damien Hirst popped in to see me with his mate Antony Genn. I hadn't seen either of them for years. He arrived with a carrier bag of goodies for me and a mystery present in a white cardboard box. The goodie bag contained a colouring book of monsters, a courgette, a cuddly toy and some Percy Pigs. With the possible exception of Jim, Damien is the funniest male in the UK. He has a way with words and imagery like no other I have ever met. This is the text conversation we had prior to my operation, when he contacted me out of the blue:

DAMIEN: Was just thinking about you walking past a fella holding a box of lightbulbs and a sack of chimp offal

ME: That's Leslie my bulb supplier . . . good man . . . Hey just found out my heart is fucked. Have to have a quadruple heart bypass next Tuesday . . . come and watch if you want

DAMIEN: Shit man. Its standard these days tho . . . gives you years

ME: I'm shitting myself . . . will I still be able to fight

DAMIEN: You will be better at it . . . maybe leave it a day or two before you kick off

ME: I'm a level 6 fighter at the moment . . . would love to be a 7 one day

DAMIEN: You will be way above that in about 6 weeks . . . your head butt will be back too

ME: I'm just about to make a will . . . going to leave you my cock

DAMIEN: Balls please . . . where there's muck there's brass . . . whose going with you next week . . . Bradley Walsh?

ME: Just the wife

DAMIEN: You're going to be fine Boss . . . I can feel it.

I opened the mysterious cardboard box that Damien had brought for me. Inside was an old-fashioned sweet jar. Inside the jar, floating in formaldehyde, was a crimson-red ox heart with a silver crossbow arrow fired through it. On the side of the jar Damien had written: 'Get well soon ... for little Bobby and his amazing centipede, Damien XXX'. Such a beautiful gift and a constant reminder to me of the day that I found hope for the future.

It was so good to see them. Damien made me laugh so hard. I was crying with laughter and yelping in pain as every chuckle stabbed my chest like a knife. I was so happy. It was my first indication that life could still be fun. I suppose that ever since my dad died I have been, in the most general sense, quite a sad type of bloke. These little moments of unthinking spontaneous laughter are when life seems worth living to me. Without them or without the prospect of their occasional presence, I am at a bit of a loss. It had been many days since my face had cracked a smile. It happened again the following day.

My first rehabilitation target was to get out of hospital, and my second was to be fit enough to perform the second half of our national tour, which started in just twelve weeks' time. My surgeon, Chris Young, set out my criteria for discharge from hospital: have a shit, have a shower and walk the whole hospital floor corridor and up one flight of steps under my own steam. Every patient on the floor had the same set of discharge requirements, so the corridor was constantly full of blokes shuffling along in their slippers trying to beat their previous day's distance.

If I passed a fellow heart walker, I would always stop for a chat. One bloke was about fifty years old, Scottish I think, and clearly fit as a fiddle before his heart packed up on him.

'Alright, mate. You're shifting well.'

'I haven't had a shit for three days and I'm eating like a horse. Something has got to give. Have you had a shit?'

A stranger swearing straight to my face in formal surroundings has always amused me greatly. I laughed out loud and immediately regretted it. My breastbone creaked and delivered a brief sharp pain, as if a lung dweller was nailing a picture to the lining of my chest.

He remained stony-faced.

'No,' I replied after I'd recovered myself, 'I sat on the pot for a while but nothing doing. I think they are going to give me something to get it moving.'

'I've got some figs. Do you want some? Supposed to make it like rush hour down there.'

'Yeah, thanks, that would be great.'

'So what are you in here for?'

'I had a triple bypass.'

'Oh, I had a quadruple – much, much worse.'

'And how are you getting on?'

'Pretty shit. This fucking coughing is doing my head in.'

'Yeah, is it hurting your chest?'

'Oh man, my chest is moving about like a fucking shipwreck . . . I think soon it will break open.'

'My nurse told me that you should try not to cough but to "huff".'

'Huff? What the fuck is "huff"?'

'It's like you just expel air from the bottom of your lungs and push it out. You don't actually form a cough on your throat. It puts less pressure on your chest. I'll show you.'

I started huffing and he joined in.

'Come on ... Huff ... Huff ... Huff ... Huff ...'

We both stood there in the corridor, holding on to our walking frames, huffing and puffing in unison like two boxers recovering from heavy body punches. Soon, a nurse came from her station to check what was happening.

'Are you two OK?

'Yeah, we're fine,' my new friend replied. 'You can Huff off.'

I laughed again and suffered. My mate didn't laugh and continued with his huffing as he walked away. He never did bring me any figs, but I would occasionally hear him passing outside my door. I knew it was him because as far as I was aware we were the only two Huffers on the ward.

I spent the rest of the week walking the ward every hour on the hour. I was very slow, shuffling rather than walking. It wasn't that I didn't have the energy or was in too much pain. It was simply the psychological barrier of putting too much strain on your heart. In my head I would imagine the stitches in my arteries bulging and leaking, just waiting to burst open and destroy me. Despite Dr Young's and the nurses' reassurances, I just couldn't convince myself that stitches could properly secure any pipe that has liquid flowing through it. I mean, when you make a stitch, you make a hole; when you make hundreds of stitches, you make hundreds of holes.

On Monday morning, one week after my admission, I declared to the lovely Irish nurse supervising my stay that I felt ready to leave. I had had a small shit and had survived a low-flow lukewarm shower. It was time for me to take the corridor and stairs test. I walked briskly this time, hoping to impress. She asked me how I was feeling emotionally and I told her that I felt 'different' – slightly euphoric, which was very unusual for me. She told me that every heart patient feels like a slightly different person after the operation.

'Nobody is ever the same after another human being has physically touched their heart. You should always hope that it is a good and kind man that holds it in their hand, and Dr Young is a good man,' she said.

I passed my test and was told I could go home. My wife helped me into her car and we drove away. I think I had a Scotch egg on the journey. Whenever I am out and about I take some pocket meat with me, and the Scotch egg is probably the king of the portable pocket meats. It creates quite a bulge in the jacket, but I'm long past caring about that sort of thing. Other pocket meats that I enjoy are a pork pie, Pepperami sausage (especially pertinent in the summer, when it can be slipped into your jean or shorts pocket), a foil-wrapped chicken quarter and a four-slice pack of corned beef. They are all portable treats and I find it's quite a rush passing and meeting strangers with your little meat secret nestling in your pocket.

An hour and a half later, I was back in my living room, in my pyjamas, sat on my favourite sofa watching the TV. My cats Goodmonson and Mavis seemed nonplussed by my arrival but I was very pleased to see them. As I sat there luxuriating in my sick-bed status, I started to get scared. I was no longer in the hospital, just mere feet away from medical attention. Now it was just me, the wife and the cats. My cats are very adept at nursing, but their speciality is not cardiology. My heart was beating fast, butterflies were flying around my stomach, and I wanted to sit there perfectly still and not move an inch for the rest of my life.

8

1977

Meet me on the corner
When the lights are coming on
And I'll be there
I promise I'll be there
Down the empty streets
We'll disappear into the dawn
If you have dreams enough to share

Lindisfarne, 1971

It's summertime and I am on a camping holiday with Cagsy in Keswick in the Lake District. We are eighteen, and we have been there together every year, sometimes twice. We camp on a farmer's field just above Ashness Bridge. Every day we walk the three miles from the campsite into town. We have breakfast in the Golden Egg café next to the bus station and then play a round of pitch-and-putt golf by the lake. Most days we hire a rowing boat and drift around the lake, stopping off on one of the little islands and having an explore. We always take a fishing rod and some spinners so that we can try our luck at catching a perch or a pike. Some days we buy a whole chicken and some potatoes from the supermarket and take them back to the lakeside beach at Ashness, where we make a campfire in the rocks and cook up the chicken and the spuds. At night we go to the Royal Oak pub in the centre of town, where they have a live folk-music evening three times a week.

I loved these nights in the Royal Oak. They were my first experience of intimate live entertainment. The audiences would comprise no more than twenty people and as each nervous, earnest performer arrived under the spotlight I would pore over every detail of their clothing and their faces. If it was a married couple, I would try to assess whether they were happy together or not. Did she approve of his beard? Did she still fancy him? Were they swingers? Was he a teacher or was he a murderer? Did they ever get in the bath together? Did they murder together? Each performer, young or old, would have their own backstory in my mind.

The sheer bravery and gall of the performers to get on stage blew me away. Very few of these amateurs seemed confident, and they were usually apologetic in their demeanour. A part of me, deep down, well beyond my grasp, wanted to be up there on stage. If these quiet, sincere people could do it, then why not me? I wanted the audience to be making up *my* backstory. I wanted to be the centre of their universe, if only for a few minutes. I wanted to be a shared memory. I wanted to be important to some strangers.

One night, I got my chance. The compere of the evening

was a large, bearded bloke who insisted on wearing a beige cheesecloth shirt with thin red stripes about two sizes too small for him. The buttons were under great strain and the thin red stripes zoomed around his body contours like details from an Ordnance Survey map. He wore a cowboy hat and magnificent red and black cowboy boots. He was the King of Lakeland Folk and performed with a little house band made up of local hobbits. This particular night he addressed the audience and asked if anyone wanted to come up and sing a song by the band Lindisfarne. Their album *Fog on the Tyne* had been in the Top 50 of the charts for many years and most people knew a Lindisfarne song or two. My stomach immediately began to churn, not because I was worried I would be picked on, but because I desperately wanted to get on stage and my body was fighting against this never-before-experienced desire. Suddenly I was up on my feet and walking onto the stage.

'Big round of applause please, ladies and gentleman,' said The King. There was no applause from the tiny audience, just a half-arsed 'whoop' from Cagsy. I sang 'Meet Me on the Corner' as The King held the microphone to my mouth and slowly revealed that he stank of meat paste. I could only remember the first two verses and the chorus, so I just repeated them until the band stopped and The King withdrew the microphone. I went back to my seat and sat there speechless for a few minutes. It had been exhilarating, and I had the feeling that there was another, totally different, Robert Mortimer somewhere inside me just waiting to come out and replace me. How I had the nerve to get up on that stage I will never know. Booze probably.

There was, however, a cloud on the horizon. I had applied to go to university that September and my A-level results would be posted up at my school on the day we returned from the Lakes. The larger part of me wanted my results to be awful so that I didn't have to leave my happy life on Teesside. So that I didn't have to leave my mum living alone in our house on Tollesby Road. As it happened, I got the A-levels I needed and would be heading to the University of Sussex just outside Brighton to study law. It gave me no joy. I had only chosen this university because at the time I was obsessed with the album *Quadrophenia* by The Who. This was a double-album rock opera where the anti-hero, 'Jimmy', took a trip to Brighton to go and 'find himself'. Cagsy also got the results he needed and would be off to Reading University to study fine art.

The fact that I got the A-levels I needed was down to my sociology and British government teacher, Mr Bill Whittingham. Most people have a favourite teacher that heavily influenced their life, and Bill was mine. Unlike the rest of the teachers at the school, Bill had a very informal approach to teaching. He wore his hair long and slightly scruffy and favoured a sports jacket on top of a yellow or red polo neck as his teaching uniform. If he was in a good mood he would start his lessons by playing the Neil Diamond song 'Cracklin Rose' on a small Dansette record player – you know, to get us in the mood for study . . . He encouraged lively discussion and debate and introduced me to writers such as Karl Marx, Talcott Parsons and Karl Heinz Popper. I loved it; these were ideas that up until then I didn't know existed. It seemed like a secret world that had previously been kept from me. You didn't just receive Bill's lessons; you participated in them. It felt very adult.

In his cupboard he had a small remote-controlled toy lion that could either scratch with its front paw or bow its head. If you made a valuable contribution, he would place it on your palm and make it deliver a nuzzle with its head. If you messed up or handed in a duff essay, then it would 'strike' you with its paw.

Before one lesson, Harry, Cags and I had sat on the playing field at lunchtime and recorded various noises on an old Phillips cassette player. There was the sound of a fly buzzing, shrieks of the word 'Wolf!', and various other exclamations, including the F-word. Just before the lesson started we pressed play on the recorder and hid it above the ceiling tiles in the classroom. Once the sounds started to kick in, the whole class, including Bill, were very confused. It was impossible to tell where these voices were coming from. Eventually Bill lost his rag and said he was going to fetch the headmaster. As soon as he left the room, Cags climbed up on his desk and removed the recorder. Bill, of course, did not fetch the headmaster – he was just giving us a chance to stop the situation escalating. At the end of the lesson he called Cags and me back and gave us both a strike with the hand lion.

I kept in touch with Bill right up until his death a few years ago. Whenever I went up to Middlesbrough, Cags and I would have a drink with him in his beloved Little Theatre Club on The Avenue. On one such evening we were having a debate about something or other and Bill said (jokingly I hope), 'Do you know what? I'm not even sure that you like me.'

'Come off it, Bill,' I replied. 'You're practically my dad.' Now I look back, I think he probably was as near as I ever got to having a father during those teenage years.

September soon came around and I loaded myself and my suitcase onto a National Express coach bound for London. It was truly awful saying goodbye to my mum. A grieving widow for the past eleven years, and now totally alone and left to fend for herself. I promised I would write to her every week and phone her as often as I could. I still shudder when I think of how she must have felt when she closed the door behind me and boiled the orange kettle in our green and orange kitchen.

My girlfriend Helen accompanied me to the bus station. I had been going out with her for about four years. Looking back, I think she might have been the first girl that I ever spoke more than a sentence to. One day in a lesson a note had been passed to me by one of her friends. It read something like 'Helen fancies you, do you fancy her?'

I replied, 'Yes, I do, thank you very much for asking.'

Another note was passed to me. 'Meet her at the electricity substation after school?'

'I will do that,' I replied. We met at the substation and I was required to walk her to her bus stop. We ended up walking the whole way to her house in Thornaby, about three miles away. The next day I received another note.

'Do you want to be Helen's boyfriend?'

'Yes, very much so,' I replied.

So that was it: I had a girlfriend. We never acknowledged each other during school but would see each other a couple of evenings a week at her house to listen to records and prac- tise snogging. I would listen to Roxy Music; she would listen to David Essex. I think that by the time we were saying our goodbyes at the bus station we thought we would be together for ever, despite the fact that she was staying in Middlesbrough to go to art college. (In fact, I have only ever had one girlfriend who didn't go to art college. I must like art college girls. Come to think of it, all of my close male friends – Cagsy, Jim, Reece, Matt, Damien – also went to art college. I'm just an art college groupie.)

The University of Sussex is a 1960s-campus-style university a few miles out of Brighton in the middle of nowhere. It's like a small concrete town, with its own church, sports facilities, shops and accommodation contained within the site. It was a cold, rainy night when I arrived and dragged my suitcase up the 'East Slope' to my accommodation. The Slope consisted of hundreds of separate eight-bedroom, white-walled concrete units. It had the feel of a holiday camp and the look of an army barracks. I went through the front door and straight to my room, which contained a small bed, a table, a chair and a lamp. It all felt like a terrible mistake. I missed my mum, I missed my gang and I missed my girlfriend. Still, it could only get better, I kidded myself.

On my bed was a welcome pack. Tomorrow was Fresher's Day, where you could join one of the multitude of clubs that were on offer. They all sounded shit. I joined something called the Libertarian Anarchists Society (I think this was probably an attempt to make my old teacher Bill Whittingham proud of me) and also the university football club. As always, I was hoping that playing football would somehow see me through. Also, tomorrow evening was a gathering for all the law students in some refectory room where we could meet each other and have wine and cheese.

So, the following night, after signing up for football training, I went to this meet-and-greet. I felt it was important that I wore an outfit that said something about the type of person I was. So, in the hope that it might help me to meet like-minded people, I chose a Middlesbrough football shirt, a Wrangler denim jacket, skinny beige Levi cords and bright-red Kicker boots. When I got to the get-together, my heart sank. Nearly all the lads were wearing dark dinner suits and ties, and the lasses all wore what I have come to know as cocktail dresses. In one visual hammer blow, central Middlesbrough came up hard against the Home Counties. I had never felt so out of place in my life. I turned on my heels and went back to my shitty room. Things were not going to get better. And so commenced the unhappiest three years of my life.

9

NOVEMBER 2015

Hey hey the cripple creek ferry
Butting through the overhanging trees
Make way for the cripple creek ferry
The water's going down, it's a mighty tight squeeze

Neil Young, 1971

I'm at home and I'm getting better and feeling a bit more confident every day. My wife takes me for a little walk twice a day,
and my aim is to be able to do 10,000 steps a day by Christmas.
My first walk is just the thirty feet to the end of my drive and
back. We increase the distance every day and within a week or
so I am able to easily walk half a mile. The main problem at this
time is sleeping. While your breastbone is healing, it is very difficult to lie on your side, and I found that I was absolutely unable
to fall asleep lying on my back. Furthermore, if you did sneak
onto your side during sleep, you would hear your breastbone
crunching and slipping and be woken by a painful bolt across

the chest. I would say it was about six weeks before I was able to sleep properly. At around this time, I switched from walking every day to gently jogging around my local park. At first I was jogging pensioner-style, all tiny steps with chest puffed out and arms tucked into my sides. After a couple of weeks, though, I was flying round the park like a greyhound on his way to collect an MBE.

I attended my first NHS heart rehabilitation session. There I learn the basic equation for maintaining your heart health:

1. Don't smoke

2. Eat a diet low in saturated fats

3. Take a statin every day (a cholesterol-lowering drug)

4. Take an aspirin every day (which makes the blood less sticky and helps prevent heart attacks and strokes)

5. EXERCISE

6. EXERCISE

7. EXERCISE

Basically you've got to keep that blood flowing to keep your pipework flushed and clean. Heart rehab is a twelve-week course that seeks to get your body up and running again and get you to a certain level of fitness that thereafter you are expected to maintain. The heart rehab session was at a local school assembly hall, and there were about twenty people in attendance. On arrival, we all wrote our first names on a large yellow sticker then placed it on our chests. The average age was probably somewhere near seventy. I was the second youngest ahead of one young lad aged about nineteen, who had recently undergone heart-valve replacement surgery.

In the middle of the room was a large circle of chairs. The

instructor, a portly nurse, told us all to take a seat. The first exercise was to lift up your legs alternately and hold them out in front of you for twenty seconds. The next exercise was to stand behind your chair and balance on one foot while holding on to the back of the chair. Next you had to walk around the outside of the circle so you arrived back at your chair. It began to dawn on me that perhaps this class wasn't aimed at people who were already up and running. The nurse then asked us to line up at one end of the hall and jog at our own individual pace around the perimeter of the hall. We were to return to our seat on completion of the circuit. Eventually we had all returned to our seats apart from one – a skinny little grey-haired fella in purple tracksuit bottoms, huge bright-white training shoes and a grey T-shirt with his sticker proudly displaying the name TERRY.

Terry's legs were simply shuffling along like an OAP in a post office queue, but his upper body was twisting and thrusting like an Olympic 800-metre runner approaching the finishing line. A few people began to encourage him. 'Go on, Terry!' 'You can do it, Terry!' 'Come on, Terry, not far now!' But Terry does not seem to respond; he just keeps flapping and shuffling. Then the young lad two down from me shouts out: 'Get a shift on, Terry, you daft bastard!'

The room went quiet. I laughed; this lad was a maverick. Terry seemed to respond. There was a noticeable change in the speed of his shuffle.

'Go on, Terry, you bastard!' I shouted. Terry raised his left arm and gave a little thumbs-up.

'Terry, you bastard, you can do it!' shouted the lad. Some of the group started to laugh and resumed their encouragement.

'Go on, Terry, you're nearly there!' Some started to clap. A few of us started to chant 'Terry, Terry, Terry!' To which the young lad responded with 'Bastard, bastard, bastard!' Terry had now completed the perimeter and only had twenty feet or so to go from the wall back to his seat. His upper body was now slightly bent towards one side and his right arm was pumping at a much greater speed than his left. He broke into a fast walk for the last few steps and collapsed onto his chair. The room erupted with cheers and applause. Terry was panting heavily and struggling to get his breath back. The nurse went over to him. 'Are you OK, Terry?'

Eventually he spoke. 'The lad's right. I am a daft bastard.'

I didn't attend any more rehab classes. They were clearly aimed at people in a lot worse nick than me, but I will always be grateful to Terry and his magnificent shuffle sprint for teaching me a thing or two about perseverance in the face of heart fears. I hope he and the young lad are doing good.

I didn't have any visitors to my house during this time. To be honest, I didn't really want to see anyone. I just wanted to be with Lisa and the kids and hide away from the world. There was plenty of TV to be watched, too, and I became obsessed with French crime box sets such as *Spiral* and *Braquo* and Spanish and Argentinian movies like *The Secret in Their Eyes* and *The Dark Side of the Heart*. I started watching reality shows such as *Catfish* and *Teen Mom*. I watched *The Sopranos*, *The Wire* and re-watched every film that my favourite actors had been in, from Robert Duvall through to Nicolas Cage. I was becoming institutionalised in my own home. I needed a kick up the arse, and it was to come from a most unexpected source.

10

1977–1983

I've been down but not like this before
Can't be round this kind of show no more

Little Feat, 1975

University is full of strangers. Strangers are my biggest fear and my greatest challenge – a challenge I'm afraid I was not up to. I shared my flat on East Slope with seven other students, and my initial basic survival tactic was to avoid them at all costs. I had the room nearest the front door, so it was just a short few steps to get out of there and return unnoticed. I would usually have a tutorial and a couple of lectures every day, and it was easy to remain anonymous in the lecture halls before scurrying off back to my room as soon as the lectures finished, while the other students mingled and laughed and made arrangements for fabulous parties (I imagined). Tutorials were slightly trickier, as the tutor groups consisted of about six students and we had to gather outside the teacher's room before each tutorial. I was well practised at this shit though, and would just hover invisibly nearby until the door was opened. I kept my mouth shut during the tutorials too. All the other students seemed so confident and worldly. None of them spoke like me or any of my friends from Middlesbrough. They all seemed so articulate, and nothing intimidates me more than articulate people. They always make me feel small and pathetic. It's not their problem; it's mine, and still to this day, I tend to clam up when I'm in the company of 'intellectuals'. It's just not a game that I was taught and I'm very unsure of the rules. At the end of each tutorial, off I would run back to my room, like a little rat to his nest.

So that was the basic set-up of university, and I had a plan as to how to get through it. The term was only ten weeks long. Helen would come and visit me on the second weekend, I would go and visit Cags in Reading on the third weekend, and he would visit me on the fifth weekend. I would take the bus home on the sixth weekend to see Helen and my mates. Before you knew it, I would be home for Christmas.

My little room became my life. On the first weekend there, I went into town and bought myself a little portable television and a radio cassette-player with my grant money. I sat in that room for hour upon hour, working on my essays, watching TV and writing letters home to Helen and Mum. In the evening I could occasionally hear chatting and laughter coming from the communal living room or other flats on The Slope. I did of course introduce myself to the other people in the flat, but I was never able to make any real connection with them. As soon as we started to speak, a little voice in my head would be saying, 'Get back to your room as soon as possible. You are wasting your time here.'

The closest I got to making a friend was with a lad called Mark. He wore a scruffy, battered old leather jacket most days and smoked roll-ups. Of all the students I had come across, he seemed to be the one that might be 'my type'. I went to the student bar with him on a couple of occasions and we passed the time perfectly pleasantly. There was one big problem with him as a potential friend, however: he was well into drugs, and I had a great fear of all that palaver. I had never used any drug other than tobacco and booze (apart from when my mates and I once tried smoking nutmeg and banana skins). I had never even met anyone who had taken drugs. In my small Middlesbrough world, taking drugs just wasn't a thing.

One night after going to the bar with him, I went back to his room and he rolled up a joint. I took a few puffs and within minutes felt nauseous. I made my excuses, went back to my room and spewed up. Well, at least I knew that smoking dope wasn't for me. Mark remained my only friendly connection at the university, but conversation never flowed freely between us. We were from different worlds. Where were Cagsy and Harry and Stava and Helen? Many miles away.

Later that term, sometime around bonfire night, Mark declared that he had got hold of some LSD and suggested that we take it early that evening. A tiny part of me thought, *Why not? Maybe I would find a way through this awful journey via the life of a druggie.* But mainly the suggestion made me shit myself. He kept advocating the joys of this particular drug and reassuring me that it would be a great experience. I caved in and swallowed the pill.

Within minutes I regretted my decision and came out in a

cold sweat of fear. I went to the bathroom, stuck my fingers down my throat and spewed up what I thought was the entire contents of my guts. It wasn't. I had made perhaps the worst decision of my life. Eight hours later and I was lying in my bed desperately hoping that sleep might take away the awful visions and hallucinations I was experiencing. Instead, they just intensified. A huge Bengal tiger came into my room and jumped up on my bed. It started to claw at my legs. I had never known fear like it. I defecated myself and ran naked through to the lounge begging for help. There was no one there. I couldn't go back to my room. The last thing I remember was sitting on the floor of the shower cubicle rocking like a baby and begging out loud for my mum.

I woke up the next day with an overpowering feeling of loss. Sadness was pumping through every vein in my body. I had destroyed the Robert Mortimer that I knew. He was history. My spark had gone. I was fucked. At first I put this terrible feeling of dread down to the after-effects of the drug, but a week later I still felt totally lost. I wanted my old self back. *Please God, just let me return to that happy, shy, footballing boy who I had never appreciated as much as I should have.*

I went to the doctor and he prescribed me antidepressants. I hoped they would bring Robert Mortimer back, but they didn't. I would still be taking them five years later.

There is nothing much more I can say about the next three years. Cags would visit, Helen came and joined me in Brighton to study for a degree in fashion at the polytechnic, I played football on Wednesdays and I got a degree in Law. I was deeply and painfully depressed. I pretended to laugh; I pretended to enjoy people's company; I pretended to be happy. As time passed I got more and more used to it, so much so that I began to forget what it felt like to be happy and therefore didn't miss it quite so much. Apart from that first trip to the doctor, I never spoke to anyone about my depression. The old Robert Mortimer would never have done that, and if I wanted him back then I thought I should act in the same way he would.

After graduating, I returned to Middlesbrough and moved back in with my mum. Helen stayed in Brighton to finish her fashion degree. Cagsy had returned home as well and the old gang was reunited. We spent every evening in the pub and at the weekends went clubbing at Madison's or the Inn Cognito or Mandy's. Every day I would wake up hoping that the dark cloud of depression might have magically disappeared overnight, but it never did. I longed for the day when I might laugh out loud freely, and not through this veil of sadness that was slowly consuming me.

Life had to be lived, though, and I needed a job. Cags was good with a paintbrush and I had a decent set of decorating skills, so we put an advert in the local paper offering the services of 'B&M Decorators. Free estimates. No job too small. Clean and reliable.' A middle-aged lady on the Lakes estate took the bait. She wanted all her exterior paintwork done. We gave her a written estimate and she accepted. We purchased loads of sandpaper, white paint and Polyfilla and borrowed a ladder from Cagsy's dad. We loaded it all onto our bicycles and started working away on her windows and doors; Cags did the first floor and I did the ground floor. It soon became apparent, however, that the ladder we were using was too short. It only reached as high as the sills of the first-floor bedroom windows. When Cags was sanding the higher parts of those windows, I had to stand on the bottom of his ladder for him. There were years of paint layers on those windows, and the sandpaper just wasn't cutting it. Cags decided that he needed a blowlamp to remove the thick coats of paint, so he ran home and borrowed one from his dad.

Meanwhile, as I worked on the ground-floor windows, it became clear that the sills were completely rotten under the paint. The more I sanded and chipped, the more they started to crumble and fall apart. I was chasing rainbows in a clown car. There was only one answer: filler. Huge swathes, if not oceans, of filler. By the time I had finished the sills, some of them must have been 50 per cent hardened powder. The upstairs windows were to prove much more of a challenge, mainly because of their height. Cags, now armed with a blowlamp, fired it up and began heating the woodwork and scraping off the molten paint. I was at the bottom of the ladder keeping it safe. As he scraped, the hot paint strips started to tumble down onto my head and body. It was like standing beneath a giant roman candle. I looked up and shouted for Cags to stop and a hot flake hit me plum in the eye. I jumped away from the ladder and it slowly slid sideways along the sill. Cags had one foot on the ladder and one foot on the sill, and I grabbed the ladder again to stop it falling any further. He was probably only twelve feet off the ground, but it all felt very frightening. His blowlamp had fallen during the first flush of the incident and was still firing away on the front lawn, scorching the grass around it.

'Jump, Cags?' I suggested.

'Fuck off,' he replied.

The woman who owned the house appeared at the bedroom window and started to open it.

'Don't open it!' shouted Cags, worried that it might catch him and send him off balance. She opened it and Cagsy jumped in panic, falling more or less on top of the blowlamp. I ran over, picked up the blowlamp and threw it into the road. The lady appeared at the front door screaming as a car screeched to an emergency stop in the middle of the road. Cags was moaning with the pain coming from his ankle when the woman told us to pack up and leave. Meanwhile, the man whose car had stopped got out, picked up the blowlamp and drove away with it. We packed up our paints and fillers and left. That was the end of B&M Decorators. We never sent the lady a bill.

My first real job was as a bin man for Middlesbrough Borough Council. I had worked as a binny during my summer holidays from university and it was always something that I enjoyed. It's a good, healthy job that at the time offered the big advantage of 'Job and Finish'. This meant that by working our arses off we would usually have finished our daily round by midday. I was assigned to a crew of six blokes. The driver was called Archie and he was the boss. He was a thin, wiry bloke in his mid-fifties with a silvery-grey rockabilly hairstyle, and he smoked like a defective wood burner, which caused him to have a trophy 'golden' right hand. He never had to leave his cab and always looked immaculate in his faded French blue overalls and deep-tan hobnailed boots.

The rest of us wore council-issue blue boiler suits and woollen donkey jackets with faux leather shoulder inserts and cuff trims.

We were given black steel-toe boots to wear, but none of us used them as the leather was as hard as peanut brittle and would have taken many long painful years to wear in. I felt like a man – you know, a proper man who goes out to work to fetch the bacon and drinks five pints of bitter at lunchtime.

On a bin crew there are two 'whippers', who go round the back of the houses and fetch the bins out onto the street; two 'loaders', who pour the contents of the bins into the bin wagon; and two 'backers', who take the empty bins back to their starting place.

On my first day, we had to empty the bins on 'the Circle' in the notorious Sutton estate. It was the worst round in the whole of the town. The bins would be overflowing with bones, processed meats, dog food tins, nappies and dog dirt. Worst of all, the bins were also used by residents to dispose of the cinders from their coal fires. This made them incredibly heavy, especially if the cinders had soaked up lashings of bin juice. They were not the shiny aluminium bins that you would get in the rest of the town, either, but thick, dull, heavy metal bastards that were hard enough to lift when they were empty. They rusted terribly around the bottom rim and when you lifted them onto your shoulder the juices from the nappies and the meats would drip down your shoulder (hence the plastic shoulder inserts, I presume). In summer, they would be full of maggots, which gave the juice a stunning, death-like fragrance. You never got used to a maggot bin.

I was told to be a loader that first day, and try as I might I just couldn't lift many of the bins onto the rim of the wagon to empty them. I was struggling, and the other loader, Brian, took sympathy upon me. He showed me a special technique for emptying a 'Circle' bin, which involved lifting it upside down and fully vertical, whence the slurry would just drop out into the hopper. He also told me to just shout to him if a bin was too heavy and he would give me a hand with it. Brian soon became my mate on the crew. He was a big bloke and a hard man but took a shine to me. I was no threat to him and I think he quite enjoyed allowing me to call him a fat lad and a bin head and the like. I never stopped being scared of him, though. His mood could turn in a split second. He once punched a fellow crew member's lights out for farting while Brian was eating his chips.

Another problem with the Circle was the packs of wild dogs that patrolled the streets. Bin day was one of their favourite days. As soon as they heard the wagon, they would begin to gather and get into formation for an attack. They obviously saw the bin wagon as some sort of invader that they needed to repel. I am very scared of dogs – I have been since I was about five years old, when a golden retriever ran out of a driveway, knocked me to the ground and started interfering with my face with its hot, wet tongue. Brian, on the other hand, considered himself to be something of a dog whisperer and saw it as his personal mission to befriend, placate and dominate even the most devilish of dogs. One of the wild packs was led by a huge Irish wolfhound-style beast. We named him The Wedge after one particularly scary encounter with him.

On the day of said encounter, The Wedge and his boys chose to confront us on an open lawn at the junction of two roads. Brian told me to continue whipping out the bins while he dealt with the dogs. These houses were designed with a four-foot-wide brick passageway between each house that gave access to the rear. I took the bins out from behind a couple of homes and then made my way down the little passage of the houses that shared the open lawn. Brian was in the middle of the lawn talking to the dogs and offering his hand in friendship. I went round the back of another house, collected a heavy bin and carried it out of the passageway on my shoulder. The dogs were kind of circling Brian, but he seemed OK. I returned to the back of the house and put another bin on my shoulder, and as I stepped back into the passageway I was faced with a terrifying sight: there, stood right in the middle of the gap, was The Wedge. He was stock-still, staring at me with his hungry eyes and his pre-meal juices flowing down his hipster beard. There was no way around him.

'Brian!' I shouted. 'Brian! Help me!' Brian soon appeared at the other end of the passage beyond The Wedge.

'Just stand still and don't act scared,' advised Brian. He spoke some soothing wolfhound words and took a step towards the dog. The Wedge looked over his shoulder and took a couple of steps in my direction. I started to back off. 'Keep still!' shouted Brian. I stopped moving and slowly took the bin down from my shoulder and held it in front of me like a shield of tinned garbage. Brian was inching forward, still mumbling wolfhound nonsense. Then The Wedge started to bark. I farted. 'Just walk towards him,' Brian told me. 'He's feeling trapped. I've got to back off.' So Brian backed out of the passage, and it was just me and The Wedge again. I was frozen. My fear of dogs runs deep. This dog had massive teeth and looked hungry for meat and sport.

'Brian!' I shouted, but there was no reply. I lifted the bin up in my arms, preparing to throw it at The Wedge. As I did so, Brian appeared at my shoulder and squeezed past me. He had managed to get in the house and come out through the back door to save me. He then delivered what I think may be the greatest refuse-collector line that has ever been spoken. Walking slowly towards The Wedge, he spoke in the hushed tones of Alec Guinness in *Star Wars*: 'This is not the bin man you are looking for. You must give him safe passage to Alderaan.' The Wedge started to back off and turn around before sprinting out of the passage back to his boys. The Force was strong with Brian the Bin Man.

I've never minded being lightly bullied or playing second fiddle. I suppose that's what comes from being the youngest of four brothers. It's a basic tactic for getting someone to like you or at least keep them on your side. A good example of this is provided by Brian. If we were approaching a shop that sold cakes, he would offer me a challenge. Whoever whipped out their side of the road first would win a cake from the other. I would always take up the challenge and always make sure I lost. This way I knew that Brian would grow to love me.

I enjoyed working on the bins. It gave me muscles and meant I could pay Mum for my keep. It's good, honest, useful work, and at Christmas you received plenty of tips. When the wagon was driving between rounds, me and Brian would ride along stood on the back bumper with the wind in our donkey jackets singing the song from the 'Texan' chocolate-bar advert. We felt like renegade cowboys coming to clean up the town.

I was still depressed, but beginning to accept it as a state of mind that would be with me for ever. It was bearable. I stopped taking my pills and told myself to forget the old me and accept that he would never be coming back. And then he did, one Saturday at a Middlesbrough FC match.

One of the worst things about depression is that it steals away the pleasure you get from ordinary life – your breakfast, reading the newspaper, watching the TV, playing a game of pool in the pub, talking nonsense with your friends, going to the cinema, stroking your cat, having chicken-in-a-basket at a country pub, going for a walk in the Cleveland Hills, kicking a football around, mowing the lawn, drinking a pint, eating a hot dog etc., etc. You know, the things that make our little worlds go round. I still did all these things, but each and every one of them was a cruel reminder of happier times.

One thing that had always given me the greatest of pleasure was going to Ayresome Park to watch my beloved Boro. I would never miss a home match and often travelled away to support them. It was the same ritual every week: meet up with Cags and Harry in the Yellow Rose Pub, walk to the match full of hope and anticipation. Throw a half-eaten Newboulds pie at the opposition goalkeeper, sway and sing in support for the team, and then rush home for the results of the day's matches, feeling either elated or crushed.

As a kid, whenever Boro scored, I would experience the purest joy – immediate, visceral and all-consuming. Not anymore. Yes, I went through the motions, jumping and screaming with joy along with everyone else, but inside I was indifferent. This particular Saturday I was stood in the Holgate End when Boro scored. I celebrated instantly and without restraint.

When the noise died down, a flotilla of butterflies exploded in my stomach. I had experienced a rush of unbridled joy for the first time in years. Robert Mortimer was back. I could be happy again. I bowed my head to hide my tears of happiness from Cagsy and Harry. They would never know what had just happened, that I had had an invisible moment of breakthrough.

So often I had asked myself if I would ever be happy again, and how I would even know if I had retrieved my old self. Well, here was my answer. I am so grateful to my old self for persevering with his support for this club so that I would have a barometer by which to judge my mental well-being. If you have ever suffered from depression, you will know exactly what I mean by that. It was yet another Big Day to add to the pot.

I realised that being a bin man was not what I wanted to do with the rest of my life. My mum would often badger me to find a 'proper career', and I wanted to make her happy. So I successfully applied for a job as an assistant probation officer with the Cleveland Probation Service. The offices were in a small Victorian brick building in Thornaby-on-Tees, and there was a staff of four probation officers and a couple of secretaries. My job was basically to do anything I was told, from tidying up files, delivering documents to the court, cleaning the boss's car to visiting long-term probationers in their homes to prepare little reports on their family and employment situations.

My boss was a despot. He ruled that little office like an Eastern European gymnastics coach and kept a vice-like grip on any outbreak of happiness or joy. It seemed impossible to escape his surveillance. If you started to read a newspaper, his face would appear at the window. If you went into the kitchen to make a coffee, he would peep out from behind the fridge. If you were two minutes late for work, he would be stood in the entrance hall. If you dropped a chip on the floor, he would crawl out from beneath the table. Whenever he left the office, the whole building would breathe a sigh of relief.

He was well into his sixties, approaching retirement, and wore a dark-navy blazer and grey slacks. His hair was plentiful and grey, and his thick-lens spectacles made his eyes look like those of the fish after which he was named. He always had his tobacco pipe either in his hand or in his mouth, and when really annoyed he would jab the pipe into your shoulder or sometimes clonk you on the top of your head with it. He was an old-school ex-army bully boy, and on a few occasions when he had left his pipe on his desk or in the kitchen, I would take it and rub its mouthpiece into one of my sweatier creases.

The home visits are what I remember most from those days, as the people I was visiting invariably lived chaotic lives in poor housing conditions. These visits were the first occasions that I had actually been into the homes of total strangers, and I felt like an intruder from a different world.

One family that I would visit once every fortnight was the Casey clan. They were perhaps the poorest and most dysfunctional family in the area. Mr Casey could often be seen pushing three or four of his children around the streets of Thornaby in a wooden cart. Mrs Casey was the 'client'. She was short and always wore the same dark-green woollen coat, whether outside or indoors. Her greying hair was tied back in a ponytail and there was a tattoo of a helicopter on her neck.

She would receive me in the front room and always offer

me a cup of grey tea. Dogs would run in and out of the room seemingly enjoying the game of being told to fuck off. I was required to ask a set of questions about the family's well-being. Were they receiving their benefits, were the children keeping their hospital appointments, how were the children getting on at school, were the bills being paid, was the house in good repair, how was the family's health etc., etc. Mrs Casey was a dab hand at dealing with these intrusions, and if she was to be believed everything was just hunky-dory. The truth, of course, was that life was difficult, if not unbearable. The family needed money. I took it upon myself to learn all I could about the welfare benefits system and try to make sure that the family were receiving everything they were entitled to. The social security laws and regulations are pretty complicated, but I was able to get a basic grip on them, and I soon became the office resource for checking whether clients were getting what was due to them. It was nice to occasionally help a client rather than just police them. My little reports would be placed on file, seemingly a back-covering exercise to tick a box should trouble lie up ahead.

Some of the clients were terrifying, especially the parolees who had been released from long sentences on licence. The most fearsome I encountered was Ian Ferris. He had served five years or so for armed robbery, had the build of a cruiserweight boxer and was covered in tattoos. I don't think I ever saw him wearing a shirt or top. He loved to intimidate with his physique and of course I was absolutely petrified of him. He would tell me story after story of violence he had encountered both in and out of jail and would frequently grab my shoulder or my face while telling these tales. He loved seeing a lad supposedly 'in authority' literally sitting there shitting himself. He lived with his wife and their home was immaculate. I remember there were swords everywhere – lining the hallway, above the gas fireplace, along the stairwell and above the sofa.

On one occasion when I called, his wife told me that Ian was upstairs and that I would have to go up there if I wanted to see him. When I got to the top landing, I apologetically called out his name.

'I'm in here,' came the reply from the bathroom.

'OK, Ian, I'll wait downstairs, shall I?'

'No, get your fucking arse in here!' Ian would reply. I popped my head round the door and there he was laid naked having a bath. The small tub could hardly contain his bulk. On the wall above the bath were two massive samurai swords arranged in a cross pattern. 'Sit down on the pot, son. I don't get out of the bath for no fucker.' I did as I was told. 'Have you never seen a bloke in a bath?' he asked.

'No, I don't think I have.'

'I've seen so many naked blokes this last five years I don't even give a fuck anymore.' And with this, he stood up in the bath to display his full magnificence. He then took one of the swords off the wall, balanced it on top of his head, and started to bend its blade by pressing downwards on its tip and handle. When he was happy with his bend, he passed the sword over to me and told me to bend it back into shape. Again, I did as I was told. It was actually quite easy, but I made it look incredibly difficult and stopped before it was back to its former shape.

'I can't do it, Ian. Jesus, you must be strong.' This pleased him, and he proceeded to do a little muscle-man display before dropping himself back down into the bath.

'Are you sure you wouldn't rather do this after you've finished in the bath?'

'No.'

So, I took my little writing pad out of my briefcase and proceeded to ask my list of set questions.

'Are you currently in full-time employment?'

'No.'

'Are you actively looking for work?'

'No.'

'Is there any reason why you can't work or seek employment?'

'No.'

'Are you or any members of your household suffering from any health issues?'

'No.'

And so on. At the end of the form there is a general welfare question.

'Is there any problem at all that the probation office may be able to assist or advise you upon?'

'Yes.'

'What is it, Ian?'

'You, you're a problem. Now get out of my bathroom and fuck off out of my house.'

I did what I was told. The system had no real way of dealing with bruisers like Ian. They had seen a thousand do-gooders in their time and knew that they were toothless agents of a system that was geared against them. I filed my report and assume that no one ever looked at it.

I worked at the probation office for about a year, and I can honestly say that it changed me. I became something of a social injustice warrior; I wanted to help people whose lives had turned towards the shit. I came across the details of a Master of Law course at the University of Leicester that covered what is known as welfare law. It promised to turn you into an expert in social security, housing and childcare law. I applied and was offered a place.

I had also applied to Cambridge University to study for a master's degree in criminology. My mum was very excited about the prospect of me attending Cambridge. I had to write an essay and attend an interview, and the essay I submitted was something to do with paradigms of thought in social sciences. I prepared myself to answer questions on this and mugged up on some basics about criminology. The interview was held in the wood-panelled and multi-sofa-ed chamber of some esteemed professor. I felt out of my depth and intimidated to within an inch of a knife, like a hobbit sharing a shower with Richard Osman.

'Would you like a cup of tea and some toast?' he asked me.

'That would be nice, thank you, sir.'

'I'm not a sir; I'm a professor. Why would you think I was a sir?'

'I didn't mean that you were an actual sir; it's just how I always addressed my headmaster.'

'This isn't a school, Mr Mortimer. Is that how you addressed your tutors at Sussex?'

'No, we just used first names, apart from with my professor.'

'What did you call him?'

Me aged 9 with a home haircut

The pink house where I was born

Mum

The only picture we have of my dad

The 1969 Green Lane Primary School football team
(top row, fourth from the right)

1975: Sam, me, Mum, Angela, Johnny and Richard

The Pifco blackhead
removal sauna

Aged 19 with my good friend Mr Billy

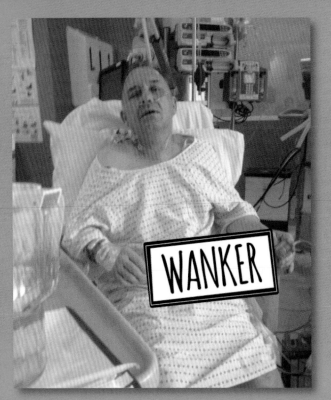

WANKER

In intensive care the day after my operation.
My wife added the caption to cheer me up

My recovery gift
from Damien

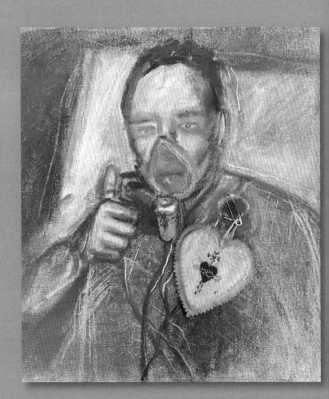

Jim's painting of me
following his visit
to the hospital

Smoking at Ayresome Park, then the home of
Middlesbrough Football Club

Me and Cags in our late teens

Blakey's famous segs
for noise generation

The homeless hostel in Peckham
with my room highlighted

Wedding day with Lisa in the registry

1984: graduating from Leicester University with a master's degree in Welfare Law. Mum wishing it was Cambridge

1990: cataloguing in Montreal with Jim, Paul and Charlie

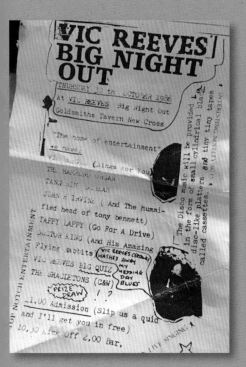

Street flyer for Big Night Out at
Goldsmiths Tavern in New Cross

1988: Jim bursts onto the stage
at Goldsmiths Tavern

Outside our first office at Helicon Mountain. Also the headquarters of the Gentlemen's Motorcycle Club

Me and Jim thinking in 1990

Comic Relief in 1995, when Jim and I attempted to drink 90 pints of beer in three minutes

This was a tricky one for me, as my professor/personal tutor at Sussex was called Mr Richard Cock (I promise that is true).

'Just "Professor" really, or "Richard" sometimes. He didn't really mind.'

'And what was his surname?'

It dawned on me that he probably knew his name from the bundle of sheets he had on his lap. He just wanted me to say it.

'Professor Cock.'

A tiny smile broke on the face of the old bloke.

'And what did you say his first name was?'

'Richard.'

'Ah, Dick Cock, how wonderful!'

We both laughed. An old besuited academic blurting out the phrase 'Dick Cock' could never be resisted as a laughter switch.

Still giggling, the professor asked me, 'And was he?' (More giggles.) 'Was he a cock?'

'I couldn't say for sure. He kept his trousers on during tutorials.'

'Excellent,' giggled the professor. 'Truly excellent.'

How easily pleased is this bloke? I thought to myself, looking around the room to see if there were any melons or jugs to which I could bring his attention.

When his secretary brought in two plates of buttered toast and a teapot and cups for two, he asked me to pour the tea. The first thing I did, as is my habit, was to pour some milk into both the cups.

'Do you always put the milk in first?'

'Yes.'

'Excellent, carry on.'

I finished pouring the tea and began spooning sugar into my cup.

'My word, you have a sweet tooth. How many spoons are you having?'

I was still taking around twelve sugars in my tea at this point, but felt it best not to reveal this.

'I have five sugars,' I lied. 'I was a lot worse when I was younger. I used to have seventeen sugars in a mug of tea.'

'Excellent. Take a slice of toast; it's buttered already. I actually prefer margarine to be honest; how about you?'

'I'm fine either way. I was brought up on Stork SB margarine.'

'Excellent. Well, tuck in and tell me a bit about yourself and your parents.'

I told him about my home in Middlesbrough and about my dad working as a biscuit salesman, and my mum being a house-wife until her husband was killed in a car crash. I told him about my love of football and talked up my abilities in that respect. He nodded along sagely and occasionally added an 'Excellent' here and there when something piqued his interest. I had barely finished my toast before his secretary returned to the room and informed us that our time was up. He shook my hand and wished me luck. Not a word had been mentioned about my essay, criminology or the course for which I had applied. I didn't understand what had just happened. I concluded that he had seen straight through me and realised I was not at the academic level required. He seemed a nice fella. I assumed I would never see him again.

A few weeks later, however, I received a letter from Cambridge offering me a place on the criminology course. I couldn't believe it. I thought back to that strange interview and the talk of margarine and whether I put milk in my tea first. It began to dawn on me that maybe it was all about checking that I had the correct 'working class' credentials to help bolster up their non-public-school statistics. I will never know for sure. My mum, of course, was over the moon, absolutely thrilled. Me, not so much. I accepted the offer and told myself that the correct choice between Leicester and Cambridge would reveal itself over the summer weeks. My mum kept badgering me to decide and encouraging me to take up the offer from Cambridge. I was worried about disappointing her; she had suffered a lot of heartbreak over the years and I had the chance to deliver her a little bit of sunshine.

The problem for me was my received perception of life at Oxbridge, probably taken entirely from old movies and TV shows such as *Shadowlands* and *The Glittering Prizes*. I pictured hordes of over-confident, highly educated posh boys riding their penny farthings through the cloisters to the refectory, where they would dine on Continental meats. I pictured them mocking me for my accent and ridiculing me in tutorials for my lack of education and learning. Posh, confident, articulate strangers. It was the stuff of nightmares for me. If I went there, I would only be doing it to make my mum proud and not for me.

On the Sunday before both courses started, my brother Sam arrived to give me a lift to either Leicester or Cambridge. I still hadn't made up my mind. I didn't have the balls to tell my mum that I wasn't going to Cambridge, and when I waved her goodbye that is where she thought I was headed. I was leaving my gang of friends and leaving my mum on her own again. As we drove off, the Madness song 'It Must Be Love' was playing on the car radio.

I never thought I'd miss you
Half as much as I do
And I never thought I'd feel this way
The way I feel
About you
It must be love, love, love

I cried.

I talked the decision over with Sam on the A1 headed south. He agreed that I might struggle to fit in at Cambridge but nevertheless thought it too good an opportunity to decline. As we approached the M18 motorway junction, it was time to decide. Continue on the A1 to Cambridge or take the M1 to Leicester.

We took the M1 and my mum's dream to have a son attend Cambridge was over. I phoned her that evening to give her the bad news. She was not best pleased. She tried to change my mind but I wouldn't shift. I had let her down and I hated myself for it.

I had a shit time at Leicester. It serves me right.

I arrived in the town and took a single bedroom in a Victorian house shared with five other students. They were all Christians and four or five years younger than me. My bedroom was tiny, only big enough for a single bed and a side table. As I had done in Brighton, I bought a small portable TV and made this room my home. I never mixed with the other occupants of the house. It was only a year-long course, and being in the middle of the country meant it was a lot easier to go back to Middlesbrough at the weekend or take a coach to visit Helen, who was still living in Brighton.

My time in Leicester was not particularly memorable. I was lonely, but I studied hard. I would have an occasional drink in the student bar with another lad on my course, called Ben, who looked like Joe Jackson, the 'Is She Really Going Out with Him?' singer. We shared a love of music and would sometimes go and see bands in the Student Union or the De Montfort Hall. One night we went to see an up-and-coming indie band called Orange Juice. They didn't arrive on stage until well after midnight and most punters had left. Ben and I stuck it out, however, and were treated to perhaps the best gig I have ever seen. Music comes and goes, shines and fades as you get older. But the Orange Juice album *You Can't Hide Your Love Forever* has never left me or faded from my view. It has been a regular uplifting companion for almost forty years.

One weekend while I was at Leicester, I took a coach down to Brighton to pay a surprise visit to Helen. She lived in a flat above a kebab shop and next to a supermarket on St Peter's Square. On arrival, I popped into the supermarket to buy something to eat. As I walked in, I saw Helen stood at the checkout with a basket of food. She looked up and our eyes met. An expression of sheer horror spread across her face. I knew in a moment that our relationship was over; she had found someone else. I was heartbroken. My fragile little world had lost one of its key members.

I felt angry, sad, rejected and a little bit scared. My relationship with Helen had lasted seven or eight years and she had been a source of constant support. I couldn't see how I would survive without her. My shitty little room in Leicester seemed more like a prison without the opportunity to escape down to Brighton to see her.

They say the first cut is always the deepest, and I think that's true. It's a big blow to the ego, getting dumped. Helen had been my only girlfriend, and I couldn't for the life of me see where I would get another one. I found it nigh-on impossible to talk to strangers, and doubly hard when it came to strange women. I would occasionally go down to the student bar and sit on my own trying to look interesting with a book in my hand, wearing a quirky hat or gloves, hoping that somehow a lady might approach me. They never did and I would become so self-conscious that I never lasted beyond a second pint. Every time I passed a phone box I desperately wanted to phone Helen, and occasionally I did. She had been kind/unkind enough to phrase the split in terms of 'I just need some time to think', which of course in my mind meant that there was still a chance that we might get back together. I even persuaded her to allow me to come and visit her in Brighton. When I saw her, she had cut her hair short and bleached it white; she looked radiant and happier than I'd ever seen her. It was the new haircut that convinced me I had no chance of winning her back. She was moving on; I was the past.

I continued to see Helen occasionally as a friend for a few years after our split, but that faded away along with pain. It always saddens me that in the mating game we so rarely continue our relationships with girlfriends on a platonic basis. We had meant so much to each other and shared so many memories growing up. If it had been a fella, we would have been friends for life. As it is, as I sit here now, it's hard to even remember her face. Sad.

Without Helen, I immersed myself in my studies and listening to music, and I visited home as often as I could. At the end of that year I obtained my master's degree in welfare law and returned home to Middlesbrough.

11

NOVEMBER 2015

I firmly believed that I
Didn't need anyone but me
I sincerely thought I was so complete
Look how wrong you can be

Rod Stewart, 1971

You left me earlier in late 2015 sat on my sofa feeling vulnerable and sorry for myself, watching Nicolas Cage movies and basically trying to deny that the world outside my home even existed. It was over a month since my heart operation and my chest bone was beginning to weld together. I was able to sleep without too much discomfort and could jog the full circumference of my local park.

The live tour with Jim was still scheduled to commence on 30 January the following year, which was now just eight weeks away. I tried not to think about it, but deep down I had resigned myself to the fact that the tour would not take place. It would be easy to cancel it so shortly after such a big operation. My doctor told me it was theoretically possible for me to tour at the end of January but that I would have to be highly motivated with my recovery to achieve this. I wasn't motivated. I was hiding away.

During my hospitalisation, my old mate Paul Whitehouse had been in constant touch with my wife. On my release he kept phoning me to chat, but when I saw his name come up I just ignored the calls. I knew that Paul would get on my back about exercising and diet, and I was happier thinking about my next box set to watch rather than my recovery. To be honest, I was ignoring calls from everyone at this time, even Jim. But Paul was very persistent and got my wife to work on his behalf. She made me promise to phone him and eventually I did.

I have known Paul for a long, long time. We first met when he and his comedy partner Charlie Higson came along to the Goldsmiths Tavern in New Cross, south-east London, to watch one of our early Big Night Out shows in 1987. I don't recall much about that first meeting other than that he was a wiry, angular, cockney bundle of energy and fun. Paul always likes to prove that he is the funniest person in the room, and he always pulls it off, as he invariably is. He is as sharp as a sea eagle's talons and a superb mimic. I remember being quite intimidated at the time and even a little frightened. I have always been scared of gobby cockneys. I think it's the accent. It gives even the most benign statement a hint of aggression. He was also very good-looking back then, and not the walnut on a stick that we see now. We met again a few weeks later when he and Charlie performed a little sketch on stage during a live Big Night Out. I think they called the act 'David Dunn and his dead dad'.

It involved Paul sitting on Charlie's knee pretending to be a ventriloquist dummy as Charlie fried some bacon rashers on a camping stove. I cannot remember the point of the sketch but I can remember the delicious smell of bacon filling the room. Perhaps there was no point other than the successful cooking of the meat; perhaps it was an advert for the versatility of that particular camping stove; perhaps it was a comment on how we ignore our children whenever free bacon is on offer. You would have to ask Paul.

On the next live show, I remember Paul and Charlie taking part in what Jim and I called the 'Tanita Tikaram Dream Sequence'. This was a visual piece where Charlie climbed up and down a stepladder dropping tins of dog food into a child's paddling pool while Paul sat on the stage trying to feed a leg of lamb into the sound hole of his acoustic guitar. As they did this, Jim and I paraded around the stage with bananas as noses to the music of Tanita Tikaram, occasionally raising our arms to signal the sound effect of heavy thunder and lightning. Again, I can't remember the point of this particular piece. It involved both fresh meat and heavily processed meat, though, which has got to be a good thing. Charlie was achieving a good height by being at the top of a stepladder and there is no doubt that a high comedian is a pleasing occurrence. As for the bananas on mine and Jim's noses, I think they represented thought. Whatever its thrust, I'm glad we did it. We would often meet up with Paul and Charlie in London for a drink, and we soon became good friends. Our respective careers have been inter- twined ever since.

I phoned Paul and we chatted for a while about the operation and my recovery. A couple of years previously, Paul had three stents inserted into the arteries around his heart. He was the nearest to a friendly expert that I had. Mostly, though, he banged on about me going fishing with him. It was the last thing I wanted to do at the time. The thought of standing on a cold riverbank in the middle of winter miles away from the nearest hospital wasn't my idea of the perfect first trip away from home since the operation. I told him I would think about it. It actually wasn't that strange a suggestion. For about the past twenty years we had been promising each other that we would go on a fishing trip together. Around fifteen years earlier we had even gone together to a posh fishing shop next to Green Park in London, where Paul had picked me out a fly-fishing rod and reel for me to use when we eventually went. It had never happened.

He kept phoning and eventually I ran out of excuses. We were to go fishing on the beautiful River Test in Hampshire. Paul would be fly-fishing for pike and I would be float-fishing for grayling. I wasn't looking forward to it and felt a little bit bullied by Paul and The Wife.

I arrived at the riverbank and there was Paul waiting for me. He had already boiled the kettle in the bankside fishing hut and we sat and had a cup of tea. He was the first friend I had seen since coming home from the hospital. I didn't look well; my new diet of pulses, grains, nuts and fruit had left me two stone lighter and very wizened in the face. My complexion was pale and I had a very ghostly presence. The fishing hut had a genuine Victorian vibe: old leather Chesterfield sofas, stuffed fish in display cases, ancient fishing rods and tackle displayed on all the walls, a wood-burning stove in the corner and numerous pictures of proud fishermen displaying their catches. Paul sat me down and asked me how I was doing. I bluffed away for a while telling him that everything was as sweet as a lizard's tits, but he wasn't about to be fobbed off.

'No, I'm asking how you are. How are you feeling?'

'Honestly, I'm fine. A few aches and pains but that's to be expected.'

'You look like shit.'

'You look like a bullied monk.'

'You look like a knackered bollock.'

'You look like a glassblower's anus.'

'You look like the outskirts of Leicester.'

We laughed. It was very pleasant to be talking to an old mate in a non-medical setting. He took me outside to the riverbank and set me up with a float rod before leaving in search of a pike on the next beat. I stood there for an hour or so, lost in the unique rhythms of the water and the gentle, hypnotic lullaby of its flow. There was no one else around and nobody keeping an eye on me. Watching a float bobbing along the surface of a river is one of the most meditative experiences you can have. All your brainpower focused on that little orange tip to the exclusion of all other thoughts and worries. This was a place that I was glad to be in, and then, *whoosh!*, the float goes under and you strike. You are immediately hit by an intimate connection, both physical and emotional, to another living thing. It's visceral and exhilarating. The play is over in thirty seconds but contains as much drama as *EastEnders* packs into a week. I've caught a small grayling, with its translucent grey scales and magnificent purple-hued dorsal fin. What a first catch. I am ecstatic and beaming like a pensioner who has just found his missing tin opener. This is what life should feel like; this is participating in the world rather than just watching it go by. I am hooked.

Paul arrives a bit later and I blurt out the details of my catch. As Paul listens and congratulates me, I notice that his hand and wrist are bleeding. He has caught his pike and the pike did not like it, giving him a few puncture wounds with its predator teeth. Its bite delivers an anti-coagulant, which means the flow of blood is difficult to stem. We retire back into the warm embrace of the fisherman's hut. It all feels like a little escape from the dread and worry of the previous months. I want to do this again.

Something about that fishing trip gave me the kick up the arse I needed. Sitting on my sofa no longer felt enough. I knew what needed to be done. I needed to get physically and mentally prepared for the live tour in January. It was a lovely act of care that Paul showed me by taking me on that trip. He is a wily old fox.

12

1983–1987

Get up in the morning and it's just another day
Pack up my belongings
I've got to get away

Bad Company, 1974

I'm back in Middlesbrough living with my mum, and I've got a job working for the Stockton-on-Tees Law Centre. This is a free advice and representation service that specialises in social security law and housing law. I spend my days helping people claim their correct benefit entitlement and issuing court proceedings against landlords whose properties are not fit for habitation. In the evening, I go out drinking and clubbing with Cagsy and Harry Harriman. Life is sweet. I still don't have a girlfriend and that feels like the only fly in the ointment. There is a girl I like working at the Law Centre, and I manage to invite her to come and have a drink with me, Cags and Harry. She comes along but takes a shine to Cags and cops off with him.

Other than her, my only chance was the nightclub. Twice, maybe three times a week we would go there looking for the lasses. It was always the same routine. The Endeavour pub first for five pints of Worthington E and then a cab into the town centre. Find a viewing perch near the dance floor and sink another five pints while trying to look alluring. Slink onto the dance floor and start comedy dancing near a likely conquest. Lady leaves dance floor full of upset. Return to perch and repeat until one of us spews up or the club closes at 2 a.m. Walk home down Linthorpe Road stopping at the Boro Fish Bar for a kebab or a packet of chips. Cross the road and watch the inevitable fights develop. Arrive home and drift off to sleep with head spinning. If only I could summon up the nerve to actually talk to a girl, it might all be so different. I had a bleached banana shape above each ear and a bleached Mallen streak in my quiff. What's not to like?

Our boozer of choice was The Linthorpe on Roman Road, which attracted the punks and the students and the trendy younger people of Middlesbrough. It had a small rear conservatory room that housed a pool table, and one night as I was playing a girl came over and placed ten pence on the pool table to secure her place as the next player. The rules were that the winner stays on and plays against the next one in line. If I won the game I would be playing with a girl. THEY MIGHT TALK TO ME!

The girl in question was about my age. She was wearing a second-hand 1950s-style flowery dress with blood-red Doc Marten boots, and she had a huge purple Mohican haircut with the sides of her head shaved as smooth as a Milky Bar's underside. I won my game and she strode up to the table and placed the balls on their spots.

'Loser buys the winner a drink, yeah?' she declared as she smashed the yellow and red rack of balls in every direction. This wasn't the normal arrangement, but was of course fine by me.

'Yeah, I'll have a pint of whiskey,' I replied.

'You can have a glass of water. I'll have a pint of snakebite,' came the reply as she blasted three balls on the trot into their chosen pockets.

'What's a snakebite?'

'Anything that threatens its kids.'

'No, seriously, what is it?' I asked, already knowing the answer but wanting the chat to continue. If there was a break in the conversation, I knew I might clam up.

'Half cider, half lager in a pint glass with a dash of blackcurrant.'

'Sounds shit.'

'Tastes shit too, but it gets you pissed.'

'I haven't seen you in here before. Do you come here often?' (Yes, I said that.)

'Not really, I work nights.'

'What, you on the game?'

'Yeah, I am. I thought I'd seen your face before.'

I was talking to a girl.

I can't remember who won the game, but I bought her a drink and we sat together for the rest of the night. We arranged to meet up again. I had a girlfriend. Her name was Mandy. She was a nurse at the local hospital. Good times.

Things were falling nicely into place. Cags, Harry, Mandy,

Stava, a couple of Mandy's mates and I rented a large house on Marton Road in the centre of Middlesbrough. It wasn't so hard leaving Mum's house this time as I would be living just down the road and could see her as often as I wanted. I loved it. It felt like I was finally enjoying the life that I should have experienced during those long years and months in Brighton and Leicester. We would play cricket for hours in the high-walled back yard, we would cook meals for each other and then watch the soap opera *Brookside* on Channel 4 every night. We would all go out drinking together most evenings, mob-handed and fervent, dressed with a slight New Romantic twist, which – believe me – was a dangerous game in Middlesbrough.

One of the residents was the boyfriend of one of Mandy's mates. He was about ten years older than the rest of us and mod-elled his image on that of an American Indian. He had straight, jet-black, centre-parted hair that grew down to his midriff and wore a beaded headband and leather bracelets on his wrists. He was invariably topless to display his smooth tanned skin and if feeling the chill he would wear an embroidered suede waistcoat. On his feet he wore brown suede ankle-high moccasins. His name was Malcolm, and he worked at a clutch-repair centre.

I was supremely happy in my home and social life, but the work I was doing at the Law Centre had become very repetitive and depressing. Client after client came in wanting their benefits checked or their homes properly repaired. At first I thought I was actually doing some good, but the problems of poverty are far beyond repair by a little fart in a suit in an tiny office on the banks of the River Tees. I was also frustrated by the fact that, not being a qualified solicitor, I was unable to issue proceedings myself and couldn't represent clients in court. My mum was continually on my back encouraging me to complete my legal training and become a proper solicitor. Taking my law exams would mean moving to either Manchester or Chester, however. I chose Manchester. Once again, I was on the move.

Law school is a hothouse of lectures and learning. There are seven exams at the end of the intensive one-year course covering all the essential areas of law and legal procedure – conveyancing, wills and probate, criminal law, court procedure, family law, commercial law and accounts. It's a massive exercise in memory learning, and the failure rate is very high. You have to pass every exam; one fail and you start the course all over again.

I rented a small attic room in a large Victorian house in Fallowfield, just off the Wilmslow Road. My days were spent attending hours and hours of lectures and my evenings preparing hours and hours of notes and papers. It was during this time that I discovered the joys of weak lager and takeaway curries. Just a few hundred yards down the road from me was the legendary Curry Cottage. It sold the sweetest, freshest and most succulent curries you could imagine. The rice was as soft and fluffy as a hipster's chin. I would go and fetch one nearly every night. Next door to the Curry Cottage was a grocery store that sold cans of Skol lager for a pittance. Skol is only 2.8% proof and I could drink it all night without getting overly pissed and therefore continue with my evening studies. The weak lager/chicken curry is an axis on which I have freely swung ever since.

A few weeks into the course I was approached by a small, friendly Scouse lad called Paddy. I was still in the habit of wearing Middlesbrough football tops at the time and he must have put two and two together and asked me if I would be interested in joining a law school football team. Of course I would. Paddy was one of those unique charming and confident lads that has the ability to bring people together. They are like manna from heaven for shy people. It's such a simple act of compassion to approach someone on the fringes of things and try to bring them in. Through Paddy and the football team I met three lovely lads: Chris from Manchester, Steve from Manchester and The Walrus from Northern Ireland. They were all on the course and it was lovely to have some friends away from home. The Wednesday afternoon football matches were the highlight of my week.

A couple of months into the course, I arrived back at my flat to find Mandy parked outside with her car full of her possessions. She was moving in. We had never discussed this and it was a total surprise to see her.

'What are you doing here with all your stuff?'

'I'm moving in.'

'But what about your nursing job in Boro?'

'I've packed it in.'

'Why?'

'I was sick of picking shit out of pensioner's arses.'

It was a fait accompli. I was doing pretty good and had my own study-based routine down to a tee. I didn't really want her moving in but there was no way I had the balls to tell her to go home. I will always avoid conflict no matter where it occurs or who is involved. Of course, there is always a heavy price to pay for this approach. Not only in the invisible and creeping build-up of resentment, but on a more practical level there was the fact that I was now living with Mandy and her stuff in a room no bigger than ten foot by eight foot.

The following term gave some relief when Paddy invited Mandy and me to join him, Steve and Chris in a large flat in the Hulme Crescents, in the centre of Manchester. These huge interlocking ten-storey blocks of local-authority flats were the most notorious shitholes in Manchester. You could rent one for six pounds a week. It was basically the case that if you were willing to live there, they would give you a flat. It was the most dangerous place I had ever lived, occupied by families and people who were at risk of falling through the net. On many evenings or during the daytime in the summer you could stand on the walkway outside the flat and watch domestic violence outbursts, drunken fighting and anti-social behaviour of every description. Police sirens were a constant background soundtrack to life in the Crescents. It had a heavily shuttered grocery store in the centre and any trip from the flat to the shop felt like a journey behind enemy lines. If you weren't mugged by one of the local street gangs, you could well be attacked by one of the packs of stray dogs that would surround you and steal your shopping, especially if you were stupid enough to carry it in a plastic carrier bag, which they would rip apart before running off with the contents.

I continued to study and Mandy got a job as an assistant on a local-authority double-decker play bus.

At the end of the year I sat my law exams and I was 100 per cent confident that I had failed. I wanted to stay in Manchester though. I loved shopping in the second-hand clothes arcades and going out into the town centre on a Friday night. It was an exciting place at the time and going to gigs at the Hacienda made you feel like you were right in the apple of the eye of British culture. I was, however, resigned to the fact that I would not be qualifying as a solicitor, so I took a job as a legal assistant at the Wythenshawe Law Centre just outside Manchester, near the airport. I knew there was no joy to be had in this work but at least it was a steady job. I would return to Wythenshawe many years later to film a one-off comedy drama pilot for Channel 4 television called *The Weekenders*. It features my most spectacular outdoor forward roll ever (and I've done a few) on the very patch of grass that I used to sit on and eat my lunch every day while working at the Law Centre. Little could I have known that one day I would be returning here with a film crew and a personal make-up artist.

Fast-forward four months and it turns out I did pass my exams. The power of weak lager and chicken curry should not be underestimated. I was free to commence my practical, in-work, legal training. Mum was over the moon. I was too. It felt like an entirely new adventure and the beginning of the rest of my life. I was on my way to London.

13

December 2015

I changed my name
In search of fame
To find the Midas touch
Oh I wish I'd never wanted then
What I want now twice as much

Mott the Hoople, 1973

I've been fishing with Paul and have determined to get myself ready for the live tour at the end of January. I start jogging a little faster and a little further every day. It's a curse. I hate it. I would rather paint my living room ceiling with an eyebrow brush than do this jogging tomcockery. As I pass by the same front-garden walls and hedges, over the familiar cracks and gradients, all that consumes my mind is the end of the run. My comedy career, such as it is, has always been about finding humour within the mundane, but I cannot find any joy in these starkly suburban streets. How I long for a squirrel to pop out from beneath a hedge and offer to show me his nuts. How pleasing it would be if a rabbit passed by in a top hat and shoulder-length cape. Even a mouse holding a handbag and smoking a tiny cigarette would add a bit of sparkle. Dream on. It's just grey skies, rotting leaves, cold winds and the constant rustle of a cheap Millets anorak. I manage to get up to about three kilometres a day.

I go fishing with Paul again, and this time we make it an overnight stay. Paul loves to fish on the River Test as often as he can, and he is a regular at the Greyhound Hotel on Stockbridge High Street. The routine is always the same: arrive late morning and have a lazy late breakfast on the high street. Drive to the river and set up the fly-fishing gear then have a nice cup of tea in the fishing hut. Paul will then give me yet another fly-casting lesson and I will attempt to listen. Funnily enough, on this second trip the first practice cast I made hooked a fish, a lovely brown trout with an extremely cheeky attitude. I was so chuffed. Paul landed the fish but I convinced myself that it was my catch. What an amazing thing. When I was a young boy, I used to sit in front of the TV when my mum was out shopping. One of the programmes I adored was *Out of Town*, presented by Jack Hargreaves. Jack was an old, white-bearded bloke with great knowledge of country pursuits and traditions. He presented the show from inside his wooden tool shed. I was always mesmerised by the sequences they shot on the River Test. The beautiful landscape, the gin-clear water and the vibrant exotic brown trout seemed like a world apart from the streets of Middlesbrough. Never did I think that I would be on those very banks with one of those dazzling fish in my hands.

Christmas feels very normal. I'm up and about buying a

Christmas tree, helping Lisa put up the decorations, pouring Disaronno over the Christmas cake every other day, popping into town for last-minute presents. I am terrible at buying presents. It's always last-minute. I remember a previous Christmas, in the mid-'90s, where I trudged around the high street in Ashford looking for something for Lisa. I went into the Tandy electrical store and it suddenly became patently and spiritually obvious to me that the perfect present for her would be a metal detector. I chose a decent model with a pleasing grip and a telescopic handle. It promised to locate all the main metals and would indicate their presence with a pleasingly scientific-sounding beep. It also came in a long cardboard box that would look intriguing under the tree. What a mistake. When Lisa opened it, she snapped the handle in half and threw it out of the back door, where it remained for a few weeks until I quietly disposed of it.

My spirits and health are good. The only remaining problem from my surgery was the lack of capacity in my lungs. The hospital had provided me with a little plastic device to help exercise them and get them back to normal. Basically it was a short plastic tube with a pipe attached to the side that you could blow into. As you blew, a little yellow ball would rise up the pipe. If you could get the ball up to the top of the pipe, your lungs were working perfectly again. By Christmas, I was about three quarters of the way there. I would give it a go about four times a day. I generally insisted that my wife and sons watched me so that they could break out into a round of applause if I broke my previous record. It was Boxing Day when I finally huffed and puffed my way to victory over the device. I celebrated with my first chocolate since the operation. I now had only my consultant's opinion standing between me and being able to go on tour.

New Year's Eve is always the same in my house. As soon as we have eaten our evening meal, I start boozing. Lisa keeps providing a rolling selection of treats, and my sons, Harry and Tom, Lisa, Granny, Grandad and I then all watch back-to-back *Practical Caravan* and *Practical Motorhome* TV shows that we have recorded from whatever obscure satellite channel they have been showing on. It's not that any of us are actually interested in caravans; it's just that the features of the caravans are about as celebratory as life gets. We all applaud in unison if a caravan features an extendable work surface, salad bowl sink, bedroom USB points, externally accessible storage options, soft-close kitchen drawers, floral curtaining, pre-installed TV mounting bracket. The list goes on, and there is a lot of clapping.

At 11 p.m. we turn on the latest *Ireland West Music TV Christmas Special* presented by Paul Claffey and Gerry Glennon. It's a live recording of a number of obscure Irish singers performing songs about journeys, structures, memories, incidents, tiny towns, cravings, mothers, urges and Jesus. There isn't a dry eye in the house. My personal favourites are Brendan Shine, Farmer Dan, 'Donkey Collision' (we use this name due to the singer's massive teeth) and Conal Gallen. At 12 a.m. I force the family to watch and applaud as I light a single firework in the back garden. It's been a strange year, and I know my family are sincere when they wish me happiness for the following twelve months.

A few days later, I attend the offices of my cardiologist. He puts me on the treadmill and inspects the print-out of the results. He asks me how much physical activity is involved in the live show. I explain that there is a lot of singing and classy dancing and that I am required to throw many interesting shapes and postures. I also get struck with a frying pan a lot and fall over at regular intervals. He declares that he is happy for me to go on tour if that is my wish, and also happy to sign me off as sick if I don't feel up for it. I make my choice to go ahead with the tour. He explains that I must always have an aspirin in my pocket in case I collapse and must not let my heart rate get over 154bpm. I must be constantly on the lookout for any changes in my blood pressure or pains in my chest. I phone Jim and tell him the good news.

We never rehearse our live shows. We prefer to just do a run-through on the morning of the first show to check all the props and musical cues. We pretty much always know 80 per cent of what we are going to say. We have spent hours writing it, so the essence is firmly engrained in our brains. The first show is at the Leeds First Direct Arena in front of a sell-out 7,500 crowd. We haven't toured for many years and as show time approaches my stomach begins to churn and my heart begins to beat faster. It is just me and Jim alone in a room in the depths of the arena. We go through our opening lines hoping to pull off a smooth start to the show, but I can't concentrate. I have a heart monitor on my wrist and it is already showing 120bpm. The tour manager knocks on the door and tells us it's time to head to the stage. I can feel my heart pounding in my chest as we make our way through the bowels of the stadium. As we arrive backstage, the auditorium lights go down and the crowd goes apeshit. Jim and I give each other our familiar pre-gig smile and walk our separate ways to either side of the huge stage. I arrive at the break in the curtains that is my entrance to the stage and have a peep through; the audience seems to go on for ever. We should have rehearsed; I should have told my consultant that I wasn't ready to tour. I check my heart monitor; it's 150bpm, just four off the maximum I am allowed. Our entrance music strikes up – the first track from *A Sea Symphony* by Ralph Vaughan Williams; dry ice starts pumping onto the stage and begins to filter back-stage, where it fills my lungs. It's all too much.

'Ladies and gentlemen, please welcome on stage Mr Vic Reeves and Mr Bob Mortimer!'

What am I going to do? My legs have turned to jelly. I can't remember the first lines of the opening song. I want to run away and hide. I want the world to swallow me up and deposit me inside a duvet on a single cloud hovering above a deserted beach. I don't think I can do this.

I suppose it's time I told the story of how I even got here in the first place.

PART TWO

In which I finally qualify as a solicitor and tell the story of how I met Jim and helped to take a little comedy show from a room above a pub onto national TV.

14

To London

I'm twenty-five years old and I've passed my law exams. It's time to continue my legal training. The first two years of practical training to become a solicitor is called your Articles of Clerkship. I got an interview for a clerkship with the London Borough of Southwark legal department in south-east London. I always try to be early for appointments. Timekeeping is a bit of an obsession with me. I've always thought that the two most unselfish things you can do in life are to turn up on time and to be quiet around a house when someone else is sleeping. They are not things you will ever be thanked for and that makes them all the more satisfying. As I wait in a backstreet off Camberwell Green, a pigeon shits on my shoulder from a great height. That seals it; a bird shit on your shoulder is a traditional good omen that I deeply believe in. If I get this job, I decide, I'm going to take it. They offer me the job before I get back to the train station and I gratefully accept. I am to start in two weeks' time.

My old acquaintance Dave (The Walrus) from Manchester Law School had moved with his wife to Wimbledon in south-west London, so I contacted him and asked if I could stay on his floor for a couple of weeks until I found somewhere to live. He kindly agreed. The daily commute to Camberwell took well over an hour, making it an eleven-hour working day. I must admit it did feel very grown up and cosmopolitan to be commuting on the London Underground. With my shitty little grey BHS suit and plastic briefcase, I half imagined that I was an important businessman in a 1950s black-and-white movie. This feeling soon passed, though, as the realisation dawned that I was more or less completely alone in this vast city.

A couple of weeks into the job, I had my first meeting with the Town Clerk, my de facto boss and the person to whom I was articled. His job was to 'instruct me in the principles and practices of the profession of Law'. He was a short, barrel-shaped bloke with a ruddy complexion and thinning, fuzzy ginger hair. He had a good set of ginger Noddy Holder sideboards, too, and wore a dark-blue three-piece suit that had become shiny due to overuse. His office was rather grand, all wood panelling and mahogany furniture, portraits of important local politicians and officials adorning the walls. Unusually, his desk was positioned on a slightly raised area, with me seated on the lower level. He was a high Town Clerk at Southwark Town Hall, which I think is to his credit.

'How are you settling in, Robert?'

'Fine, thanks, think I'm finding my feet.'

'Do you have any friends or family in London, Robert?'

'No, not really, sir.'

'It can take time to make friends. Are you a confident lad or more of a mouse?'

'Somewhere in between,' I lied, almost tempted to twiddle my whiskers and reach into my jacket for some pocket cheese.

'The council has many sporting and social clubs that might be a good place to start. What are your particular interests, Robert?'

'Well, the law obviously.'

'Boring!'

'I like football. I played a lot at university and I support Middlesbrough.'

'I thought you said you liked football, ha ha ha ha ha ha! Are you a drinker, Robert?'

'Yeah, I like a drink, especially at the weekend when I haven't got work.'

'I drink every day. I find it a joy. I'll tell Geoff Wilson to take you out for a drink. Yes, that's what I'll do. Go out for a drink with Geoff, that's the best way to oil the wheels of friendship. Have you got anywhere to live, Robert?'

'No, I haven't.'

'Are you saying you are homeless?'

'Yes, well, sort of. I'm sleeping on someone's floor in Wimbledon.'

'Well, then, what about the homeless hostel on Southampton Way? It's only about 200 yards from the town hall. A young lad like you should be able to cut it ... You interested, Robert?'

'Yeah, sounds good.'

'I'll arrange for you to have a look round this lunchtime. You working hard, Robert?'

'Yes.'

'Well, don't overdo it. You know where I am if you need

anything. I'm here most mornings but don't bother me on an afternoon. That's all, Robert, goodbye.'

'Thank you, goodbye.'

I liked him and his attitude very much and he left a deep impression on me. Twenty-five years later, I would base the character of 'The Alderman' in my podcast Athletico Mince on him as, I think, a fitting tribute.

True to his word, I received a phone call from the homeless hostel manager that lunchtime inviting me over to have a look at the accommodation. The hostel was an impressive four-storey Victorian building with a Georgian frontage. The three first-floor front rooms each had floor-to-ceiling double French windows and a little balcony.

The ground floor consisted of a lounge/dining room, a large commercial-style kitchen and various offices. There were six rooms and a shared bathroom on each of the other three floors. When I visited there was no one else around apart from the hostel manager. She was a small, thin older lady dressed in cleaner's overalls with a roll-up cigarette permanently attached to her lower lip. She showed me to the one room that was available. It was one on the first floor with a balcony. The room was empty apart from a green sink in one corner and yards and yards of hot and cold water pipes. The carpet was green and the door had a sturdy lock. I liked it. I asked the manager about the rest of the residents. She told me they were a mixed bunch and well behaved. If anyone caused trouble she would tell them to fuck off and she would do the same to me if I caused her any problems. I believed her. I took the room and she told me I could move in whenever I wanted. I did so a couple of days later with only a sleeping bag and a suitcase of clothes to my name.

A couple of chairs, a mattress and a TV later, and it felt like home. I had my London base. My fellow residents were mostly single males in varying degrees of distress: a Welsh dope-smoker, a West Country drug dealer, a Scottish boozer, a Brummie keyboard wizard and a strange, immaculately dressed silent creeper who looked a spit of David Byrne from Talking Heads. Residents came and went, and noise levels dipped and peaked. I was very wary for the first few weeks and kept myself to myself. The manager lady ran a tight ship, though, and soon enough I was settled. I started collecting glass fish and clowns from the bric-a-brac stalls on East Street Market to give my room a homely feel.

The Geoff Wilson to whom the Town Clerk had referred was my immediate boss in the Planning Law section of the legal department. And when I say 'department', I mean Geoff, a secretary and myself. He was thin and dressed scruffily in an ill-fitting jumper, slacks and a grey leather bomber jacket. I would guess he was about five years older than me. We had not spoken much since I started working under him other than when he showed me the forms and procedure required to make a tree subject to a Tree Preservation Order. He had then pointed me to a huge stack of pending TPO applications and stated, 'That should be enough to keep you busy for a while.' He would leave the office every lunchtime and return to work mid-afternoon a good few pints worse for wear. One lunchtime in my first few weeks, and obviously at the insistence of my beloved Town Clerk, he asked me if I would like to join him down the pub. I accepted. He took me to the Grove on Camberwell Grove, about half a mile away from the town hall. It was right up my street. I could immediately tell that it was the haunt for all the art school graduates and fashionables in the area. Although a man of few words, Geoff really liked his booze, and before I knew it, it was three o'clock in the afternoon and we were downing our fifth pint. I felt like a member of the South London Crime Squad out on the booze after getting a local Mafia boss convicted.

On our return to the town hall, the Town Clerk was waiting for us in our office. He was not happy. While we were on our little binge, something important had come up that required the immediate attention of his planning lawyers, but they were 'elsewhere'. We had left him halfway up the U-bend without a plunger. It would have been immediately apparent to him that we were pissed.

'Where the fuck have you been, Geoff, like I need to ask?'

'I took Robert for a drink like you asked me to.'

'You've been out for three hours. *Three fucking hours*, Geoff!'

'Yeah, sorry, but it's no worries, we'll soon catch up with what we have to do. We'll stay late, won't we?' He looked at me for confirmation.

'Yes, we'll stay for ever,' I responded. The Town Clerk looked at me without interest, as if I was an advert for PVC windows.

'That's no help to me, Geoff. I've had the chief executive on to me wanting to know if we've lodged our objections to the Globe Theatre development and I couldn't give him an answer because my planning team was out on the piss!'

'It's all good, boss,' replied Geoff, and again looked at me for support.

'Yeah, it's all good, boss, we've got this.'

The Town Clerk looked at me with total disdain then barked: 'Get out, Richard [*sic*], I don't need your smart-arse comments.'

I left the room and wandered around the corridors until it was safe to return. Geoff explained that the Town Clerk usually slept all afternoon in the basement and that we had been really unlucky to have been caught out. We both received formal written warnings about our behaviour. If only the mobile phone had existed. I never went out for a drink with Geoff again and it was also the last time I ever had any dealings with the Town Clerk.

One evening after work I returned home to the hostel and a familiar sight. Mandy was parked outside with a car full of her belongings and an apologetic look on her face. We hadn't discussed her moving down and she didn't intend to discuss it now. Truth is, I was pleased to see her. It was getting lonely, and my old curse of social inadequacy was suggesting that it wasn't going to get better any time soon. We started to make the Grove pub in Camberwell our local, and would also often go to local pub comedy nights in the area. A lot of the comedians at the time were middle-class and heavily educated, mostly doing political comedy. It was bang in the middle of the Thatcher years, so I suppose that's no surprise. It wasn't for me, though.

If I think back to what made me laugh growing up, it was always the clowns, the fools, the idiots. Laurel and Hardy arguing and hitting each other. The Three Stooges, bickering and lamping each other to within an inch of their respective lives. Norman Collier and his permanently faulty microphone. Spike Milligan in tights, arsing about and corpsing with a comedy rubber nose and a price tag on his shirt. W. C. Fields playing golf with a bendy golf club and a circus acrobat tumbling around the putting green. Jacques Tati playing long-distance table tennis and falling off his bicycle without reason or purpose. Tommy Cooper repeating 'Spoon jar, jar spoon' until tears of laughter streamed down your face. And of course Monty Python, with its twisting and bending of our comedy expectations. Michael Palin was my favourite. The sketch where he asked policeman John Cleese, 'Do you want to come back to my place?' had been re-enacted by me and Cagsy hundreds of times.

None of these new alternative comedians tapped in to this rich tradition of tomfoolery and slapstick. Perhaps it was gone for ever. Despite not being my cup of tea, I was still transfixed by their performances. They seemed to be making it up on the spot and most of them had their audiences eating out of the palms of their hands. How must that feel? How elated must their brains be when they have a room of strangers laughing at their command? The only time I had come anywhere near that circumstance was when I did a best man's speech at my brother Sam's wedding, and sadly my elation only lasted for seconds. The wedding party had gathered for the reception in a restaurant on Harborne High Street in Birmingham. I had prepared a heartfelt and genuine tribute to the couple, but on the way to the reception an old friend of Sam's had told me a joke he had used when he recently did a best man's speech. He told me it had gone down very well. I decided to open my speech with it. Sam's bride was pregnant at the time of the wedding and came from a large Irish Catholic family. I got up to make my speech and the room fell silent in anticipation.

'It's lovely to see them together. The bride's legs, that is!'

The groom's side of the room laughed loud and hard, but the reaction from the bride's side was much more muted. As I continued with the speech, I became aware that the guests on the bride's side of the room were all getting up off their seats and making their way out of the restaurant. I looked across the table to my mum. 'Sit down!' she hissed at me. I did as I was told. My eldest brother Jonathan was sent out onto the street to apologise to the bride's guests for my faux pas and the guests slowly returned to their seats. I never got to finish my speech, but it had been exhilarating for those five seconds. So, yeah, that was the start, and I presumed the end, of my stab at stand-up comedy.

My work at the town hall was deadly dull. I spent most of my time just smoking cigarettes and staring at the old school clock on the wall. The only piece of work of note that I remember doing was preparing the list of documents for a planning inquiry concerning the proposed Globe Theatre development on the South Bank of the Thames. The Labour-controlled council was doing everything it could to slow down and hamper the application. One of the tasks that the council legal team had to do was to provide a list of documents relating to the case for the lawyers representing the applicants. The documents ran into the thousands and I was tasked with preparing the list. We did not have computers in those days. The council had a system where you dialled up a machine in another part of the building and dictated via the telephone. Your voice was recorded on a vinyl twelve-inch disc and then listened back to, and typed by, a member of the typing pool. The hard copy was then delivered to your desk a day or so later by one of the internal mailmen. I would sit at my desk with the latest pile of documents and dictate as follows.

Item 346, Letter to chief executive from Borough treasurer dated 2 May 1981, Subject: Relocation of bin storage lockers in Sawn Street SE1.

Item 347, Letter from CP Wilson Environmental Services to United Utilities dated 17 January, Subject: Deviation from agreed purchasing procedures.

Item 348, Letter of 15 March 1979 from Town Planner to Ayeford Architectural Consultant, Subject: Change of Use application no 116734210.

Item 349 . . .

And so on. Hour after hour, week after week. It drained my very soul and each new batch of documents was like being punched in the guts by an ape. I decided I had to find a new job away from the malaise in the town hall. I lasted about five months in total and then transferred my Articles to Philcox Gray and Co., a firm of high-street solicitors in the centre of Peckham.

Peckham was at this time one of the poorest and roughest areas of London. Lots of high-density social housing and lots of crime. Criminal defence and housing law was to be my bread and butter. It was a complete change of gear; this work required my full attention ten hours a day and I had to be on call in the evening. The offices were on the first and second floor of an old bank, and it was a rabbit warren of rooms. I had my own office on the second floor, and my fellow workers were all lovely, particularly the two senior solicitors, Claire Turney and John Butler. I particularly liked John for his stubborn refusal to ever speak to an estate agent on the phone. I never socialised with anyone in the office, however; we all very much went our separate ways at the end of the day. I wasn't a very good lawyer, but my clients seemed to like me.

I think it's time for another Would I Lie to You? chapter, concerning my time as a solicitor. See if you can guess which ones are true. None of the names are real.

15

Would I Lie To You? Part 2

Brian Peters

A lot of my work at Philcox Gray was as a criminal defence solicitor. If the client told you they were guilty, then you would do all you could to get them a light sentence. If they told you they were not guilty, then you would prepare their defence and do your best to pick holes in the prosecution's case against them.

Brian Peters was in his early twenties. He always dressed in a black or grey hooded tracksuit and was a regular face around the meeting points on Peckham High Street. Visually there was something of the boxer Nigel Benn about him. He certainly shared his build and physique. He was a scary charmer, in and out of Camberwell and Peckham police stations on what some-times seemed like a weekly basis. Whenever he was arrested he would use his one phone call to contact Philcox Gray, and I would usually be sent out to attend. If it was the evening then I would be contacted via my pager. (No, we still don't have mobile phones!) He was usually arrested for possession of drugs and/or committing a mugging. Mugging seemed to be really catching on in the '80s; I don't remember it being a thing before then. Brian would often be high as a kite and adamant that he was innocent. I would always insist that he kept his mouth shut during his police interview and would sit by his side to ensure that is what he did. His interviews were always fun and invariably went something like this:

OFFICER: Are you Brian Peters of Flat 15, Priory Estate, SE15?

BRIAN: Absolutely not.

ME: It's all right, Brian, you can confirm your name and address or you'll never get out of here.

Silence.

OFFICER: Are you Brian Peters of Flat 15, Priory Estate, SE15?

BRIAN: No fucking comment.

ME: Brian, you can answer the detective, we all know your name and address.

BRIAN: But you said I had to answer 'No comment' to all the questions?

ME: Yeah, but not this one. It's OK, I promise.

BRIAN: I want that promise in writing, right now.

ME: I'm not going to do that, Brian, but if you want to get out of here before tomorrow you need to confirm your name and address.

BRIAN: OK, bro, I'm ready.

OFFICER: Are you Brian Peters of Flat 15, Priory Estate, SE15?

BRIAN: Absolutely fucking not.

ME: Brian, if you don't answer, the police can charge you with a separate offence of failing to give your details. I strongly advise you to confirm your name and address.

BRIAN: What if the address they are saying is wrong?

ME: Then give them your current address.

BRIAN: What if they've got my name wrong?

ME: Have they?

BRIAN (to officer): How are you spelling that name?

OFFICER: B-R-I-A-N P-E-T-E-R-S.

BRIAN: OK, I'm ready. Ask me again.

OFFICER: Are you Brian Peters of Flat 15, Priory Estate, SE15?

BRIAN: Abso-fucking-lutely. Now that was easy, innit? These coppers don't know their arse from their elbow, man. They need to get some proper filing system incorporated into their business.

OFFICER: Thank you for that advice, Brian. Now, can we get on with the interview?

BRIAN: Absolutely fucking not.

And so on.

One evening I was with Mandy and a couple of lads from the Grove queuing outside a pub on Peckham High Street to get into a club that was held on the first floor. Suddenly there was a little commotion in the queue just as the rest of my group had got through the door. I was jostled to one side and pushed up against the pub wall. My assailant was wearing a hoodie to conceal his face and had a knife in his hand.

'Give us your fucking money!' I was frozen scared but managed to reach into my pocket to search for whatever cash I had in there. 'Fucking hurry up,' said the bloke.

'You can have whatever you want,' I said. 'Please don't use the knife!' At this juncture he pulled down his hoodie and gave me a big, beaming smile.

'Hello, Mr Mortimer, I didn't realise it was you.' It was Brian Peters. Never had I been so pleased to see one of my clients. I was out of danger. I think I even thanked him for being so understanding. I represented Brian many times over the next few years.

The Cockroach King

The vast majority of my clients were advised and represented for free on legal aid. I hardly ever saw anyone who earned enough money to be above the legal aid threshold. As said before, Peckham had an awful lot of high-density social housing, a fair percentage of which was infested with cockroaches. The residents seemed to consider it as just something you had to put up with, and before long it became routine for me to ask my clients if they had a problem with a cockroach infestation. If they did, I would arrange a home visit to carry out an inspection of the property. I always took my damp meter along with me on these visits, too. This little hand-held tool has two sharp prongs you push against the internal walls of a home to give a moisture percentage reading. It was rare to find a property that was correctly ventilated and therefore free from condensation, dampness and mould – all of which are potentially damaging to people's health, especially children's.

It wasn't hard to find the cockroaches. They don't like the light, so under the fridge or inside the cooker were good places to start. In some flats they would be everywhere: under the carpets, in the bedding, inside the drawers and cupboards, and even in the baby's cot.

When I had been working in Manchester, I had heard of some lawyers attempting to use Section 99 of the Public Health Act 1936 to bring criminal proceedings against local councils where their houses were subject to a cockroach infestation. I thought that I would give this a go. I chose a lovely lady called Mrs Graham to be my 'test' case. She was a single parent with three young children living in a two-bedroom flat on the North Peckham estate. She had been trying to get the council to do something about the cockroaches for over five years. The stock response was to arrange for the flat to be sprayed with insecticide and then to install special cockroach traps that would make the female cockroaches infertile. This was no more than an Elastoplast. The blocks of flats were huge and for the treatment to be even temporarily successful every single flat in the block would have to be treated, preferably on the same day. This was not something that the council had either the desire or the wherewithal to organise.

The first step was to have experts conduct a survey and have a report prepared. I instructed a public health professor from the University of Cambridge to prepare a report confirming the infestation and that the presence of cockroaches was damaging to the health of the occupants. His report estimated that the flat was home to between two and three thousand cockroaches. I forwarded the report to the council's legal department with a letter threatening to issue a summons against the council if they did not carry out an entire block treatment or offer my client new accommodation. In return, I received a standard pro forma reply stating that the council was aware of the problem and doing everything within its power to eradicate it. They also expressed doubt that the Public Health Act was applicable in these circumstances.

I decided to go shit or bust and issued a summons at Camberwell Green Magistrates Court. At the first hearing a solicitor and a housing officer from the council attended. I was young and newly qualified, and before the hearing they tried to intimidate me with talk of requesting costs from my client if the case proceeded. They questioned whether the Public Health Act was applicable in this case and advised me to drop the case and just go through the normal channels. The housing officer, Mr Rodgers, went as far as to say that the extent of the infestation was being grossly exaggerated by my client. Mrs Graham hated this particular housing officer, who had persistently blocked her requests for help. She instructed me to proceed. The council requested an adjournment so that they could prepare their own report. It was granted and the case would be heard in five weeks' time.

A couple of weeks later I received a letter from the council offering to rehouse Mrs Graham in a different flat on the North Peckham estate. She was not interested. The whole estate was infested and, besides that, it was probably the most crime-ridden, neglected estate in the whole of south London (it was demolished and redeveloped some ten years later). Then another offer came for a flat on a different estate. They were clearly panicking. Mrs Graham declined the offer; she wanted a flat in a converted Victorian house, not on an estate. The council then went silent until the day before the hearing, when they offered Mrs Graham a three-bedroom flat in a Victorian house over-looking Peckham Rye Park. She was delighted but still wanted to go to court. She would give them their answer there.

On the day of the hearing, the council had instructed a barrister to appear on their behalf. I explained that my client was happy to accept their offer and that I would agree to the proceedings being adjourned until a date after she was safely installed in her new flat. After the brief hearing, Mrs Graham and I were approached by a local journalist for our version of events. He took a photo. The next day, a copy of a South London local newspaper was handed to me. There I was on its pages under the headline 'The Cockroach King'. I felt like a warrior in humanity's continuing battle with the insect world.

Daniel

In a solicitor's office, you often need to employ the services of a private investigator. Most frequently this is for the serving of court summons, witness summons and domestic violence injunctions. It can be very time-consuming work and so is rarely carried out by the solicitor. The firm that we used was called Southern Investigations, which is the outfit that has now become notorious for its involvement in telephone hacking and the bungled investigation into the murder of Daniel Morgan.

Daniel was the person I always used to serve my documents. He would be in the office two or three times a week picking up papers and delivering statements, and loved to have a chat and a cup of tea. He had a childlike enthusiasm for his work and was always happy to spin a yarn or two about the world of private detecting. One night at the close of play, he invited me to go for a drink with him in a nearby pub. I could tell there was something on his mind. After a few drinks he came to the point. Would I like to come and work for Southern Investigations? He would pay £30,000 a year, which was not far off double what I was being paid as a solicitor. I told him I would think about it and get back to him. We never did have that follow-up chat. Shortly afterwards, he was found murdered with an axe in his head in a pub car park in Sydenham.

The investigation into his murder is still ongoing some thirty-three years later. It looks like it may never be solved. Whenever I hear his name on a podcast or see his face in the latest TV documentary about the case, I can't help but remember what a charming little bloke he was. It seems he was potentially involved in some very shady dealings, and I sometimes wonder what my fate might have been if I had taken him up on his offer.

Witness for the Defence

You deal with a lot of shoplifting cases in any criminal defence practice. Rarely is there any room for dispute, as the defendant has usually been caught on CCTV or arrested in the shop with the stolen goods about their person and the absence of any proof of payment.

Tanya Wilson had been arrested and charged for the theft of a small box of Lady Esquire shoe dye from Boots the chemist in the Elephant and Castle shopping centre. Value: approximately three pounds. There was no CCTV footage of the theft. She had been stopped and searched by shop security just after leaving the shop. They had found the box of shoe dye in her handbag and no receipt for it. She was adamant that she had not stolen it. She just happened to already own some, and was carrying it around in her bag. She had opted for a jury trial in the Crown Court.

The only exhibit in the case was the unused bottle of shoe dye, still in its little box. The box was notably creased and damaged, but had never been opened. The main witness for the prosecution was the senior security officer from the store. When he was asked about the condition of the packaging of the dye, he explained that it is very common for the packaging of such goods to become tatty because customers often inspect the item with great intensity. It would not be unusual at all for a good percentage of the display products to be damaged in this way.

The Inner London Crown Court is only a stone's throw from the Elephant and Castle, so that lunchtime, out of curiosity, I walked down to Boots and checked the display of Lady Esquire shoe dye. All of them were in perfect condition. This directly contradicted the evidence of the store security officer, so I got out my credit card and bought the lot. I reported my find to the defendant's barrister and he asked if I would be willing to get in the witness box and give evidence about what I had found. I readily agreed, and Tanya was found not guilty. I felt like I was the founder of the UK's No. 1 detective agency.

A Local Incident

I always liked appearing for a client in the County Court, not least because a solicitor is allowed to wear a gown and collar when representing a client there. County Court is where they deal mostly with financial claims between organisations and individuals, and I would most often be representing clients who had fallen behind with their rent or mortgage payments. It was usually just a case of coming clean about their financial situation and agreeing a manageable debt-repayment schedule. If they kept up these reduced payments, they would not lose their home.

One such client was Tony Ellard. He was your typical muscle-bound, tattooed, cockney wide boy that much of the rest of the country would simply refer to as a Millwall fan. A self-employed painter and decorator, he had fallen on hard times due to back problems that stopped him working as much or as often as he would like. One of the major building societies had applied to the court for repossession of his house.

Lambeth County Court is a purpose-built Victorian court-house with fancy feature windows and marble staircases. Tony arrived there on a pair of crutches, gasping and moaning in pain. We sat in the sombre wood-panelled corridor together, finalising the details of the repayment scheme we were going to suggest to the judge. Eventually the solicitor representing the building society, a Mr Duggan, came over to chat. He was a regular face at Lambeth Court and a very difficult man to negotiate with, a company man with no sympathy for the debtor's plight. He wore a cheap silvery-grey suit with a fancy multicoloured tie. His shoes were brown and pointy and his hair was thick and bouffant-styled. There was something of the David Dickinson about him. He declined our offer, stating that he had no faith that Tony would actually stick to the proposed payments.

At this point Tony threw away his crutches and grabbed Duggan around his midriff and pushed him into a small room off the corridor, kicking the door shut behind him. Nobody seemed to have noticed. I should have immediately run to the other end of the corridor and alerted the court bailiff, but for some reason I didn't. Instead, I politely knocked on the door and spoke.

'Tony, are you alright? It's only me, Mr Mortimer.'

'Fuck off, I'm thinking.'

'Is everything OK in there?'

There was no reply. I was still unsure about what to do. Tony was a decent bloke whom I had known for a few years. I had handled the conveyancing when he purchased the house and had looked after his eldest son when he was arrested for assault earlier that year. He would be in serious trouble if this went on and I felt it was worth another go at trying to diffuse the situation. I knocked on the door again.

'Tony, this is really stupid, please just let him go? You'll be in deep shit if this continues.'

There was no reply. I knocked again but he didn't respond. I decided to chance it and slowly opened the door. The first thing I saw was Duggan standing petrified by an open window. As the door opened further, all I could see in the room was an office desk and some filing cabinets. Tony was nowhere to be seen.

I looked at the solicitor again and he nervously pointed at the office desk. Tony must be under there, I assumed. I indicated to the solicitor to leave the room and he scurried out like a snake being released back into the wild.

'Tony, come out from under there. It's just me.'

'Has that solicitor bloke gone?'

'Yeah, but I'm sure he'll be back any minute, probably with a couple of bailiffs.'

Tony slowly emerged from the cubby hole beneath the desk.

'I'm fucked now, aren't I?' he said.

'I don't know, Tony. Did you hurt him or anything?'

'No, I never touched him. I didn't even say fuck all to him. I don't know what I was thinking. My wife's going to kill me!'

'We need to get out there and apologise to him, see if we can smooth it over.'

I told Tony to stay quiet. We walked out of the room together. Duggan was sitting with his head in his hands.

'Mr Duggan, I am so sorry for my client's behaviour. He doesn't know what came over him and wants to apologise for any distress he caused.'

Duggan looked up at me. He was crying.

'Can I get you a glass of water or anything?'

Duggan shook his head.

'My client wants you to know that nothing like that will ever happen again. Would it be OK if he came over and apologised to you?'

Duggan nodded his head. I beckoned Tony over.

'Mr Duggan is ready to hear your apology, Tony.'

'Look, I'm really sorry, mate. It all just got too much for me, you know, the thought of losing my home and that ... What can I say? I'm really, really sorry.'

Duggan nodded tearily, then slowly got up and walked away. Tony and I sat together nervously expecting the arrival of the bailiff or police, but they never came. Eventually our case was called and we went into court. Duggan was nowhere to be seen. If the plaintiff's representative does not make an appearance, then the suggested repayment schedule goes through unopposed. It was a great relief to Tony, although as we walked out of the court we still both half expected a policeman to come and grab him. Nothing happened, though, and Tony went back home to give the good news to his wife.

I never saw Duggan again at Lambeth County Court. He must have had some sort of breakthrough that morning and decided to take a different career path. I was glad to have played a part in that decision.

The briefcase

One day I had an appointment with a Mr Greenwood. I had never seen him before. The note in my appointment diary simply read 'land dispute'. When he entered my office he was wearing a light-coloured mackintosh with a checked shirt and a green woollen tie. His hair was thick and greying. He wore thick-rimmed spectacles with powerful lenses. He had in his hand a bulging briefcase, which he immediately placed on my desk. He was not one for pleasantries and small talk.

'Are you a solicitor? I mean a proper, qualified solicitor?'

'Yes, I am. How can I help you?'

'You seem awfully young to be a solicitor. Do you have a certificate or something?'

'Yes, I do. It's on the wall there, above the fireplace.'

He got up and inspected my practising certificate. Happy with its contents, he sat down again. He stared intently at me while chewing his cheek.

'Forgive me for being cautious but I've been to several solicitors before you and none of them have been of any help. I'm hoping you might be different.'

'I hope so too. Now, how can I help you?'

'I've lived in the same house for the past thirty years, which backs onto a piece of land that I believe is owned by the council. About seven years ago my neighbour moved his rear fence back about twenty feet and incorporated some of this land into his garden. It's theft if you ask me, but no one will do anything about it.'

'What have you tried to do since the fence was moved?'

'Well as soon as I saw what he had done I reported it to the council. After months and months they finally told me that it was a matter between themselves and my neighbour and they would inform me when the issue was resolved.'

'Do you have copies of your correspondence with the council?'

'Yes, we'll come to that. I then got in touch with the local MP, who fobbed me off by saying it was being dealt with by the council, which of course, as far as I'm concerned, it wasn't. That's when I went to a solicitor for the first time. They informed me that a small strip of the stolen land might actually belong to me.'

'Do you have any of the correspondence from those solicitors?'

'Yes, I'll come to that. Can you please stop interrupting me? Now, the land registry searches revealed that the main portion of the stolen land actually belonged to British Rail on some sort of lease from the council. When my solicitor wrote to British Rail they referred him back to the council saying that they had the right to enforce the boundaries.'

'It would be really helpful to see those land registry searches and the correspondence with British Rail.'

'Why don't you listen instead of just interrupting? I have all the relevant papers in my briefcase but you need the general picture before you get stuck into them.'

Around this point the telephone rang on my desk. It was my boss, Claire.

'Are you with a Mr Greenwood?'

'Yes.'

'Has he got grey hair, big spectacles and a tatty brown briefcase?'

'Yes.'

'I'll be up there in a minute.'

I put the phone down and Mr Greenwood continued.

'The problem is that the council are now point-blank refusing to correspond with either myself or my solicitors. I've sacked my solicitors on account of them being useless and now I want something done.'

At this point Claire entered my office.

'Hello Mr Greenwood. I thought we had agreed that you wouldn't make any appointments with this firm?'

'Well, yes, kind of. I couldn't quite remember.'

I had no idea what was going on. Claire asked me if I had

seen the contents of the briefcase. I told her I hadn't and she invited me to open it. I pressed the two clasps and pulled the lid. Inside were forty, maybe fifty, used cardboard McDonalds chip and burger packets all pressed tightly together in a lump.

'Come on, Mr Greenwood. I'll see you out,' said Claire and led the slightly sheepish and deflated Mr Greenwood out of my office.

Every legal aid solicitor will be familiar with the Mr Greenwoods of this world. Law offices attract them as do many other public offices. They are harder to spot than you might think and he certainly had me fooled.

16

Yet Another Big Day

My life as a fully fledged solicitor is ticking along. I don't find the work easy. Mornings are in court, afternoons are spent with clients new and old, leaving only the evenings to do any actual casework. It's a slog and a challenge to keep on top of it all, and I'm too knackered to go out much. Mandy now has a job working on a play bus in Brixton. She is similarly drained. We watch the television, order take-out meals and occasionally go down to the Grove pub, where we are on talking terms with a little gang of regulars. At the weekend we go to East Street Market and never return without buying yet more glass clowns or fish. We become increasingly obsessed with the movements and lifestyle of the David Byrne look-a-likey who lives silently in the room above us. Every morning we see him leave in his silver suit carrying a cheap shiny briefcase. He walks bolt upright and with his steady, even pace seems to glide along the pavement. There is always a low light at his window, but never any movement or sound. What is he? What scheme is he composing? What is he building in there?

One morning Mandy and I were in the downstairs kitchen cooking processed meats, when we were joined by another resident, called Frankie. We were slightly wary of him, as all of our net-curtain spying on him seemed to suggest he was a drug dealer. There would be a constant stream of visitors to his room early morning, early evening and late at night, and occasionally, when visitors rang the intercom late at night, he would open his French windows and tell them to fuck off while brandishing an electric chainsaw. As we talked with Frankie, we heard the front door of the hostel open and close and then watched as David Byrne floated away down the road. We mentioned to Frankie how fascinated we were with him and how much we yearned to get a glimpse inside his room. We should never have said it. Frankie marched us upstairs to his room and produced a key that fitted Byrne's lock.

He opened the door and then walked away. We couldn't resist, and took a step into the room. What we saw sent a chill down my spine. The bedding had been removed from the bed and replaced with a large board of what looked like plywood. On this board were two tea trays, on each of which were four or five candles burning away. At various points around the floor were lit candles, and there were more on the dressing table, sink and shelves. The curtains were drawn, and on the ceiling was a huge, hand-painted red spider. Had we chanced across the very heart of a satanic cult? It felt like something that we should never, ever have seen. The following day we heard the first sounds of life in the room above us. David Byrne was changing his locks. We felt uneasy, now convinced that this dark master would know exactly who had been in his room. He would often look up from the street at our window as he left the building, and we just hoped he didn't have any rituals planned for us.

As work was so busy, it was not my habit to go home during the day, even though I only lived about half a mile from the office. One day, however, I finished my court hearings by mid-morning and so thought I would surprise Mandy and pop home before going into the office. When I opened the door, I was met with the sight of Mandy in bed with what looked like a Hells Angels farmer. I felt pathetic in my cheap grey suit, holding my pretentious plastic briefcase.

'Hi, Mandy, I'll leave you to it,' I said. I closed the door and went into the bathroom on the other side of the corridor. I felt angry, confused and empty. Mandy came into the bathroom and said she was sorry, really sorry. I told her I would like her to leave and went back to work.

When I got back home that evening she was gone. All I was left with was a gut-wrenching feeling of heartbreak. I felt very lonely. I had failed to establish a life beyond my relationship with Mandy and my little room in the hostel. We had suffocated the life out of each other and she had escaped while a handful of air remained in her lungs. A few days later there was a knock on the door of my room. I thought/hoped it might be Mandy. It wasn't. Instead, it was face I hadn't seen for some ten years or maybe more: Alan King.

Alan had been at the same school as me in the early '70s back in Middlesbrough. We had never been close friends, but we had always had a friendly relationship. In truth, I had long forgotten him. He explained that he had heard I was living in London and had phoned up my mum to get my address. We chatted for a while. It seemed he was making a living as a professional horse-racing gambler. I was glad to see him and have his company, but in my current malaise was mostly itching for him to leave. He suggested that we go out for a drink sometime, and I gave some sort of non-committal reply. Just as he was leaving, he asked me if I fancied meeting up for drink that Thursday. He was going to a comedy show in New Cross.

'Yeah, maybe. What's the show?' I replied.

'It's called "Vic Reeves Big Night Out". It's a lad from our neck of the woods, really funny. It's at the Goldsmiths Tavern. Just come along if you fancy it?'

'Yeah, I might do that – you know, depending on work and stuff.'

When he left, I shut the door with no intention of seeing him again or going to his odd-sounding comedy night. Over the next couple of days, my life continued to feel shit and panic was beginning to set in. Maybe it was time to do a runner and go back home. I couldn't eat. I couldn't sleep. Men are so shit at coping with break-ups. Well, at least it appeared that this one was. The only tiny flickering flame of hope for contact with the world outside my room was this invitation for a drink with Kingy. It wasn't much, but at least it was something. So, that Thursday I dragged myself onto the number 12 bus and made my way down to the Goldsmiths Tavern for a slice of 'Vic Reeves Big Night Out'.

This decision would of course turn out to be the most pivotal moment of my entire life. What if my mum had refused to give Kingy my address? What if Kingy hadn't been such a decent bloke as to seek me out? What if I hadn't been home when he called? Above all, what if Mandy hadn't left me? I would never have taken up this invite if she was still around and I was happy. It always feels to me that fate was playing its part. I have never had the chance to thank Mr Hells Angels Farmer.

17

1988: A Big Night Out

When I arrived at the Goldsmiths Tavern, there was no sign that any comedy night was on offer. I asked at the bar and they informed me that it was being held in the room upstairs. I bought a pint and walked up the stairs into a small dark room with a makeshift stage at one end. Only three or four audience tables were occupied. Kingy was at a table with about five other lads, all around my age. I sat down and waited for the show to start. I fully expected it to be like all the other comedy shows I had ever seen: a mildly funny compere introducing a series of posh lads and lasses doing their twenty minutes of stand-up. How wrong could I be? From backstage came the PA announcement:

'Ladies and gentlemen, please welcome live on stage Britain's top light entertainer, dancer and singer . . . Mr Vic Reeves!'

A spotlight hit the stage and a backing track of the song 'Fly Me to the Moon' struck up. Then he emerged.

Fuck . . . Fuck . . . FUCK . . . **FUCK!**

What is he? Where am I? Who sanctioned this? I have been

transported, in an instant, to a world of entertainment far, far away from anything I have ever witnessed before. A tall, handsome man, with jet-black high-quiffed hair, bounds onto the stage. He is wearing a beautiful toothpaste-white suit with a white shirt and black tie. His shoes are shiny black and unfeasibly pointy. He kicks his slender leg high into the air, fashions a stance that is part cockerel, part lion, and begins to sing. Who is this entertainment warrior? It really does feel as if Elvis has just entered the building. He begins to sing, and boy has he got the voice to back up the chutzpah. I am transfixed. I have found a very happy place. This is magnificent. This is Mr Vic Reeves.

After finishing his song, the audience of fifteen people erupts into applause. It is impossible for me to remember all that I saw him perform that evening, but I know at one point he pulled a hideously misshapen handmade fox puppet out of a battered old suitcase and had a chat with him.

I remember him and his mate Johnny Irvine on the stage tap-dancing with short planks of wood nailed to their shoes. Their faces were covered with picture masks of Brian Ferry and the tap-shoe noises were provided by a recording of pans being hit with a wooden spoon.

I remember him donning a ZZ Top beard and examining some woodworking tools.

I remember him seated behind a cardboard box mounted on thin wooden legs with 'Hammond Organ' written on it, and he mimed playing a tune from a Hammond Organ party album playing over the PA.

I remember he beckoned a member of the audience on stage and asked him various nonsensical quiz questions such as, 'True or false: Cliff Michelmore's favourite harness was made of meat.' The prize at the end of the quiz was to 'Meet John Wilson'. John was just a shy little local lad whose hand the contestant got to shake.

The show ended with Vic singing along to the theme from the TV series *Star Trek* while a disco ball shot a thousand starry lights across the stage and the audience. He didn't sing any words. He just 'aaarh aaarred' along with the melody.

Although I don't remember the entire contents of the hour-long show, what I do remember is the extraordinary feeling of witnessing something truly unique and important. I felt like I had seen the past, the present and the future of comedy. It was right up my street, even though I had never walked its pavement before.

When the show was over, Vic came to our table and sat down to enjoy the rest of the evening with his mates. Kingy introduced me to him (revealing his real name was in fact Jim Moir), but I could hardly speak. I have no idea if he even noticed me. His old mates at the table had known him for years and treated him as just one of their gang. Johnny Irvine, Jack Dent, John Wilson and Alan Davidson were lifelong friends of his from Darlington. Fred Aylward and Dorian Crook were mates of his from art college. They were really friendly blokes and I felt at home in their company. I suppose it probably did cross my mind how nice it would be to be a part of this gang, and on the way home with Kingy I couldn't help but ask the questions that everyone would ask when they first saw Vic perform: 'What is the show all about? What is it meant to be? Is it a spoof of something from the past?'

Kingy was ready with his reply: 'No, it's not a spoof. It's what comedy was always meant to be before it was diverted by arseholes.' Bit harsh but I knew what he meant.

I couldn't wait until next Thursday and my next dose of 'Vic Reeves Big Night Out'. In the meantime I chanced a visit to the Grove to see if any familiar faces might allow me to join them for a drink. I was in luck. Nick the Cabby and Andy Blackburn were in there having a drink with some other mates. I told them about Vic Reeves and they agreed to come to the next show. I was evangelical about it, and waxed lyrical to anyone who would listen. I think this was the usual pattern for any newbie who attended the show, as the audiences kept doubling every week. About four shows later, it was transferred to the 10 p.m. slot in the big room on the ground floor (Paul O'Grady had the 8 p.m. slot).

The week before the move downstairs, Jim was anxious to make the show longer and fuller. I had been to the past three or four shows and Jim now knew who I was and we had spoken on a few occasions – just little chats; we weren't really friends. Nevertheless, he asked me if I would come on stage and present him with a cheque for £10,000 for helping the daft kids. I, of course, agreed. He asked Johnny Irvine to ramp up the production on the musical numbers and add an extra layer of sound effects. Some speciality acts from the local talent-show circuit were added to the bill: a 6ft 7in giant who sang easy-listening songs while smoking a pipe, and a tiny little old fella who dressed in lederhosen and played *oom-pah-pah* songs on his accordion.

The following Thursday, I made my Big Night Out debut.

The big room could hold an audience of around 150 people. Half of them sat at tables boozing and the other half stood around boozing. I think admission was £2. My part in the show was tiny, but it was a massive deal to me. I got to take the hallowed walk to the backstage area, where Jim had his pile of homemade props and costumes – a tiny little room with flaking paint and the smell of damp. A cheap mirror leant against the wall and was covered with little messages and graffiti from previous performers – 'Prepare to die a thousand deaths'; 'I'm pissed again despite all the promises'; 'I used to be a half decent tyre fitter' – and hundreds of signatures from long-forgotten hopefuls.

Taking that step backstage was like taking my first step into showbiz. It really does feel like you are crossing an invisible line between the real world and some other alien experience. It is very enticing. When my cue came, I strode onto the stage, gave Vic his cheque and congratulated him on his charitable achievements regarding the daft lads. I think some people laughed. I was probably only up there for a minute. Afterwards I sat back down in the audience and watched the rest of the show. People were telling me I had done well, but better than that people were actually talking to me: people I didn't know. The dreaded strangers.

Over the next few weeks, the audiences got bigger and bigger. There would be a large queue forming from about 9 p.m. and lots of people were unable to get in. The place was packed and the atmosphere was bordering on the Hogarthian. Big Night Out was very much a night out, not a stand-up comedy show. It lasted two or three hours, during which huge amounts of booze were consumed.

The audience wasn't necessarily transfixed by what was happening on stage; they would dip in and out of the show as they felt fit. There was absolutely no requirement to remain quiet during the performance, although when Jim was on stage they usually did. Jim booked a few stand-ups from time to time but they could never get their heads around the fact that the audience wouldn't really give them their full attention. It never bothered Jim. He just did stuff that he considered entertaining and it was up to the audience to either enjoy it or reject it and go to the bar or talk to their mates.

The show was entirely new every week, though certain characters and items, such as 'Vic's Big Quiz' or 'The Hammond Organ', would appear in every show. Local celebrities started to attend: Chris Difford and Glen Tilbrook from the band Squeeze (significant heroes of mine), Tim Roth, Danny Baker and Jools Holland. I think one night Paul Gascoigne came along. God knows what he made of it. I started to do more and more little appearances. Jim always needed something to be happening on stage while he got changed or had a break for a pint and a fag. Kingy would go on stage as Doctor King and his Flying Rabbits. He would tell jokes and after each punchline would frantically twirl a couple of toy rabbits attached to a string around his head. He would also perform as 'Les Pantalons'. He would wear a French blue-and-white shirt and erect a washing line on the stage, on which he would hang different coloured damp trousers. As he did this, some French café music played, and with every pair of trousers that was successfully pegged onto the line, a sound-effect voice stolen from a French-language teaching tape would say, '*Le pantalon gris*', '*Le pantalon noir*', '*Le pantalon vert*' and so on.

Jim's mate Dorian Crook would come on stage wearing a tweed suit and a cravat and tell one-liners. On every punchline, the audience would shout, 'Fuck off, Toff!' and Dorian would reply, 'Why, thank you.' But aside from Kingy and Dorian, I was the only one who seemed up for getting on stage and speaking. Some of the cameos I remember doing were:

The Butcher

Vic would introduce me from the stage and I would come on with a huge paper helmet covering my head and face in the shape of a bishop's hat. On the hat I drew pictures of the various cuts of this week's guest meat. For example, if it was beef, I would illustrate the hat with shit drawings of its various cuts: topside, fillet steak, flank, shin, tongue etc. We would chat about the cuts and pick a favourite or two. The helmet with the drawings on would return at a later date as the preferred headgear of The Man with the Stick.

Judge Nutmeg

I would wear my legal gown and collar and act as the judge of the climactic Vic's Big Quiz. I would try to come over all legalistic and bullying, and would even occasionally be slightly confrontational with Vic. This was a bit of an accidental revelation. The audience seemed to enjoy Vic Reeves receiving a bit of pushback. Jim had created Vic to be a super self-confident, even occasionally pompous character, full of bluster and self-assurance. He was, after all, as Jim's flyers posted around New Cross declared,

'Britain's top light entertainer'. Underneath all that swagger, though, there was definitely an idiot and a clown who had been given the keys to the castle. Jim made sure that Vic never ever allowed his cover to slip, though he let Judge Nutmeg pick away at Vic's confident façade, and I suppose in that simple dynamic the seeds of a double act were sown.

Tinker's Rugsack

These two were a folk-singing duo from the Lake District. For this, Jim and I would dress up as two fell walkers with red cagoules, huge bushy beards and walking sticks, and would chat about our latest walks. Jim was always slightly more enthusiastic about our rambling activities and there was also a suggestion that I was having intercourse with his wife behind his back. His character was always keen to suggest that 'it's not all walking.' For example, he would wax lyrical about a nativity scene that we had fashioned from root vegetables, or a broth we had cooked using only topsoil and the softer barks. A sample:

VIC: I noticed you disappeared upstairs whilst the broth was simmering.

BOB: Yes, I was just searching for that OS map of Arthgarthenthaw.

VIC: Did you find it?

BOB: No, but I found what I was looking for.

VIC: Great news, praise the Lord. So as you can see from this wonderful broth, it most definitely is not all walking.

BOB (under breath): It fucking is.

We would then sing our Tinkers Rugsack theme song:

I remember the summer of '75
I was your husband
And you were my wife
We lived in a tent made of parsley and sage
And we looked at each other and smiled
I played the drums
Whilst you played the flute
Crash bang wallop
And root a toot toot
We ate thousands of turnips never asking why
In the summer of '75
Oh reflections of you in the waterfall
Cascading through my mind
Oh reflections of you
Still waters run deep
In the summer of '75
My eyes were blue
Whilst my eyes were black
I spoke to the churchwarden
While I smoked some crack
You murdered my wife and buried her alive
In the summer of '75
We slept in an orchard on a tapestry rug
And drank fine mead from an old Saxon jug
We gazed in wonder as Frampton came alive
In the summer of '75

Lyrics and music were by Jim. The show was 95 per cent his work and I was just a bit-part Rodney. As I recall, I would just sit with Jim for, say, twenty minutes before the show and he would tell me what was required of me. We didn't have a script; we just needed to have a general idea of what needed to be said and we could then wing it once on stage. I was just having the time of my life being part of a wonderful, vibrant, exciting evening. It made my whole week as a solicitor bearable, knowing that I had my Thursday-night adventure up ahead. I had no more aspirations for the show than that.

My favourite memories of these Goldsmiths Tavern days are quite simply sitting in the audience allowing the genius of Vic Reeves to wash over me like a huge wallowing chocolate button. He would sing like a handsome prince serenading his favourite stallion. He would dance like a crab scuttling his way to a Portsmouth boot sale. He would perform intricate magic tricks with unfathomable denouements. He would present characters that had only been previously imagined in the discarded handbag of Dr Yusef Chicago. My favourite was probably Davy Stott and his dancing bott. On his head he wore a wig made of half a plastic football, inverted, with some wiry hair attached to give the impression of a comb-over. He wore a tweed jacket and a big gold bow tie. Down below he wore a green tartan kilt and on his feet shoes with the pointiest toes you can achieve while still being able to walk. He spoke with a high-pitched Geordie accent and would tell very funny Tommy Cooper-style jokes, such as: 'I put so much petrol in my car the other day that I couldn't get into it!' and, 'Talk about fat! It's ideal for cooking with.' At the end of the joke he would pick up two sticks, each with a small football on the end, bend over with his back to the audience, and produce the balls from under the kilt to represent the two cheeks of his arse. The buttock balls would then 'dance' to some old-fashioned children's party music as Jim manipulated them with the sticks.

The shows were chaotic and sprawling. All the props were purchased from Deptford flea market or made by Jim in his kitchen. I don't think Jim and I could be described as friends at this point; we had only known each other for about twelve weeks, and I didn't really see him much away from the Thursday-night shows. When we did meet up at one of the pubs in Deptford or New Cross, I was still a bit in awe of him and found it tricky to separate Jim from my passionate admiration for the character of Vic Reeves he played on stage.

The show kept attracting more and more people, mostly via word of mouth, and was even starting to get attention from listings magazines and London newspapers. A reviewer from the *Evening Standard* wrote a piece about the show basically saying it was the most inept, confusing, anti-comedy show he had ever seen. I think Jim sensed otherwise and felt the show had a bright future. He stopped booking the Goldsmiths Tavern and arranged a run of eight Sundays on the trot at the nearby Albany Empire Theatre in Deptford. The Albany was a 400-seater. The show would need to have proper production values and be less chaotic and rambling. In a word, it would need to be 'proper'. Jim had about six weeks to get it all together.

18

From Robert to Bob

I doubted I would even be involved in the new show, and reckoned that my contributions were unlikely to make the cut. My guess was that Jim would probably book established acts to fill the gaps when he wasn't on stage, and I wasn't too upset at the thought. Big Night Out had already given me my first set of mates in London, and, perhaps just as importantly, a new girlfriend.

There were a lot of attractive and seemingly single ladies that attended the shows, and my tiny little sprinkling of celebrity, which only existed during the three-hour bubble of Big Night Out, meant that occasionally one of them would come up and talk to me. This was my dream of thirty years come true. From the pubs and clubs of Middlesbrough to the student bars of Brighton, Leicester and Manchester, all I had ever yearned for was the occasional female to approach me with a friendly smile and an easy outlook. Now it was a reality, and probably the greatest gift to have ever been bestowed upon me.

I would chat and have a laugh with them, but the one thing

I still couldn't do was actually ask any of them for a date. There was one girl in particular that I was getting along with. She enjoyed her booze and loved to smoke – two of my all-consuming passions at the time. We could make a tight smoke and booze unit, I surmised. Her name was Emma, and we would sit together long after the shows had finished, but I could never drum up the courage to ask her out. She was a dancer and, like Mandy, wore '50s dresses and Doc Martens boots. She had a boyish mod haircut that would have laid sweetly on the head of any of The Small Faces, and we talked a lot. I enjoyed her company, but we were in danger of becoming 'just friends'.

At Easter that year I went up to Middlesbrough to be with Mum. She was sixty-seven years old now and had been living on her own for the past five years. She was as fit as a fiddle, though, and her house was still an orange and yellow palace. My brother Sam was living in Birmingham and Johnny was in Southend. Rick still lived in the North East, near Northallerton, and Sam, Johnny and I would stagger our visits up north so that she always had a visit from one of us on the near horizon. Rick would see her nearly every day. Mum now had three grandchildren: Sarah, Charles and Helen, and they were the new loves of her life. She would look after Rick's baby daughter Helen during her parents' working hours and continued to do so until she went to school. I owe a great debt to Rick and his lovely wife Angela for looking after Mum. Without their commitment to her, I think the guilt would have been too difficult to bear.

I returned from my trip up north early evening on a Sunday. When I got to the hostel, the front car parking area was covered with burnt furniture, mattresses and debris, and the façade of

191

the building was grey with smoke. There had been a fire and the place was uninhabitable. Maybe one of David Byrne's rituals had got out of hand; maybe some of my leftover processed meats had dried up and spontaneously ignited; maybe the Hells Angels farmer had left a splash of diesel oil on an electrical fitting. I will never know. I phoned up Kingy and he said I was welcome to come and stay in the spare room at his flat in East Dulwich. The only items I bothered to salvage from the hostel were my glass fishes and clowns.

While staying with Kingy, I confided in him that I fancied Emma. At the next Big Night Out, when we were all milling about outside the venue at the end of the evening, Kingy grabbed me by my collar and dragged me over to Emma. He then crushed us together declaring, 'You two have a fucking snog and stop fannying about.' And we did. Not all my own work, of course, but I had a girlfriend. Soon after, I more or less moved in full-time to Emma's flat in Deptford, which was in the block next to the one that Jim lived in with Johnny Irvine.

One day Jim phoned me to chat about the upcoming Albany Empire show and asked me what I wanted to be called on the publicity material. I was really taken aback.

I was going to be in the show.

He reckoned that 'Bob' Mortimer would sound better than Robert. What did I think? I agreed. He also mentioned that we should meet up and properly write some material we could perform together. Again, I agreed. I was really chuffed.

I had never been called Bob before, but 'Vic and Bob' . . . it definitely had a certain ring to it.

19

The Albany Empire

I started to get to know Jim a lot better. He is 100 per cent committed to making other people laugh. Even today I will look up from my seat backstage or in a hotel bar and he will be with people, sometimes strangers, and they will be laughing. It's his calling and his gift to us all. There is hardly a day that I've passed with Jim in the past thirty years when I haven't buckled in two with laughter, and I have spent many, many days in his company. A quick calculation would be about 8,000 – or 64,000 hours if you prefer larger numbers.

I started to go round to Jim's flat and sit in his little kitchen with him, writing down ideas and helping him cobble together a show. He knew that I was a huge fan of his comedy and sensed that I found the same things funny as he did. Because of this, I think he trusted me as a reliable sounding board. I was just helping him sort out which sketches should be in the show, how long they should be, and occasionally reminding him of things that he had done which were 'must dos' and things that could usefully be dropped. I suppose I was acting as amateur producer. The most important thing when working with Jim is to keep him talking. He spews out ideas ten to the dozen and then forgets them in an instant. You listen and make a mental note of any crackers. Then, when you have a couple of these crackers, you stop him and force him to elaborate and develop one of these ideas.

For example, Jim might mention that he believes a simple crushed tin-foil helmet is all that you need to convince people that you are from the future. You ask what sort of clothing would enhance this futuristic vibe. He replies with great certainty: 'A red boiler suit.' You ask what message such a person would have from future generations that he has already lived through. Jim replies: 'You cannot achieve racial equality by putting trout in a bucket.' You ask what music this person would listen to. 'Clown music,' comes the reply, without hesitation. So you suggest that these people go on stage at the Albany Empire and deliver their message to the world. 'Yeah, we should do that,' says Jim. You ask what they should be called: 'Talcumpowder and Turnips.' And thus a new act for Big Night Out is born. Talc and Turnips would become a regular feature on the TV version of *Big Night Out*, too. Whenever Jim and I talk about the good old days, we always remember them as our favourite characters to perform. If you watch them carefully, you can hear us laughing all the way through our performances. No other characters express so well the sheer joy, gall and childishness of our work together, and all I had to do was just keep Jim talking.

Jim had a new format for the show when it moved to the Albany. He would present from a large desk positioned at the side of the stage, instead of standing in the centre as he had done

at the Goldsmiths Tavern. The desk would make a clear statement that this was an entertainment show of the type you might
see on your TV, and not a stand-up comedy parade. It would
also be essential for the hiding and displaying of props. The
backdrop would be black stage curtains displaying the words
Vic Reeves Big Night Out. Each individual letter was just a few
inches of white card pinned to the cloth. It served as a constant
reminder that although Vic Reeves seemed to consider himself
the king of entertainment, his budget and his actual status was
not as bloated as his ego.

The basic flow of the show was that Vic Reeves would
perform for five minutes or so and then invite his next guest
on stage. This might be a novelty act he had booked such as
Easy Listening Man, or Malcolm X, an old bloke who played
the saxophone with such ferocity that small toy snakes started
to stream from the end of his instrument. It might be Johnny
Irvine singing his electro rap 'The Evil Bull' while dangling
a papier-mâché bull's head from a string on the end of a stick.
It might be Dorian as The Toff, once again being roundly
encouraged to 'Fuck off'. It might be Jim himself playing one
of his characters, such as Mr Dennis the Shopkeeper or Peter
Rosewood the Perfumer, whose magical tinctures could heal
you of all your personal qualms.

The rest of the show would be me and Jim performing
together in character, or one of my characters assisting Vic in
progressing the show. These are the items that we would write
together. We would go to the Birds Nest pub on Saturday
night and discuss possible material while drinking, and then
the following day would write down those items that we could

remember having discussed. If any new props were needed we would pop over to the massive junk market just off Deptford High Street and buy them for pennies. We would then perform the show that evening. Some of my favourite characters that came from these writing sessions were:

The Man with the Stick

This was me with a large paper helmet covering my head. Jim wanted me to carry a large stick on stage with something attached to its end inside a carrier bag. He could then encourage the audience to shout, 'What's on the end of the stick, Vic?' On the first night of the Albany shows, the only stick we could find backstage was about fifteen feet long, so that was what we used. When the audience shouted, 'What's on the end of the stick?' Vic asked me to show what it was. Unfortunately I had forgotten to put anything in the carrier bag and so had to refuse to reveal its contents. From that day forward the Man with the Stick never revealed the secret within the bag. On the front and back of the helmet I would do terribly childish drawings of things I claimed to have seen that particular week, e.g. The Who setting fire to a tomato in an alley round the back of the shops, or Seb Coe eating a family of spiders. Jim would read out these sightings and comment upon them. We gave The Man with the Stick permission to be a bit cheeky to Vic and gently poke at his authority. During the first Albany show I asked Vic, out of the blue, if he was still eating the very cheap cuts of chicken such as the nose and the hands. For a moment Vic didn't know what to say and stared at the paper helmet as

With Mark and Ulrika-ka-ka-ka on set of *Shooting Stars*

With Paul, Jim and
Mark Williams filming
Slade on Holiday

Donald and Davy Stott.
Our favourite characters

Filming a *Masterchef* sketch for
The Smell of Reeves and Mortimer

Motorcycling through France on our way to the menu gastronomique

Preparing for our scorpion hunt on
location in southern Spain

A nice pie. One of the
loves of my life

2001: on the set of *Randall and Hopkirk
(Deceased)* with Jim, Emilia and Tom

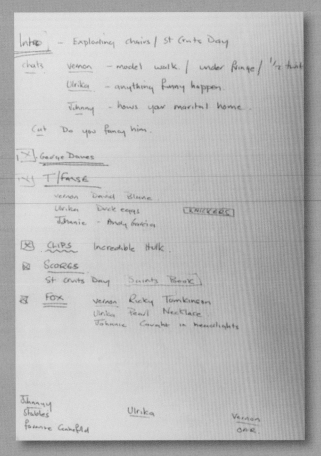

Intro - Exploading chairs / St Cruts Day

chats   Vernon - model walk. / under fringe / ½ thin
         Ulrika - anything funny happen.
         Johnny - hows your marital home.

Cut   Do you fancy him.

[X] George Dawes

[Y] T/FALSE
    Vernon   David Blune
    Ulrika   Duck eggs   [KNICKERS]
    Johnnie - Andy Garcia

[X] CHIPS   Incredible Hulk.

[X] SCORES
    St Cruts Day   Saints Book

[X] FOX   Vernon   Ricky Tomkinson
             Ulrika   Pearl Necklace
             Johnnie Caught in headlights

Johnnyy
Stables   Ulrika   Vernon
foamre Centrefold   CAR.

This is the script we would have on our desk for
Shooting Stars. We have never used autocue

2002: having a fight with Les Dennis

The cast of *Catterick*. The best bunch of people you could ever meet

2014: the *House of Fools* cast

Chris Rea sent me this wonderful photo after I told the story of him insisting on putting an egg in my bath on *Would I Lie To You?*

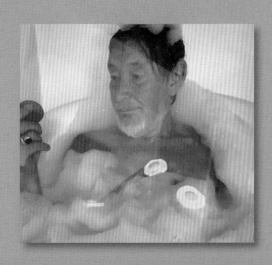

2018: me and Cags still supporting
The Boro after 50 years

Lung exercise machine

Moments before Paul caught a fish as I fell over and the true
essence of *Gone Fishing* was discovered

Terrible photo but, as you can see, we will never
be defeated

2018: backstage at *Comic Relief*. Jim and Matt cracking me up as always

For all those who have supported me

if it contained his sworn enemy. Then, after a brief silence, he said, 'You wouldn't let it lie, would you? You just couldn't let it lie.' The timing was perfect and the audience laughed. In that moment a catchphrase was born that is still shouted at us in the streets to this day. We hadn't written it and I had never heard Vic say that phrase before. Like I said, you just have to keep him talking.

Crown Court Capers with Judge Lionel Nutmeg

We both thought that somewhat tart relationship between Judge Nutmeg and Vic was worth pursuing, so decided to hold a mini trial on stage with an unsuspecting member of the audience as the defendant. The charges against them would be trumped up, such as 'fannying about on a yacht after sunset' or 'blocking the spout of Rod Stewart's teapot'. They would be forced to take an oath of truth by swearing upon an old album book of the TV show *Daktari* starring Clarence the Cross-Eyed Lion. The defendant would invariably plead guilty and Nutmeg, Vic and the entire audience would chant: 'Terrible man, terrible man, terrible man.' His punishment would be decided by Vic spinning the Wheel of Justice. This particular prop is a great example of Jim's mind working at maximum power. It was like a large Catherine wheel, encircled by pink fun fur, with a foot-long piece of string attached, at the end of which was a hair comb. Many potential punishments were written on the wheel, e.g. 'Walk like a crab while carrying a bucket of urine', or 'Spend the rest of the evening wearing a Brillo-pad helmet.'

On revealing the wheel to the audience, Jim would ask,

'What do we do to the Wheel of Justice?' 'Comb its hair!' they would command. Vic would then give the pink fun fur a little tidy up with the comb, then spin the wheel on its centre pin while singing:

Spin spin spin the Wheel of Justice
See how fast the bastard turns

The whole audience would join in and cheer happily as the defendant learned of his or her punishment.

Donald and Davy Stott

We decided that it would be fun if Davy Stott had a straight-man sidekick, to develop Davy's character beyond just being a joke-teller and magician/illusionist. Donald would have a similar comb-over to Davy but would wear a grey leather bomber jacket and super-tight yellow slacks. We found a pair of bright-red multi-buckled Chelsea boots at Deptford market to complete the look. We would sit in Jim's kitchen and both talk in high-pitched Geordie voices. Soon enough, a pattern developed. If Donald asked a normal question like, 'Do you have a car?', Davy Stott transformed into a deluded, boastful liar. 'My car is a bright-green Aston Martin with a shark's fin and a periscope for when I am going through tunnels.' Or: 'My house was built by a team of golden eagles and has a roof made out of German diamonds.' We decided that on stage he would make up any lie he could think of on the spot. I would not share these questions with Jim before the show so the performance would be natural, and I would invariably crack up at his answers. When we eventually performed Donald and Davy on

TV, there is one episode where you can see that I have actually wet my tight yellow slacks through laughing. At the end of our little chat we would perform a magic routine to the soundtrack of 'It's a Kind of Magic' by Queen. An example of this would involve me lying down across two chairs with a long thin cardboard box over one of my legs. Inside the box we secreted a mannequin's lower leg wearing an identical red Chelsea boot to Donald Stott's. Davy would pull this lower leg out, creating the illusion that Donald's leg had been stretched by four feet. That's magic.

In later life the Stotts would interview the likes of Sting, Michael Winner and Sinéad O'Connor during *The Smell of Reeves and Mortimer*. How extraordinary it seems now to think that these two half-baked idiots would end up sharing a stage with such luminaries.

Les

Fred Aylward took the character of Les to a new level in the Albany shows. Wearing his thick, black-rimmed spectacles and a white laboratory coat, he would parade the stage between acts, clean up the mess or entertain the audience with mute mime and slapstick curios. He would impersonate the dance moves of Bryan Ferry or Mick Jagger with pinpoint accuracy, and always be available to demonstrate his love for chives and his hatred of spirit levels. We didn't really have to write anything for Fred; he was just a natural clown with a great instinct for what would please the audience. Silent clowning must be one of the hardest skills in the comedy world, and Fred was the king.

The Living Carpets Lunch Club with Les

For this one, Vic and I would sit centre stage behind a table, both wearing masks made out of a beige carpet tile with holes cut for the eyes and the mouth. As we spoke, Les would bring out a tea trolley with various foliage on it and serve us lunch. We would then make outrageous claims and exaggerations to each other: 'I once booted a hoover all the way to the moon'; 'You know the Eiffel Tower? I'm employed by NASA to lick it clean every month.' After each statement the other one would say, 'I know, I heard that rumour,' and the other would reply, 'I know, I started it.' The Living Carpets are a good example of how we would find a way to put a funny image into the audience's minds without having to bother with a set-up or a purpose. These little images are usually our 'punchlines', but they dissolve if you try to put them into any context or search for any meaning. If we had the visuals of Les fannying about and the carpet-tile masks, we reckoned it was enough just to present the images naked and unadorned.

Action Image Exchange

For this, Jim and I pretended to be members of a local left-wing performance-art group. We were both called Nick and wore T-shirts with 'Action Image Exchange' on the front. We spoke with the estuary-English intonation that was sweeping the media world at the time, and our obsessions were having meetings in rooms above pubs and preparing and distributing unwanted pub-licity leaflets. We hated the police and adored squatters. We often professed our love for dope cake, and each week we would present a dance that we thought might have a chance, by its very existence, of changing the world for the better. We would seek to end police brutality by stuffing a Mars bar into a trumpet or applying goose fat to Ronnie Wood's dancing glove to a soundtrack of light swing KPM library music from the '50s and '60s. (Vic remains obsessed with KPM music to this day.) Before performing the dance, we would don identical masks that featured a fully front-on and life-sized portrait photograph of a celebrity's face. These days you can find these masks in novelty shops all around the country, of everyone from the Queen to Peter Andre. Every time I see one of these masks, I proudly remember that the whole phenomenon was invented by Jim.

As the show was different every week, the response varied. Although occasionally the audience were ecstatic and transfixed, more often they were bordering on the indifferent. It never really concerned us; we were having the time of our lives. It's hard to nail down what the show actually was: part variety show, part a total law unto itself.

On stage, Jim and I felt very much like a straightforward double act. We would bicker and undermine each other and try to make each other laugh. We would set each other up for punchlines and occasionally strike or kick each other in a nod to slapstick. Maybe in our subconscious we were mimicking the vibe of the great double acts that we had watched on the TV: Abbot and Costello; Laurel and Hardy; Morecambe and Wise; and were heavily influenced by Monty Python and Spike Milligan. We're often called surreal, but I prefer to think of us as childish, stupid and nonsensical: a couple of idiots who you have permission to laugh at.

After twelve nights at the Albany we were signed up by Channel 4 to bring the show to television. This is how I think that happened.

20

FROM THE STAGE TO THE LIVING ROOM

The Albany run started to attract attention from London's media types. It put us on the map, and as a result Jim got a few opportunities. Jonathan Ross asked Jim to appear on the Channel 4 series *Last Resort*, on an episode that featured a studio-based market stall. Jim would man the stall and show Jonathan how to make a nativity scene using only root vegetables, as well as construct a perfectly serviceable shoe from a marrow. Jools Holland invited Jim on his hit show, *The Tube*. Then Jonathan came to see one of our performances.

I have to assume he liked what he saw, although he has since told me that when he first met me, he assumed I was Jim's boyfriend. Jonathan was a huge star at that time and I was completely unable to speak to him. I was totally star-struck. (I have of course subsequently met many famous faces and no longer find myself fazed by them. The only exception to this being professional footballers, whom I still consider to be 'untouchables'. I remember in 1994 filming a piece for a TV show where I had to attend a Middlesbrough vs Crystal Palace match at Ayresome

Park with Sean Hughes the comedian. When Sean and I arrived at the stadium, film crew in tow, we spotted the Boro player Paul Wilkinson on the concourse. The director instructed me to approach him and have a chat. I got to within a few yards of him, but as soon as I saw his face close up, I instantly shat myself and walked away in a different direction. I just couldn't do it; the man was a god.)

It is one of my many regrets that I have never got particularly close to Jonathan as a friend. He is one of the most charming, charismatic, talented and funny people I have ever met. I often wonder if it is because he was the first superstar I ever met that I've never quite lost that feeling of awe when I am in his company. I can never quite relax and be myself. It's a shame really, because Jim and I owe him such a great and career-defining debt.

Jonathan had a new chat show starting, and he wanted to include a segment called 'Knock Down Ginger', where an audience contestant would face eight front doors, and behind each would be either a comedy character or one of the guests from that evening's show. The contestant would choose a door number and whoever was behind it would emerge and ask the contestant a question. Jonathan asked if Jim and I would like to play two of these characters.

A couple of weeks later, we went to Jonathan's production office in central London along with Paul Whitehouse, Charlie Higson, Kathy Burke and Rowland Rivron. We all pitched our ideas for little characters. I would alternate between playing Graham Lister and Benji the social worker, a bearded little house husband who was desperate not to offend. Graham Lister was perfect for the item as he was as rude and undermining to Jonathan as he had always been to Vic. Charlie Higson would be 'Ken Tussle', an overweight and under-muscled veteran British wrestler who was obsessed with antiques. Kathy Burke would play a young cheeky schoolboy asking questions you might hear in the playground. This character would later develop into Perry, the schoolboy whom Kathy played in *Harry Enfield and Chums* and later in the movie *Kevin and Perry Go Large*.

Paul wanted to play a character called Mike Smash. He was a pastiche of a 1970s Radio 1 DJ who employed outdated phrases such as 'poptastic' and 'popadoodledoo', while referring to his audience as 'great mates' and 'good chums'. He performed this character for us in the office and I took him to one side and said, 'Paul, that character is shit. It will never work, you shouldn't do it.' How wrong could I be? Mike Smash went on to become one of the defining characters of 1990s comedy.

So, completely out of the blue, this anonymous, grey-suited local solicitor was to appear on the nation's television screens. I simply could not believe it. I had never had any show-business aspirations. It was just a wonderful little oasis of pleasure in an otherwise dull and dreary life.

The shows were recorded on a Sunday at the LWT studios on the South Bank of the Thames in central London. We would all turn up mid-afternoon and hang about in the green room waiting to rehearse our little segment for lighting and cameras. The room was massive, with a wall of glass overlooking the Thames. It was lined with huge comfy sofas, and had a free bar and constantly replenished platters of food. These were magical times, as we shared the green room with some of the most famous faces in the world. Talking Heads were the musical guests for one episode. Jim, Paul, Charlie and I were in the green room before the show, and apart from the barman, the room was empty. Suddenly the door opened and in walked David Byrne (yes, the real one), much taller and thinner than I had imagined, wearing baggy trousers and a white shirt and tie. We said hello but he didn't acknowledge us. Instead he slowly walked to the far corner of the room and stood with his face just a few inches from the wall. He stared deeply into the corner for about five minutes then turned around and glided back out of the room without saying a word. Can you imagine a more perfect meeting with one of your heroes?

Another highlight was when Paul Gascoigne came into the green room and said a cheery hello to everyone. He never sat down and was constantly fiddling with the food or walking back and forth from the windows. He just couldn't keep still. As a climax to this particular fidgeting session, he picked up an orange and began playing keepy-uppy with it as if it were a miniature football. We were all transfixed. It was totally effortless and it seemed he could have kept it up forever if he so wished. Eventually he tired of doing it and kicked the orange up into the air, when it was caught by one of the members of the rock band The Cult, who thanked him and immediately began to peel the orange. We all applauded. Jim was a massive fan of The Cult and asked the lead singer, Ian Astbury, if he could come up on stage at the end of their live performance with half a lamb carcass for Ian to jump over. Ian agreed and sure enough later that night he was captured live on screen jumping over that lamb.

We met loads of famous faces those Sundays. Phil Collins was there one week and was an absolute gem: so down-to-earth and normal. I think he was the only celeb that ever came into the green room and actually queued up at the bar to order his own drink. I was new to this world of celebrity, and I didn't always get it quite right. One week the musical guest was Natalie Merchant from the group 10,000 Maniacs. Their album *In My Tribe* is one of my all-time favourites. It features a track called 'Verdi Cries', which is a hauntingly beautiful song that is sung with the accompaniment of just a piano and cello. I sneaked into the studio to watch her perform the song for her sound check. There could only have been about ten other people there. It felt like I was getting a personal rendition of one of my favourite songs ever. It very nearly moved me to tears, and I felt very privileged. After the evening show I saw Natalie standing alone in the hallway outside the green room. I knew I would never get another chance and so I sidled over to chat to her. She was holding her cello in one hand and a drink in the other.

'Hi there, Natalie.'

'Hello.'

'You going to be OK getting that onto the bus home?'

'I'm not getting a bus; I've got a car to pick me up.'

'Oh, right. Just open the sunroof and stick it through.'

'No, it's a big vehicle, like a van.'

Silence.

'When did you start playing the cello? Ages back or just this last week?'

'I've been playing since I was a little girl. Anyway, excuse me, I have to get going. Bye.'

'Bye!'

She was absolutely lovely and I was an absolute wanker. I can only plead nerves in my defence.

Towards the end of our second run of shows at the Albany Empire, Jonathan and his producer Alan Marke had arranged for Alan Yentob from the BBC and Michael Grade from Channel 4 to come and see the show. Jonathan and Alan both know their television onions and realised that the show we were doing on stage could very easily be transferred to TV without much fiddle-faddle at all. It had never even crossed my mind. I think Michael Grade came backstage after the show to say hello. He was small like me and very charming. Jim and I said very little. I felt like I was back in the headmaster's office. Jonathan looked after us and guided us through this impromptu meeting. The very next day, Jonathan phoned Jim to tell us that Mr Grade wanted us to put Jim's show on Channel 4. He was also waiting for a phone call from Alan Yentob. His secretary had contacted Jonathan to say that Alan would also like Jim to come and do his show on the BBC, and he would be in touch very soon.

I wasn't really involved in anything that happened over those next couple of days. Jim tells me that Jonathan and Alan advised very strongly that Channel 4 was the correct home for the show, and unfortunately Alan Yentob had to attend a family funeral and couldn't get in touch. So Jim and Jonathan bit the bullet and accepted the offer to go with Channel 4. The following day Alan did get in touch and offered to take it for the BBC, but it was too late. I remember thinking at the time that Jim would probably not need me to be part of the show. It would only be twenty-six minutes long and Jim had more than enough material to fill that time slot. I continued with my soliciting and just hoped I might be able to play the odd part in the TV show. I figured that if Jim needed someone to play The Man with the Stick, Graham Lister or Donald Stott, he would get someone proper.

The first hint I got that Jim did want me to be a part of the show was when he phoned me to say that he was meeting an agent in London and that I should come along. I took a sick day and met up with him in the offices of PBJ Management in Soho. They looked after the likes of Rowan Atkinson, Harry Enfield and Lenny Henry and had been recommended to Jim by Paul and Charlie. We met Peter Bennett Jones and his business partner, Caroline 'Chiggy' Chignell. Again, I hardly said a word. God knows what they made of me. I can only assume they trusted Jim's judgement. We were signed up on the spot and have been with PBJ ever since. Chiggy has advised, encouraged and chastised us through all these years and we would be lost without her.

Channel 4 commissioned us to write a pilot episode, so Jim and I started meeting up in his kitchen at the weekend and I would help him formulate a show that would showcase the essence of his talents. To be honest, it was incredibly easy. Whether by design or other accident, Jim had already created a perfect little TV show on the stage of the Goldsmiths Tavern. The hardest task was to select the characters and items that *wouldn't* make it into the show. We didn't have a computer at the time, so Jim simply wrote down a running order and drew pictures of any props that were required and posted them to the production office in central London.

We didn't send in an actual script. We had never worked with a script and didn't want to change that habit. The producers got anxious about this but we said that they could see the show on the afternoon of filming and give us any notes at that point. We had no real idea of how television worked and how difficult this would make it for the director to plan the shots, lighting and sound. We stood firm, however, and so the producers agreed that they would simply hire as many cameras as possible and just try to cover the action as it unfurled. We were sure this was the right way to go. We wanted the show to feel live and to include all the mistakes and unexpected stage movements that occurred. We also asked to record it with an audience and in real time. In the event, because of problems getting props on and off the stage, we recorded the half-hour show in just under an hour. The pilot show, although pretty good, was never broadcast.

One of the comedy producers at Channel 4 at the time – I shall call him Rich Bilberry – didn't think we were funny at all. He thought we should have been given a little slot in a comedy compilation show that he had commissioned instead.

(A few years later I was one of four judges at the Edinburgh Festival's new comedy talent show *So You Think You're Funny?* It was a prestigious competition and a big leg-up in the business for the winner. Rich Bilberry was a fellow judge. The first person up on the stage was a young lad from Bolton called Peter Kay. I thought he was magnificent. When we retired to our judges' room, I instantly declared that Peter was the clear winner. Bilberry's response? 'Why? All he did was tell jokes.' It was a three-to-one decision in favour of Peter.

A year after that, I went to the Edinburgh Festival to see my mate Dorian 'The Toff' Crook perform in the Gilded Balloon. He just told one-liner jokes and I was in hysterics. Seated in front of me was The Bilberry. After the show he approached me and chastised me for laughing 'at' rather than 'with' Dorian. He simply couldn't believe that I found Dorian's jokes so funny. He clearly didn't. Comedy commissioners are the gatekeepers to the TV comedy slots. Some of them have a sense of humour, some of them do not; it's just the luck of the draw and I shudder to think of some of the talented people that have had the door shut firmly in their faces by them.)

Fortunately for us, Michael Grade stood firm and insisted that we be given a series of six half-hour shows to be broadcast at 10.30 on Friday nights.

Of course, this meant that I had a big decision to make. It had taken seven years of hard graft to become a qualified solicitor and I was well aware that it would provide me with a career for life. I don't think either Jim or I thought that *Big Night Out* would ever last beyond one series. It was too specialist in its outlook and likely to have only a limited appeal. On the other hand, I wasn't a very good solicitor and always had a nagging doubt about whether I was really cut out personality-wise for a career in Law. The day-to-day grind of representing clients and taking responsibility for their problems was quite relentless. Just as when I had worked in the probation office and Law Centre, I had an underlying feeling that what my clients really needed was more money to be able to live their lives in peace. All I was doing was exploiting their predicaments for a few shillings in my pocket.

Being the type of character that I was at this time, my instinct was to keep the security that a career in Law offered. I knew that's what my mum wanted. But the lure of a being in a TV show was very powerful, so I approached my boss and explained my predicament. She was very understanding and suggested that I take the twelve weeks required to write and make the show as unpaid holiday and then return. I snapped up the offer; it was just the type of fudge that appealed to my indecisiveness.

Meanwhile, Jim had made an agreement with Jools Holland to rent an office above his recording studio in Blackheath. This is where we would write the series together. We bought an Amstrad word processor and got to work. We had six weeks to write the whole series. This should be more than enough time, as we had around forty hours of material from our live shows.

After five long years of getting up at 7.30 a.m., putting on my grey suit and tie and walking to a cold, dreary office, I could now rise at 9 a.m., put on my motorcycle leathers and ride over to Blackheath on my motorbike. Jools's studio was, and is still, called Helicon Mountain. It is a beautiful refurbished and re-imagined old Victorian railway station, and our little office, on the first floor above Jools' recording studio, had wood-panelled walls, a large Victorian mahogany desk with a green leather top insert and two comfortable leather chairs. As we sat working, we would hear the wonderful sound of Jools' piano drifting up from beneath us. Some days Glenn Tilbrook would be singing along; on another day it might be Cher. The view from our window stretched over south London to the towers of Canary Wharf.

Our working day would typically start at 10 a.m. and end at 3 p.m. I had learned to type reasonably quickly in my legal work, so I sat at the keyboard. We probably wrote an entire show every three days and then dutifully faxed an outline of the contents and Jim's drawings up to the production office.

These were joyful times. With the money I had been paid for the pilot show, I had purchased more glass clowns and fish and a 1959 Ariel Leader motorcycle. It was turquoise and cream with a tall Perspex windshield, and always reminded me of two-wheeled ice-cream vans. Jim was riding a silver Norton Café racer and Jools had a beautiful black Velocette Venom. We decided that we should start a motorcycle club – specifically, a motorcycle club for English Gentlemen. It would be the antithesis of the usual biker gang. We would wear tweed suits, follow the Highway Code to the letter, and adhere to a strict code of manners and etiquette, which we drew up on fancy paper using an elaborate font. Jim wanted the rules to reflect those of the Hells Angels, but with a gentlemanly bent. So, for our initiation ceremony, rather than have to bite the head off a chicken, we would go for a sit-down roast-chicken dinner. We would always lift our helmet visor if we passed a lady and we would always remove our gloves before entering commercial premises. You had to ride an English motorcycle, and swearing or fannying about in public was discouraged. The bikes had to be regularly serviced by a man of fifty years old or more, and on formal occasions we were to refer to each other by our surnames. We would never discuss politics, religion or ladies. Membership was by invitation only.

One day Jools was due to record in his studio with the singer Paul Young. He had mentioned the Gentlemen's Motorcycle Club to Paul and invited him to come down to the session on

213

his bike and be interviewed for membership. Paul duly arrived riding an American Harley Davidson. He was wearing a dark-brown leather bomber jacket and light-tan leather trousers that had seams that looked like shoelaces all the way up the outside of each leg, from the bottom to the top, and a full-face helmet without a hinged visor. We chatted to Paul for about half an hour about his biking history and his attitude to litter and road manners. He was a lovely bloke. After our chat, he went downstairs to record with Jools. About an hour later Jools came up to our office and asked us what we thought about Paul joining the club. For us it was difficult, if not impossible, to see beyond the light-tan shoelaced pantaloons. Add to them the American motorcycle and it became more problematic. We decided to put it to a vote. We would each write yes or no on a scrap of paper and place them in a hat. Jools read out the results. It was three nos. He had the difficult job of telling Paul. A little later we heard the thrum of his Harley leaving the premises. We never saw him or his hat at the studios again, and I still to this day feel awful about our decision. Rules are rules, I suppose, but it doesn't make it any easier.

Every other day, Jools, Jim and I would have our lunch at Eddie's Café on the Woolwich Road. It was just a completely ordinary-looking end-of-terrace house with no indication that food was being served inside. The downstairs front room was the dining area and the back room was the kitchen, and there was a hatch in the wall between the rooms where you ordered your food. The menu was straight out of the 1950s: stuffed ox heart, liver and onions, steamed steak-and-kidney pudding, and corned-beef pie, all served with a huge dollop of mash and two veg. The dessert was always steamed suet syrup pudding with custard. Eddie's is long gone now, though whenever I pass the house I can still smell the gravy, the cabbage and the sweet, sweet meats.

Powered by beef and puddings, we finished writing the six shows, which were to be filmed at Ewart Studios in Wandsworth, south London. I remember Ainsley Harriott, the light-hearted chef, was the cook at the studio canteen. There was an audience of around 150, the majority of whom were regulars from our days at the Albany Empire, so they knew all the characters and catchphrases off by heart. The shows were recorded at 7.30 p.m. and we would generally be out of there and sat in the next-door pub by 9.30. All the costume changes were done in real time and if we fluffed a line or missed a camera shot, we just carried on. We never did any retakes. If nothing else, this gave the show a real energy and a feeling that you were watching a live recording. It also led to many unforced errors and unexpected delights.

During one show, I was parading around the stage as Graham Lister, celebrating my victory in Novelty Island, and I forgot that the world's biggest diamond with a puppy inside it was about to swing down over the stage from the lighting rig. It hit me full on the face and knocked me clean out for a few seconds. Thankfully, it was the end sequence of the show, so I just laid on the floor until the cameras stopped rolling. I had a headache the length of a football pitch for the following few days though.

On another occasion Jim had to attack me by ripping off the top of his desk and striking me with it. In preparation, the top had been cut in half so that one side of it was actually balsa wood, which meant the impact would be minimal. Jim unfortunately picked up the wrong side of it and smacked me over the

215

head with what was a rather large piece of solid wood. I had a lump on my head the size of an angry plum for days.

In another episode, I had to bend down and hide behind Vic's desk so that my appearance would be a surprise when it eventually occurred. Vic was performing at his desk with Morrissey the Consumer Monkey puppet, and as I knelt there listening to Vic speak, I began to notice that he was punctuating his words with little tommy squeakers from his arse. I couldn't shift my position, as any movement could be caught by the cameras. Unfortunately, my nose was only about six inches from the source of the squeaks and I had no escape. Each individual squeak evoked a different aspect of a rotting corpse. Eventually I could take it no more and rose up from behind the desk in the middle of Vic's lines and declared that I was surrendering to the most powerful enemy I had ever faced: Vic's show gas. The audience laughed and Vic denied his involvement. It didn't make the final cut of the show because the pain on my face was too real and distressing for a comedy show.

Mentioning Morrissey the Consumer Monkey reminds me of the time that Jim and I actually met with the man. Jim was a big fan and in 1991 he received an invite from Morrissey to come to his manor-house recording studio in Oxfordshire and record some backing vocals for the song 'That's Entertainment'. I had no real interest in his music at that time, but Jim was pretty insistent that I come along with him. I think he was excited by the prospect of meeting him. When we arrived, early evening, there was no sign of Morrissey, however, and we were put into a holding room to pass the time. A couple of hours later we were ushered into a large, wood-panelled dining room to have our dinner, where Morrissey joined us at the table and his chef brought in various vegetarian dishes to eat. He was extremely quiet and reserved, only coming to life when talking about a ghost he believed walked up and down the stairs of the manor house at night making a racket and disturbing his sleep. After we had eaten, we went through to the actual recording studio where Jim entered the singing booth and did his backing vocals. While he was in there, Morrissey remained silent, so I thought I had better try to start a conversation with him. I plumped for this winning question:

'Morrissey, do you like brown suits, or do you prefer something a bit more formal?'

He gave me a hint of a smile, then answered, 'I never wear suits. They make me feel like I'm in trouble.' I thought it a good answer and we chatted for a while. He told me you should always wear clothes that reflect your default mood and make you feel comfortable. You should never wear clothes that make you feel like a character or are intended to suggest a personality that you don't possess. After Jim had finished his vocals, Morrissey went up to bed, clearly preferring the company of his mischievous ghost to ours. When I got up for breakfast, I could see Jim and Morrissey strolling around the misty manor-house gardens together. Both were wearing deep-blue Crombie coats, jeans and boots. Their hairstyles were almost carbon copies of each other's but their personalities couldn't have been more different.

The shows were edited and delivered to Channel 4, and we waited for them to be broadcast – though not with bated breath.

We knew they would find a small cultish following, but that would be it, we thought. At best, the publicity would mean that we might be able to tour the show around the country and then return to the Albany Empire to carry on with the fun. I'm convinced that neither of us thought at the time that there would ever be a second series.

Then, a couple of weeks before the show was due to be broadcast, we were asked to do an interview for the *New Musical Express* to promote the show. The editor, James Brown, had been to some of the Albany Empire performances and was a big fan. I don't remember any other media interest in the show. James was something of a visionary and it was very reassuring to have him on our side even if every other news outlet gave us the cold shoulder. We certainly didn't do any other newsprint interviews. At that time, the *NME* was a very big deal, with a circulation number in the millions, and it very much spoke to what would be our target audience. The interview was with a bloke called Danny Kelly, and when he came into the room at Jonathan's production office to record the interview, the first thing he did was ask why I was present, as he had come to interview Vic Reeves. I immediately felt like an intruder and a spare part, because of course this was Jim's show, it was his vision and his baby, which had taken him years to perfect. So I mostly kept my mouth shut and let Jim do the talking.

And then, the week the show was to be broadcast, the interview was published. I had read the *NME* avidly every week since about 1982. I had gazed at those icons that adorned its cover and pontificated in its pages. It was a cultural driver, a style and thought dictator and there, *on the front cover*, was Mr

Vic Reeves with the brash headline 'This is the funniest man in the UK'. I was so proud of Jim, and chuffed for myself that, by association, my show was on the cover of this esteemed and respected rag. It also made me wonder if we did perhaps have a chance of making it. We owe a great debt to James for his support in those early days.

In May 1990, the shows were broadcast. They were not watched by many, but each week the audience grew and the media were increasingly intrigued by this strange, post-modern take on comedy entertainment. Most people hated it, but a hardcore minority couldn't get enough. One person who felt so angry about the show that he telephoned Channel 4 and put his feelings down on the complaints log was a certain Mr Matt Lucas. He thought the show was childish and lacking any semblance of humour. He complained that the host, Vic Reeves, kept promising that guests would be appearing on the show but they never turned up.

Overall, the show was a minor hit, and a second series was commissioned. It went on to win numerous comedy awards and a BAFTA, and thirty years later Jim and I are still working together and still loving it. *Vic Reeves Big Night Out* is the fundamental reason I found myself backstage at the O2 Arena Leeds in January 2016 shitting myself and wishing the earth would eat me up in one greedy swallow. Between Big Night Out and this moment is something that might at a stretch be called a career. Let's have a look at it and let's have a sniff around it too.

PART THREE

In which I drop the chronological approach in favour of discussing the work that might interest the reader most.

21

SHOOTING STARS

Jim and I have made many TV shows since the two series of *Big Night Out* in 1990–91. Here is a non-exhaustive list for reference, and date confirmation if that's your cup of soup:

THE WEEKENDERS (1992)

POPADOODLEDANDY (1992)

THE SMELL OF REEVES AND MORTIMER (2 seasons, 1993–94)

SHOOTING STARS (8 seasons, 1995–2011)

BANG, BANG: IT'S REEVES AND MORTIMER (1999)

FAMILIES AT WAR (2 seasons, 1999–2000)

RANDALL AND HOPKIRK (DECEASED) (2 seasons, 2000–2001)

CATTERICK (2004)

MONKEY TROUSERS (2005)

HOUSE OF FOOLS (2 seasons, 2014–15)

Out of interest, I just phoned up Jim and we discussed which of our shows are our favourites. We agreed that the following were our top five:

Catterick

Bang, Bang: It's Reeves and Mortimer

Vic Reeves Big Night Out

House of Fools

Shooting Stars

Without doubt the most popular of the above with the British public was the quiz show *Shooting Stars*. This was our version of the comedy-panel-show-genre nonsense, and it came about through a mixture of laziness and necessity. In 1993 we had moved from Channel 4 to the BBC and had success with a new show called *The Smell of Reeves and Mortimer*. It was a jazzed-up and fancified version of *Big Night Out*, with a whole new cast of characters and routines. Only Donald and Davy Stott remained from the old days.

The move to the BBC had been triggered by the indifference of Channel 4 to a comedy drama pilot we had made with them called *The Weekenders*. They didn't think much of it but said they would allow us to make it if we gave them two more series of *Big Night Out*. We were a bit torn. We really wanted to make a series of *The Weekenders* but we felt that the *Big Night Out* format was spent. In the light of this dilemma, our agent Peter Bennett Jones arranged for us to meet Alan Yentob, boss of the BBC, to see if he was interested in taking us on. We attended Alan's office with Peter and waited in his secretary's office for about an hour. Eventually he beckoned us through to his grand chamber and Peter explained to him that we wanted to make a whole new studio comedy show and also a comedy drama series. This could not be *The Weekenders*, though, as that idea was owned by Channel 4. Once Peter had finished his pitch, Alan's telephone rang and he talked to the caller for ten minutes or so. As soon as the call was over, he left the office without a word and disappeared without explanation. We sat there for about fifteen minutes before asking his secretary what was happening. She explained that he had left the building but was sure that he would be in touch. I don't suppose Alan had said anything more to us than just a simple hello at the start of the meeting. We didn't know what to think.

A few days later, however, he contacted Peter and told him he would commission a series of our new studio show and a script for our proposed comedy drama. We decided to take him up on his offer. This silent, seemingly indifferent approach to meetings is something that I have encountered a lot within the upper echelons of TV executives. Sometimes I just put it down to a lack of personality; sometimes to the idea that if they don't say anything they won't give away their lack of ideas; sometimes to the insecurity that many executives have because they have never actually gone out there in front of a camera and put themselves on the line. The upper-management levels of the BBC have traditionally been a playpen for Oxbridge graduates. It's slightly more glamorous than going into finance or politics and certainly less demanding, and yet I think many of them are slightly embarrassed when they come face to face with the actual so-called talent. They know that we know that they know that they are just the guardians of the money bag and not really creators of entertainment. The Oxbridge clubhouse vibe has begun to fade these days and many of the senior people we work with have long histories of making successful shows. Back in the '90s, though, it was akin to a secret society.

Our first work for the BBC was *The Smell of Reeves and Mortimer*, in the autumn of 1993. Not long after, we were asked to curate a whole evening of entertainment on BBC Two for their Christmas schedule. It was to be called *At Home with Vic and Bob*. This was quite a task, as they wanted lots of original material from Jim and me, along with a selection of some of our all-time favourite TV shows. We built the evening around our personal favourites: Eric Idle's *Rutland Weekend Television*, an episode of *Dad's Army*, a famous meerkats documentary and Mike Leigh's *Nuts in May*. We had to fit sketches of our own into the programming, and what we needed was a decent half-hour chunk of Vic and Bob. We didn't have the time, the budget or the inclination to record a one-off special *Smell of*. We needed a half-hour format that could be written and in the can in less than a month.

The only element of our live shows that we had never exploited on TV was Vic's Big Quiz, and Jim still had note-books full of all the nonsense questions that he used to ask the contestants live on stage. Lots of these were in true-or-false format, such as:

'True or false: Karl Marx had a sister called Onya.'

'True or false: Kerry Katona doesn't actually own a cat.'

So we had Round One. Many of Jim's questions involved much-loved celebrities such as Benny Hill and Thora Hird, so Round Two could be a clips round, where we would show archive footage of these stars and ask a question about them. Jim and I would often entertain ourselves when writing with useless impressions of famous people, and we had just about enough passable ones to make a third round. Now we just needed a device to allow us to ask some of our favourite Big Quiz questions. We decided that for the final round the contestants would choose random phrases that were written on a huge blue suitcase suspended from the roof of the studio.

Finally, to give the quiz some sort of climax, each member of the winning team would be given a 'prize', such as a Mars bar sellotaped to a toilet roll. A member of the winning team would then be invited to take 'The Final Challenge'. This would be similar to the punishments handed out by Judge Nutmeg at the end of 'Wheel of Justice'. In this particular show, it would be: survive inside a large metal bin while Jim and I thrash it with cricket bats. If the contestant wished the thrashing to stop, they had to eject a turnip out of the bin's chimney.

When Jim hosted the Big Quiz live on stage, much of the pleasure was in seeing the contestants struggle to give any answer to the questions. We didn't know whether this would translate to TV and so we decided that half the questions should actually be real quiz questions. There was no doubt that the experience would be difficult for our celebrity contestants. It could go either way; people might think we were just being cruel and using them as props. We hoped that viewers might accept it if it seemed like the celebrities were in on the joke and happy to be there, though, so for this reason we asked our mates Jonathan Ross, Danny Baker, Martin Clunes and Noddy Holder to be four of the guests. One morning while we were writing, I saw a clip of Ulrika Jonsson corpsing as she read out the weather report on GMTV. She seemed like someone who didn't take herself too seriously, so we asked her to be a guest. Finally, we secured Wendy Richard from *EastEnders* as well. Quite a line-up for a half-baked one-off quiz show.

The recording of the show was a pain in the arse. It took over two hours because of all the stopping and starting for re-takes and changes of camera angles. It was not what Jim and I were used to and it didn't feel very funny as we were filming it. Wendy Richard got very impatient with the process and threw a bit of a strop. Jim told her to cheer up and stop acting like she'd just received her gas bill. I remember talking to Jonathan and Danny afterwards and we all agreed that the show was a disaster and in a perfect world would never be broadcast. We didn't have that choice, though, and just hoped that the rest of the evening's entertainment would overshadow this half-hour pool of dross.

In the event, *Shooting Stars* was the most-watched segment of the evening, and came and went without criticism or derision. Jim and I were grateful to have got away with it and it quickly faded from our memory. Fast-forward to 1995, and celebrity panel shows are all the rage. Jonathan and Alan Marke, who were producing our shows at the time, approached us and asked if we had any interest in making a full series of *Shooting Stars*. We didn't, but said we would have a look at devising a new version of it that would give us a bit more joy than the original.

We needed to make some changes; none of the rounds quite worked yet. We believed that the bones of the show were there, but did we really want to do it? We decided that we did – as long as we could make it 100 per cent pure Vic and Bob's world. We didn't want it to be a pastiche or spoof of other panel shows, but a stand-alone, different approach to the genre, the antithesis to shows like *Have I Got News for You?* We went into a frenzy of writing and ended up with a sparkling new version of the original. We made every aspect of the show as daft and childish as we possibly could. It was a joy to write and at the end of the process all we needed was to cast a couple of team captains and find someone who could be our on-screen scorekeeper.

At around this time I had taken a trip up to north London to watch and support my mate Dorian Crook performing his set in a pub basement comedy club. At the top of the show the compere introduced three 'try-out' acts who would perform short five-minute sets without payment. One of these acts was a shortish bloke, around forty, wearing a tweed jacket and slacks and sporting a thick mop of unruly reddish hair. He bounded onto the stage and declared in a deep, rich, 'posh actor' voice: 'Hello, how do you do? I'm a c**t. Didn't you know? I thought you did? Yes, I'm an absolute c**t. You didn't know? How strange, I thought you knew I was I c**t, because I am a c**t. I honestly thought you must know.'

I could hardly breathe for laughing. This was right up my street. He continued in the same manner for the rest of his set and then, to top it all, he scratched his head and in doing so dislodged his wig and left it to fall to the ground. He was completely bald and only around twenty years old. It was a triumph in my mind, though I don't remember that the audience really went for it.

During the interval I went upstairs to the bar and there, propped against it, was the young man who had so earnestly declared that he was a c**t just half an hour earlier. He was quite the reverse. He wore a permanent beaming smile and was as polite and charming as you could ever desire. He introduced himself: 'Hi, I'm Matt, the c**t you saw on stage. I heard you laughing. Thanks very much, it means a lot.' But the thanks should really have come from me, as I instantly realised that we had found our scorekeeper for *Shooting Stars*. I said to Matt that we were looking for someone to play a part in our new TV show and would he be interested in playing a great big baby in a nappy. 'Make that a romper suit, mate, and I'm in.' I took his details and said we would be in touch. George Dawes, The Man with the Scores, was born that evening. I told Jim and he liked the sound of it. The next time I was to see Matt was at rehearsals for the show.

This left us only needing our two team captains. Ulrika had been great on the original show. She was really game and unfazed by what was going on. She was also extremely beautiful and we reckoned this would be a rich source of material. Jim would fancy her rotten and always get knocked back, and I would flirt with her and seemingly get a bit of encouragement. It was also lovely, and crucial for the show, that she really cared about winning. Without Ulrika's competitiveness, the show could have fallen apart at its seams.

We were nearly there, but with only a couple of months to go before the show was to be recorded, we still hadn't found our other captain. By chance we were booked as guests on the late-night Channel 4 show *The Word*, presented by Mark Lamarr, and it was to be the last-ever episode of the show. Mark interviewed us and did not give us the usual easy ride. Mark has the very sharpest of minds; I have never met another comedian who is so quick-witted and inventive. After the show there was a wrap party. I wandered over to Jim, who was talking to Mark.

'Hey, Bob, Mark hasn't got a job on straight after this. Why don't we ask him to be team captain on *Shooting Stars*?'

'Fine by me,' I replied, and that was that. I didn't know Mark at the time, but trusted Jim's instincts. It turned out to be one of the best decisions we ever made, both for the show and me personally.

When *Shooting Stars* was broadcast, it was the first show of ours that attracted a mainstream audience, and we went on to record seventy-two episodes over eight series. Our humour hadn't changed, but it was being presented in a familiar, accessible format that was easy for viewers to get their heads around. By surrounding ourselves with famous guests each week, the audience was reassured that the programme was not operating in an alternative universe. Jim and I would write down a wish list of guests for each series, and it always contained Rod Stewart, Meatloaf and John Prescott, but we never got them. In the earlier series we always tried to fill the guest slots with celebrities that we either knew or had a connection with, since they were always a lot more open to the gentle ribbing that they were subjected to – people like Martin Clunes, Jonathan Ross, Paul Whitehouse, Robbie Williams, Hale and Pace, Caroline Aherne, Patsy Kensit, David Baddiel, Stephen Fry, Noddy Holder, Chris Rea and Neil Morrissey. As time went on, high-profile guests would agree to appear simply because their children were fans of the show.

One of the most important aspects of *Shooting Stars* was the way the celebrities were treated in the studio. We never told them what questions or tasks they would be facing, and I think many of them had an almost visible feeling of dread as they took their seats at the start of the show. The format didn't allow them to easily maintain their celebrity persona.

I remember when I was young watching Michael Parkinson interviewing some of the most famous people alive on his chat show. It felt like a wonderful privilege to hear these people speak and to try to assess what they were 'really' like. Since those days, though, celebrity interviews had become ten a penny and could be watched every day, on breakfast television through to late-night chat shows. The celebrities had become adept at presenting themselves with a lovely sheen and a personable demeanour. Celebrity-watching had become a bit boring.

On *Shooting Stars*, however, it was very difficult to maintain a showbiz persona, and the mirror would occasionally crack and a glimpse of the real person would emerge.

There were lots of other dynamics in operation. The female guest nearest to Jim would always be subjected to his juvenile sexual advances and rubbings of his legs. Some of them, such as Christine Lampard and Carol Vordeman, would lap it up. Others, such as Katie Price and Belinda Carlisle, were not so impressed. And then there was the obvious frisson between Mark and the entire show. Mark played the part of a reluctant participant to perfection. He would often undermine the content of the show and point out its frailties. If he seemed grumpy at times, it might well have been because he was grumpy. The format gave him little room to shine and sometimes he was just a disinterested observer. You could guarantee, however, that on every show he would come up with two or three monumental lines, and also, when required to perform, he would do so with full commitment and vigour. If I ever see an old show, my favourite moments are invariably when Mark finds himself actually and genuinely laughing at the material. From my point of view, it always felt like a hard-won and important victory to get Mark on our side, even if it was only for a few brief moments.

Matt Lucas, as George Dawes, The Man with the Scores, was absolutely essential to the show's success, not least because he always provided a welcome break from my and Jim's wittering. He was a hit from the first moment he ran on stage dressed as a baby in a romper suit, proudly displaying his bald head. Matt developed and nurtured this character with great skill. He gave him different voices and characters to inhabit and always seemed to be having the time of his life. We basically said to Matt that he would have five slots on the show and he could use them to do whatever he liked. He would never tell us what he was going to do beforehand, so we were seeing his performances for the first time just like the audience at home, and our laughter was always genuine. Matt would order his props and music separately so that we never even had the chance to guess what he might be up to. I used to love his songs.

Once, we were with Matt in the dressing room trying on wigs from a dressing-up box. Throughout our career Jim and I have relied heavily on a box of wigs to complete or invent new characters. Sometimes 'The Look' is often the very root of the idea, the starting point from which the character develops. When Matt tried on this particular wig, both Jim and I cried out, 'You've got a Look!' We told Matt he should immediately purchase the wig from the make-up department and put The Look to good use at some later date in his career. He took our advice and a couple of weeks later emerged onto the set of *Shooting Stars* shouting the word 'Peanuts' over a jaunty children's-party-style tune. We were in hysterics at the sight of him and laughed all the way through his performance. Matt, of course, could hear us laughing and throughout his turn has his hands behind his back, where they were furiously giving us the 'V's. As always, there was never the option of doing a second take; what happens is what you see. Later, he would use the Peanuts wig as his look for wheelchair-bound Andy in his sketch show *Little Britain*.

The recordings of the *Shooting Stars* shows were some of the funniest nights of my life. A lot of the guests were chosen from friends we knew from late-night drinking sessions at the Groucho Club in Soho. This was very much the popular venue for media types throughout the '90s, and there was a bit of a gang of us that were regulars. I would probably go there two or three nights a week, usually with Mark Lamarr. Mark was the best company you could wish for, and incredibly knowledgeable about any topic you cared to raise; the Swindon Stephen Fry. We could make each other laugh like a couple of chipmunks who'd just discovered a takeaway nut-and-seed outlet.

We used to dare each other to play the Herbert in front of some of the big stars that would be in the club. One night Brad Pitt was in there drinking and I asked Mark to go up to him and ask him how many people were killed in the movie *Seven*. Mark, who literally couldn't give a fuck about celebrities, strode straight up to him and asked. Brad was very charming and tolerant and told him there were seven murders. Mark then asked him if he thought that was why they had chosen the title for the movie. Brad told him he suspected it was. On another occasion Jennifer Saunders was eating at a table and we took turns to dare each other to walk behind her while practising various sporting moves such as striking a cricket ball or heading a football, grunting like feeding hogs. If Van Morrison was in, we would take turns sitting next to him so we could be told to 'fuck off'. Some of the happiest times of my life were spent with Mark.

In 1996, Jim and I were asked to present a trophy at the Brit Awards. We shared a Portakabin dressing room with Jarvis Cocker. The actual awards show is quite dull and sweaty, and so at some point I abandoned watching it and hung around the backstage bars. Suddenly Anth, the Pulp guitarist, rushed up to me.

'Bob, Bob, Michael Jackson's goons have arrested Jarvis – they've got him locked up! You're a solicitor. You've got to help him!' he begged in his rich Sheffield accent.

'Hold on, Anth, what are you on about? It doesn't make any sense. Michael Jackson's people can't arrest anyone; they're not the police ... What's Jarvis done anyway?'

'I haven't got a clue, but come and look. They've got him surrounded!'

I followed Anth back to where our Portakabin was and sure enough its doors were shut and there stood six goons all dressed in black suits and ties guarding the entrance.

'Are you sure he's in there?' I asked Anth.

'Yes! I watched them march him in.'

'Is he on his own in there?'

'Yeah, I reckon.'

'And you have no idea what he's done?'

'I haven't got a clue.'

The Kabin was my dressing room, after all, so I marched up to what appeared to be the lead goon.

'I need to get into my dressing room.'

'That's not possible at this moment in time, sir.'

'Why not?'

'I'm afraid the room is being used for security purposes. Now could you please move away, sir, and just let us do our job.'

'But I need to get some stuff out of there.'

'That will not be possible at this moment in time. Please move away.'

I was surrounded by goons. These blokes were massive and looked like they possessed a full set of adult fighting skills. We retreated back to the nearby bar. As we stood watching the Portakabin and the goons, we both began to feel angry about these American blokes acting like they were above the law. Jarvis was likely to be pretty scared trapped in that room on his own. I thought I would have a go at coming over all legalistic. We walked up to Daddy Goon again and I declared that I was a lawyer acting on behalf of Jarvis and I wished to have immediate access to my client. If such access were to be denied then I would consider the situation to be false imprisonment and would seek the assistance of the police to gain access.

Daddy Goon told me to fuck off.

We searched around and I managed to find a lovely WPC. I think the news of Jarvis's 'arrest' had begun to spread and there were more and more people beginning to gather on the concourse near the Kabin. I explained to the WPC that Michael Jackson's security men had trapped Jarvis in our dressing room and that they wouldn't let him out nor me in. She told us to stay where we were and she would go over and talk to them. When she returned from speaking to them it was clear from her face that she was furious. She told us that they were holding Jarvis because he had assaulted Michael Jackson and some of his stage dancers. They would not let anyone see him until they had spoken to the person in charge of the awards. We were all getting an increasing feeling of 'Who do they think they are, coming over here and arresting our lead vocalists?' I told the WPC that despite the fact that I was reasonably pissed, I was a solicitor, and asked if she could secure me access to see Jarvis. She agreed to give it a go. A minute later she returned and said they will let 'the lawyer' in but no one else.

She walked me through the goon fence and I entered the cabin alone. Jarvis was sat on the edge of a sofa, nervously rubbing his hands up and down his thighs.

'Alright, Bob?'

'What the fuck have you done, Jarvis? What has happened?'

Jarvis looked up at me with his puppy-dog eyes.

'I showed me bottom to Michael Jackson.'

I laughed, half in disbelief. 'What do you mean? Did you moon him or something?'

'No, it wasn't me bare bottom. I just pulled the back of me trousers down and pointed it at Jackson.'

'You promise me that's all you have done?'

'Promise.'

I told him that he had nothing to worry about and that he

hadn't committed any offence. I said I would do anything I could to get him out of there as soon as possible. By the time I left, some more police had arrived. We watched as they negotiated with the goonerage. Eventually a more senior officer came up to me and asked if it would be OK if they arrested Jarvis and took him to the nearby police station. They wanted to get him out of the building and away from Jackson's people. They assured me they would release him as soon as he was at the station. I agreed; it seemed fair enough. A few of us followed the police car on its journey to the station. We sang 'Free Jarvis Cocker' all the way there.

The police were as good as their word and Jarvis was released after making a brief statement. We all went back to a posh hotel to celebrate Jarvis's freedom. The Gallagher twins were there, Liam was with his girlfriend Patsy Kensit.

At some point Liam started to accuse Jim of not being working-class and demanded that Jim arm-wrestle him to prove which one of them was more working-class. That sort of malarkey is right up Jim's street, so he immediately agreed. A table was cleared and the arm wrestle began, with me supporting Jim and Patsy supporting Liam. The 'wrestle' lasted about two seconds with Jim slamming Liam's hand onto the table with a minimum of fuss.

Liam immediately jumped up and barked at Patsy. 'Right, that's fucking it, we're going to bed. I'm right out of form,' and off he strode, utilising his always famous superwaddle. I think Patsy did eventually follow him.

So that's my Jarvis at the Brits story.

*

Noddy Holder is another *Shooting Stars* guest who conjures up a happy memory.

Sometime in the mid-'90s, we were touring the country with a live *Shooting Stars* show. It was the whole gang: me and Jim, Ulrika, Matt Lucas and Mark Lamarr. For our show at the Manchester Apollo, Noddy had agreed to be one of the guests. After every show it was our habit to get very drunk in the bar of whatever hotel we were staying in, and this night was no different.

After about an hour or so we were joined by Alex 'Hurricane' Higgins. I think Noddy had met him before, but no one else had. Higgins was very drunk, his speech more or less incomprehensible. I somehow got stuck with him and indulged his drunken bullwater for about half an hour before saying as politely as possible that I had better go and sit back with me mates. Higgins was very slight and small but he had with him a bald bulldog of a minder. Higgins didn't like the fact that I was moving away and started calling me every name under the drunken sun. As I backed off, he took a drunken swing at me and missed. I could see his ape mate watching from behind his shoulder, just waiting for me to respond. Higgins came at me again and from nowhere Noddy appeared and grabbed hold of him.

There is no way a person can remain violent when they find themselves in the loving embrace of Noddy Holder, but Higgins remained fidgety and angry. Just as things might have kicked off again, a foot and half a leg burst through the ceiling just above us, sending fragments of plaster crashing onto the floor. Another foot and leg followed and then a whole person fell through the ceiling and landed not five feet away from us.

It was Mark Lamarr. He got up in an instant, brushed himself down and made his way straight to the bar to order a drink.

It was enough to reroute the circuits in Higgins' brain and his attention turned to discussing the incident with Noddy. If my memory serves me right, Mark had locked himself in some cloakroom above the bar and decided his only way out was through the floor. (In Jim's version of this incident, it is not Mark who falls through the ceiling but a tramp-type character who, on falling, retreated out of the bar making monkey noises. Either way, I avoided a potential beating from Higgins's ape.)

I am often asked who our favourite guest was on *Shooting Stars*. It's a tricky one to answer. The Americans were always good fun largely due to their complete bemusement as to what was going on around them. Larry Hagman, who played JR Ewing in the American soap *Dallas*, was perhaps the most bewildered. At one point I gave him a gift that was half a dead partridge attached to a small plastic bag filled with air. I explained to him that it was a 'fartridge' on account of it being part fart and part partridge. He accepted the gift gracefully but I noticed when I returned to my seat that he was giving his agent, who was stood in the wings, a look like daggers. I asked him if he was still happy to be on the show. 'Yes,' he replied. I then asked him if he would be sacking his agent at the end of the show. 'Yes,' was his instant reply.

Robin Gibb was another guest who I think regretted his participation. As part of the deal for him to appear, his management insisted that we played his latest single during the show. We told them that it probably wouldn't work within the show's framework but they insisted it was done. About halfway through, after Robin had answered a question, Jim announced, 'And now, ladies and gentlemen, Robin would like us all to listen to his latest record.' The song was played over the studio sound system and the whole audience and all of the guests just sat and listened in silence. It was excruciating. At the end of the song, the silence carried on until it was broken by Matt, who, using his Marjorie Dawes voice, said to Robin: 'That was really nice, Robin, you should be really proud. You've done ever so well.'

A special mention must also go to all the ladies who gamely endured Vic's advances and his unusual courtship rituals. My favourite was probably Christine Lampard. Jim had decided that he would try to impress her with a tattoo he had drawn at the top of one of his arse cheeks. However, in showing the tattoo to her, he would pull the back of his underpants outwards, revealing that they had significant stainage on them. Jim prepared the stained underpants in his dressing room using sachets of instant coffee and a bit of water. He made three pairs and asked me to decide which pair was the most realistic. I chose the most soiled ones, which to their credit did look very authentic indeed. As the show proceeded, Jim whispered to me that he was worried we had gone too far in choosing that particular pair. Too late now. When Jim presented the soiled pants to Christine, the look on her face was priceless. It was like she had encountered a gremlin sticking its head out of the bathroom plughole. Sometimes less is not more.

22

THE ACTING CURSE

By 2000, without really knowing how I'd got there, I officially had a seat at the lucky table. Jim and I had never expected to get further than the Albany Empire, yet we were cast to play the leads in a Saturday-night primetime revamp of the 1960s detective show *Randall and Hopkirk (Deceased)*. We were having a sniff around the Big Time. I would be playing the ineffectual private detective Jeff Randall and Jim the ghost of my former detecting partner Marty Hopkirk. We requested that the scripts be written by our old friend Charlie Higson.

However, as exciting as it sounds, I couldn't shake the feeling that it was a mistake. From the moment we agreed to take the job, I had a sinking feeling way back in my mind, just beyond its outer perimeter, that I might have bitten off more than I could chew. I was not an actor, and if nothing else this role was going to require a good amount of acting. I was just a chancer; if the spotlight was put on me, surely the cracks would quickly show? I never expressed these doubts, but they grew and grew the closer we got to filming. Eventually I confessed to Jim. He reckoned I would be OK. He said that when I was playing Graham Lister, Donald Stott, Judge Nutmeg or any of my characters, I was acting, so what was the problem? I felt temporarily reassured.

Then we came to our first read-through of a script in a rehearsal room. I was surrounded by proper actors, the real deal: Emilia Fox, David Tennant and the like. I think it was the most scared I had been in my career. It was immediately apparent that without the crutch of a comedy accent or character, I had absolutely no voice whatsoever. All I could do was read out the words on the page, with no more authenticity or verve than a trainee vicar at his first marriage-guidance session. I was in trouble, and I think the production team and Charlie realised it.

The problem, of course, was that my part couldn't simply be re-cast, as the project was basically a 'Vic and Bob' vehicle. Everyone kept their head down and decided to ignore the elephant in the room. I was playing the part of 'Bob', but saying words and trying to express emotions that 'Bob' had never said or tried to express before. I could handle setting up jokes and feeding lines, but I couldn't handle presenting a fully developed and rounded version of myself. To be honest, such a thing didn't exist. When I read out a line such as, 'Marty, I'm really going to miss you, I don't know how I'm going to cope without you,' it just sounded like a joke, or at best a set-up for a punchline. I don't think Charlie had factored in, when writing the script, the possibility that I couldn't act, and that my skills went no further than the little skits I performed in our sketch shows and *Shooting Stars*.

Sure enough, my first big test as an 'actor' came a couple of days into filming. The scene was just me standing alone beside

Marty's grave, speaking my final words of goodbye to him. I was meant to be devastated and lost. I had to establish in just this one speech the unbreakable bond that had existed between the two friends. It was a night shoot, and the whole world was eerily quiet as I stood by the gravestone awaiting the director's command for Action. On the first take, I fluffed my lines completely. I was nervous, Charlie was nervous and I could sense that the director was in panic mode. As they reset the scene, my make-up lady took me to one side and asked me if I would like to use a tear stick. I had no idea what she was talking about. She explained that it's a little lipstick-type device that you rub under your eyes and it makes your eyes water and tear up. I would have tried anything to help me get through this ordeal and so readily agreed. I took my place at the gravestone with tears already running down my cheeks and managed to get through my lines with at least a hint of emotion. As we proceeded to repeat the scene from different angles, I got slightly more convincing each take. On completion, it was no better than passable, but for me it was a triumph and I could sense the relief among the crew.

Filming took about ten weeks or so, and every other day I would have a sinking feeling of dread whenever an 'acting' scene came up for me. On one occasion I had to suddenly express my undying love for Marty's girlfriend, Jeannie, played by Emilia Fox. The first shot to be filmed was my close-up. As I remember, my lines were something like:

'Listen, Jeannie, I can't hold this back any longer: the truth is I love you, I've always loved you. I can't live without you in my life. Marty's dead – you have to forget about him.'

When you are filming your close-up, the other actor in the

scene will stand next to the camera lens to provide the correct eye line. On Action, I went for it: 'I love you, I've always loved you. I can't live without you in my life!' Emilia burst out laughing, as did large chunks of the crew. She apologised and I tried again. 'I love you, I've always loved you. I can't live without you in my life!' Emilia buckled again, this time with tears of laughter rolling down her cheeks. She apologised again and Charlie saved her embarrassment by suggesting that he stood in to provide the eye line. I tried for a third time. 'I love you, I've always loved you. I can't live without you in my life!' Charlie snorted as he tried to supress his laughter. In the background I heard Emilia giggling like a baby in mid-tickle. Charlie apologised and asked Jim to step in as my eye line. I tried again. 'I love you, I've always loved you. I can't live without you in my life!' Jim walked away, hand against his mouth, trying to conceal his laughter. Emilia and Charlie burst out giggling and the crew joined in.

Charlie kindly suggested we take a quick break. Then he had the bright idea of asking a total stranger if they would stand in as my eye line. He found a middle-aged lady who was part of the catering unit to take on the task. The crew realised that the scene needed finishing and the atmosphere turned towards the serious. I went for it again, telling the stranger, 'I love you, I've always loved you. I can't live without you in my life!' The cleaner burst into laughter and, like dominoes, the rest of the crew joined in. The director gave up the ghost and we moved on to Emilia's shots. When that scene was edited, only about two seconds of my close-up made the final cut.

I persevered on through the filming, giving it the best I could muster. I just tried to convince myself the scripts and the talent involved would somehow see us through. It was great fun being on a working film unit and having your own Winnebago, as well as make-up and wardrobe people to make a fuss of you. I also got to work with some incredible people. In one episode our adversary was an old wheelchair-bound master criminal called Colonel Anger, played by Derek Jacobi. In my first scene with him we met in the middle of a studio-set jungle about the size of a tennis court. For whatever reason, I hadn't had the chance to meet Derek before the filming of the scene. From my and Jim's starting position we could see him sitting quietly in his wheelchair, waiting for us to approach. Our eyes didn't meet. We had to go in cold. I had the first line of the scene: 'Ah, Colonel Anger, I presume. How nice to meet you.' On Action, Jim and I strode towards him.

'Ah, Colonel Wrangler, I presume.' I had fluffed it, and Derek's reaction was instant and cutting.

'Oh, you fucking c**t.' I was mortified. Thankfully, then he burst into laughter and told me to take no notice of him because he himself was the only c**t on the set. He turned out to be the loveliest of men and a willing and hilarious gossip.

In another episode, our adversary was a certain Dr Lawyer played by Hugh Laurie. Hugh was a wonderful presence on set. He is extremely self-effacing and it's joyous to watch him continually slagging himself off, before, during and after every scene. One lunchtime, he was sitting on the step of his Winnebago playing a game of Boggle with Jim and Emilia. They were talking about comedians and at some point the name of Lee Evans came up. They were talking about his merits versus some other comedian. A couple of years earlier, Lee had starred in a movie called *Mouse Hunt*. I pitched in on the side of the other comedian by saying, 'Yeah, but at least he didn't make a movie about a fucking mouse.' Hugh, Emilia and Jim looked at me as if I was an advert for a donkey sanctuary. I had clearly said the wrong thing, but I couldn't put my finger on what. I went back into my caravan, and then it dawned on me. Hugh had just starred in the movie *Stuart Little* – in which he adopts a talking mouse as his son. Oh man, if I could have pulled those words back into my stupid mouth I would have done it quick time with a ladle and hammer. I immediately went back outside and tried to explain myself, that I had made an innocent mistake. I don't think any of them believed me. It's eaten away at me ever since, largely, I suppose, because of how deeply I have always admired Hugh's work, from *Fry and Laurie* to the present day. I personally believe that his performance as Dr House is up there with Bryan Cranston in *Breaking Bad* as the best we have ever seen on our TVs.

Night shoots are always a challenge. Spirits get a bit frenzied and it's hard not to indulge in a bit of alcohol. On one night shoot I had finished my scenes by around midnight and so turned towards the booze as they set up for that evening's big set-piece scene. This involved Simon Pegg being hoisted up by a wire so that he could be positioned high on the frontage of a huge glass office block. Once in position, he was 'attached' to a large window pane with suction pads worn on his hands. On Action, he would have to release the individual pads and 'walk' down the glass pane a bit like Spider-Man might. The episode was being directed by Charlie. I was just hanging around having a drink, watching events unfold and generally getting on Charlie's nerves. The scene was ready to shoot and all the required safety checks had taken place. When a potentially dangerous scene like this is being filmed, there is always quietness around the set, born from nervous anticipation. Out of the silence, Charlie shouted, 'Action!' I, in my slightly boozy state, shouted, 'Suckers off!' (Cleverly linking a sexual act to the removal of the suction pads.) It was a once-in-a-lifetime chance to deliver that line and I just couldn't resist. The crew started to laugh, I felt like Geoffrey Amusing, and Charlie shouted 'Cut!' He briefly acknowledged the validity of the joke but asked me to behave. I was acting like a prick and I knew it. The cameras were reset and once again Charlie shouted 'Action!' I followed up instantly with another 'Suckers off!', quickly followed by 'Cut!' from Charlie.

He told me that if I did it again, I would be removed from the set, and I assured him that I had now got it out of my system and he had nothing to fear.

'Action!' shouted Charlie.

'Suckers off!' I bellowed.

'Get him off the set,' barked Charlie to the assistant director. I was marched away from the set and never got to see those suckers come off. I also missed out on the pre-dusk corned-beef hash, which was the regular night-shoot treat. I hate missing out on any corned beef opportunity, especially a hashed one.

Despite my shortcomings, the series was a success, peaking at 12 million viewers, and a second season was commissioned. By the time we started filming the second series, the excitement of working with a film crew had faded, and it was perhaps the least enjoyable filming I have ever done. There was always a scene on the horizon that was going to challenge me and cause me worry. Perhaps the most frustrating part of the process was that we nearly always had to stick to the script. The other actors had all learned their lines and it would have been bad form to throw them off balance or insist on line-changes too close to filming. Jim and I, however, had spent the past fifteen years enjoying the excitement of changing and adapting our lines right up to the very shout of 'Action!' Without this freedom of thought, it all became slightly mechanical. I often thought to myself that they would have been better with a proper actor playing my part. I wasn't really bringing anything of 'Bob' to the role. The writing was of the highest quality, but it wasn't written as my voice. It's really odd to be saying things as 'yourself' that you would never say in real life. I suppose I'm just not an actor.

So, by the time we came to film the comedy drama *Catterick*, in 2003, I had learned my lesson about the limitations of my acting abilities. I would play my part as a character and not try to be myself. The show follows the efforts of two estranged brothers to re-establish their relationship as one of them searches for his long-lost son. Jim's character was a woolly-haired and bearded bloke who lived on his own with his pet turkey. My character was a softly spoken, world-weary bloke who had just left the army and had returned home to rediscover his roots and reconnect with the real world. I made sure I had a wig and a different accent from my own so that I clearly wasn't playing 'Bob' again.

At the time of writing the scripts, the TV series *24* was a big favourite of ours. It was an action thriller show that spun its tale in real time, and we thought it would be an interest-ing challenge to make a comedy drama in real time, hoping it might give it a certain energy and oppressive sense of urgency. As always, we looked towards our mates when casting the parts: Matt Lucas; Tim Healy; and Morwenna Banks, whom we had worked with since *The Smell of Reeves and Mortimer*, would play the femme fatale, Tess. (Morwenna first appeared with us in the *MasterChef* sketch from *The Smell of.* She played a crazed lady who had cut off her ears in praise of Jesus. It remains probably our most famous-ever sketch.)

The only part we couldn't fill with familiar faces was that of my son, Tony, and a casting session of 'unknowns' was arranged for the part. I found this sitting in judgement a very uncomfortable experience, especially as I considered myself one of the most average actors in the business. Those auditioning were all aged between about twenty and thirty, all desperate for their first leading role in a BBC drama. They were all so earnest and dedicated and hopeful. You could almost smell the nerves and the peril. I just wanted to give the job to each and every one of them. A young lad called James Corden read the allocated scene, and he was very good. Others followed and I was impressed by them all. I wasn't cut out for this job; as soon as they left the room, I voted yes to the vast majority of them. I didn't want to have to live with the guilt of their rejection. As a back-up plan we had also invited Reece Shearsmith along to the casting. He read the part and just blew it over the moon and then walked across its tits. There could be no dispute the part belonged to him.

So Jim and I found ourselves acting again, but this time

speaking lines we had written and surrounded by friendly faces who were as happy as we were to busk around a script when the fancy took us. We filmed over a long hot summer in Kent and Sussex. They were magical times. Jim was at his magnificent best. As well as playing my brother Chris, he also took on the role of Detective Inspector 'Kinky' John Fowler. The American Eagle. This character had first appeared in the series *Bang, Bang: It's Reeves and Mortimer*, where he was the bookings manager at the third most popular nightclub in Hull. At the end of the day, when the dust has settled under the final ray of sunlight, 'Kinky' John Fowler is my favourite of Jim's many inventions. When we filmed him at the club in *Bang, Bang*, he wore a cheap shiny 1950s rock-'n'-roller jacket and impossibly thick glasses, and would fill out his cheeks with toilet paper. He spoke with a thick, chocolatey New York accent, and the glasses were so thick that he literally could not see a thing through them. We rarely bothered to write him any lines. He inhabited this character so deeply that they really weren't needed. I would just stand behind the camera and ask him any questions that came to mind. Jim loved it. He would have the whole crew in hysterics with his improvisations. We all just lapped it up and made him talk for much longer than was required.

At certain moments in the series the characters would break out into song. As filming progressed, I liked this aspect more and more and suggested to Jim that we incorporate some extra musical numbers. I think Jim was a bit indifferent either way, but said that if I wanted to, that was fine by him. Having Jim agree to let me look after a tiny section of the show by myself was a big moment for me. Usually, everything was either Jim's original idea or something that we had written jointly. I doubt Jim even remembers this little episode, but for me it was really important. I felt that he now trusted me and might even be accepting me as a near equal. When you are a double act, the dynamics between the two individuals can be very complicated, but I don't ever remember Jim and I having any disagreements when we are writing or performing together.

On the face of it, in all these years, the process has never seemed to change. We sit in one of our kitchens. I sit at the computer keyboard opposite Jim. We chat about last night's TV and Jim might tell me about his cooking plans for that day. I'm usually the one who then says, 'Right, Jim, we need to write [for example] twenty true-or-false questions today. Let's do it.' We then just throw ideas at each other until one of them makes both of us laugh.

JIM: True or false: Jimi Hendrix has an engine attached to his mattress to assist night movements.
Silence
BOB: True or false: The hottest part of a horse is its hands.
Silence
JIM: True or false: There are over seven hundred fence posts in the UK alone.
Silence
BOB: True or false: Lemons *are* the only fruit.
Silence
JIM: True or false: Dog the Bounty Hunter is actually allergic to coconuts.
I laugh. Jim doesn't

BOB: True or false: O. J. Simpson is a murderer.
Silence
JIM: True or false: Muesli is a by-product of coffin-making.
Laughter

I write it into the script and we carry on until the day's task is done. So on the surface it's a collaboration, where the only criteria for inclusion is whether a bit of material makes us both laugh. However, Jim has always been the unspoken boss. In our early years I was really just there to assist and to help organise the material. You never lose that basic dynamic. I would never bring my own material in to work or do anything while filming that hadn't been worked out first with Jim. If Jim felt the urge to do that, then he would. That is how our relationship had started, so why wouldn't he? I never objected and it would invariably be quality material. I suppose it must have eaten away at me a bit somewhere in the back of my mind or I wouldn't have been so chuffed when Jim agreed that I could put some more songs into *Catterick*. Morwenna and I sang 'Hot on the Heels of Heartbreak' by the Beautiful South. Reece sang 'Satan Rejected My Soul' by Morrissey. Morwenna also performed an extraordinary version of 'The Sire of Sorrow' by Joni Mitchell. They are among my favourite memories from my career, and I think that's largely due to the fact that they mark an important moment in the growth of the relationship between me and Jim.

If you have never seen *Catterick*, I recommend you at least give it a go. It's a mix of darkness, light and humour that has much more depth than anything else we have ever done. My performance is somewhere around passable, which, when compared to *Randall and Hopkirk*, is significant progress. It was a massive help to be working with people I was comfortable around and who believed in what we were doing. All the members of the cast have often said that they would jump at the chance to film a second series.

In 2014, the BBC were asking us for another show. We mentioned a second series of *Catterick* but it didn't gain any traction. We also toyed with bringing back *Shooting Stars* for a third time, but our hearts weren't in it. There are only a certain amount of times you can coo a dove down from above or chant 'we really want to see those fingers' before all sincerity and passion is lost. The one remaining comedy genre that we had not investigated was the sitcom. We thought we should give it a go. The result was *House of Fools*.

We decided on a set-up we'd always been tempted to try, where Vic and I lived together as best mates, inspired by the likes of Morecambe and Wise, and Rik Mayall and Ade Edmondson. (The last time I ever saw Rik was at some awards ceremony or other. We had a quick hug, and while doing so he grabbed my crotch and declared, 'You didn't have much to eat for lunch then.' I didn't know Rik at all well, but whenever I was in his company he was a force of nature and a joy to be around.)

Once again, we surrounded ourselves with friends and familiars. First up, Matt Berry would be playing our best friend, Beef. I had first met Matt back in 2005, when we filmed some sketches for *Monkey Trousers* together. Since then he had gone on to star in major hit TV shows such as *The Mighty Boosh*, *The IT Crowd* and *Toast of London*. Matt is not even remotely like his screen persona in real life. He is a pip, a gentleman and a hoot. He is an actor, a comedian, a musician and a writer of great significance. He is a bucket of warm cuddles with a happy laughter topping. We were so chuffed to have him agree to join the cast, along with other absolute luminaries, such as Dan Skinner, Daniel Simonsen and Ellie White, all of whom I'd come across by accident, when I stumbled into their live gigs. They are each uniquely talented and we were very lucky to get them involved in *House of Fools*. The final piece of the jigsaw was to cast the magnificent Morgana Robinson as our crazed next-door neighbour.

With the cast assembled, the same old problem once again reared its head: I was the only one who couldn't act. When we wrote the scripts, it was apparent that the stories would only work if one member of the cast played it straight and drove the narrative. It provided some genuine emotion and jeopardy. In the course of writing, that person became my character. When Jim and I are either side of the table writing, we speak all the potential material in our own voices. It's most often the correct choice to give Jim the funny lines and me the feeder lines. So, just half a script into the writing, I was already saddled with the exposition and story progression. I didn't blink an eye at this, because when it's just me and Jim either side of a desk, it always seems natural and satisfactory when we perform the lines.

Come rehearsals, though, and I tend to collapse. My confidence evaporates and I sound like the weakest member of the school play cast. I also have terrible difficulty learning my lines, and so tend to put it off until the very last moment. In rehearsals, I carry my script around with me, referring to it every other line. It must be very frustrating for everyone else involved. I think the reason that I never commit to learning the lines is that the very process brings home the hot reality that I cannot actually perform them. The only way to get through it is to make a joke of my inadequacies. Matt, in particular, enjoyed my suffering. Whenever it came to a scene where I had to do 'the acting', he would announce with great joy, 'Oh, here we go, folks, it's a pressure scene for Porky.' The cast would laugh at my efforts, but it was all done in good spirits and they were all on my side.

At the actual studio recordings, we would perform the show once in the afternoon and once in the evening in front of different audiences. The evening shows were always more fun to perform as the audiences were more lively and responsive. When it came to the edit, though, about 95 per cent of the afternoon performance would make it through to the final cut. Each performance took about an hour to film and, as always, we hated any breaks in filming for retakes or set-changes, as they always seemed to interrupt the flow and the energy of the recording. It can tend to make the finished product a bit rough at the edges, too. You can often spot continuity bloopers, and the shows are riddled with characters laughing when they shouldn't be (Matt and Morgana were the worst for this). I like to think of that roughness as our house style. Much credit or criticism is thrown at shows that break down the fourth wall by acknowledging the audience that is watching. This is usually achieved by a look or dialogue being delivered directly into camera or by deliberately showing the mechanics of the show in operation. We like to think of our filming method as breaking down the fifth wall – that wall being the unspoken agreement between the production and the audience that the filming will be carried out to assumed industry standards. It's not laziness or indulgence; it has taken us thirty years to perfect this technique. One of the most common statements Jim would make during rehearsals would be: 'Can we stop now? We are in danger of overlearning this scene.' It's actually quite a brave approach to filming. It keeps everyone on edge and encourages crew and actors alike to bring their 'A' game.

House of Fools was a big success with our fans and we ended up recording two series and a Christmas Special. My acting was dreadful but it didn't really seem to matter in the overall flavour of the shows. When Jim and I wrote them, our aim was to break the record for the number of actual gags in a studio sitcom. I think we achieved this while maintaining sufficient narrative to keep the viewer involved. I hope my performance just got lost in the sheer weight of tomfoolery. The press, of course, labelled it as 'surreal' and 'anarchic', but in truth it had its roots in Laurel and Hardy, the Three Stooges and *Dad's Army*. It was just a sitcom presented in a style that had not been seen before.

The most surprising 'acting' I've done has been appearances on the show *Would I Lie To You?* This is a comedy panel show where the guests tell a little tale that is either the truth or a lie. The opposing team must guess which one it is. I have appeared on this show about seven times and it has been an unexpected success for me, especially as it is watched by an audience that, largely speaking, wouldn't touch me with a long, bent, infected stick. I mention the show here because my appearances on it are something akin to 'acting'. The show has a lovely atmosphere generated largely by the friendliness and generosity of its hosts,

David Mitchell, Lee Mack and Rob Brydon. It is also one of the few shows where everyone is batting on an even pitch. Most panel shows are actually largely rehearsed and prepared, and some guests even bring their own writers.

On *Would I Lie to You?*, you genuinely have no idea what's written on the card you turn over before reciting the story. Everyone is slightly nervous about this and therefore very supportive of the other guests. By all accounts I'm pretty successful at throwing the audience off the scent. It seems that maybe the one context where I can actually act is where there isn't any script – just good, old-fashioned storytelling.

Before the show, you're interviewed by a member of the production team, who asks you to tell them some true incidents from your life. They probably end up with a list of ten truths. One of these will be used on the show. For your 'lie', however, there is very little you can do by way of preparation. I generally think up a few ridiculous names, such as John Caramel or Ron Waffles, and give these characters a little backstory that I can use to liven up my lie. I also generally try to think up some excuses as to why my recollection of the lie is a bit sketchy: 'My memory of these events feels very distant and out of reach, a bit like a fingerprint on an abandoned handrail.' Other than that, it's just a question of bullshitting, using the seat of your pants for traction.

My favourite appearance is probably the one in 2019 where I turned over my card and read the words, 'Following advice from Chris Rea, I always crack a raw egg into my bath.' This was a lie. Luckily, I did have a connection with Chris Rea (the blues singer) as we had made a record together back in 1996 to mark the appearance of Middlesbrough in the FA Cup final. This meant I had a sniff of a context for the story. Sadly, I made a terrible error by blurting out that Chris had actually run a bath for me and cracked an egg into it. Surely that would not be believed – but I couldn't backtrack. That's the beauty of the game. I got a sinking feeling and just had to hope that David wouldn't get too forensic on me. Luckily, David and his team got diverted by a discussion of whether the egg white would actually solidify in a hot bath. Before you knew it, they were no longer questioning the idea that Chris Rea had cracked an egg into a bath for me. It is such a joy to see the frustration on David's face as he battles with himself to call the outcome correctly. He plumped for 'True' and then proceeded to have a short mental breakdown when the answer was revealed.

Just as an aside, the wonderful Chris Rea had been an inspiration to me from a very early age. He was the only vague contemporary of mine who had made the journey from Middlesbrough to stardom. He sang about places that I knew, as in his song 'Stainsby Girls', which is about the lasses from Stainsby School in Middlesbrough, where my mum used to teach home economics. When I recorded a version of his song 'Let's Dance' at his recording studio on the Thames, we had a right laugh. The backing track is in the correct key for Chris, which is somewhere deep down beyond even Barry White. I couldn't reach this key and so tried to adjust by making my voice higher and higher up the singing scale. In the end I was singing it in a deeply distressing falsetto that would attract more dogs than human listeners.

As soon as I finished a take, Chris would call up his mates and play it back on his monitors so they could hear my efforts on their phones. Chris had tears of laughter falling down his face and I couldn't help but join in. Eventually he sat me down and told me that the only way through this hell was if I shouted the lyrics as if addressing a small crowd of protesters at a planning inquiry. It kind of worked and we finished the track before retiring to a curry house for the evening. We were both very taken by the doilies being used in the restaurant and agreed it was very pleasing to see doilies utilised in such a savoury context. About six months later, a huge, elaborate, single gold-foil doily arrived at my home in the post, with a note from Chris attached: 'Saw this and thought of you!'

In 2020 Chris appeared as a guest on *Gone Christmas Fishing*. He was struggling with terrible bad health but was as charming and positive as ever. He was kind enough to gift me a large framed photograph of himself enjoying a bath that contained numerous poached eggs.

So that's my brief visit to some of the TV shows I have made, but there are many others, and I have worked with many other lovely people. I think it's only fair that I give a few of them a brief mention.

In 2001–02, Lisa Clark and I produced a couple of celebrity boxing matches as part of the BBC's *Sport Relief* shows. In the first show I had a fight with Les Dennis, the comedian. I was 'trained' by boxing legend Barry McGuigan. I will never forget that, after a particularly rigorous workout, where he had blackened my eye with one of his super-fast jabs, he offered me the chance of revenge in the form of hitting him across his bare stomach with a baseball bat. I was a bit hesitant at first, but with his encouragement I started striking his stomach with harder and harder blows. He didn't even flinch. Although retired, he had maintained his stomach of steel. I like the fact that when the need arises, I can truthfully say that I once attacked Barry McGuigan with a baseball bat.

The other fight we produced was between Ricky Gervais and TV presenter Grant Bovey. I followed Ricky around during his training at Maloney's gym on the Old Kent Road. Ricky was a spirited worker and really packed a punch. He was quietly confident that he would win the bout and therefore did not want to bother with a proper practice fight before the actual event. His trainer, Eugene Maloney, was worried that entering the ring without experiencing a proper sparring session might be dangerous for Ricky. He considered withdrawing Ricky from the fight. As a last-ditch attempt to solve the situation, I asked Ricky if he would be willing to fight me. With one of his lovely wicked smiles, he nodded his head and agreed.

Our fight was set up at the gym in a full-size ring and with an audience of about fifty. We had a proper referee and a glamourous lady parading between the three two-minute rounds. When Ricky came out of his dressing room and stepped into the ring, I shat myself. He's a big, sturdy bloke about twice my size. He proceeded to kick my head in over those next long six minutes and earned an easy victory. I did somehow manage to land a lucky punch at some point and at the end of the fight he had a bit of a black eye. I like the fact that when the need arises, I can truthfully say that I once gave Ricky Gervais a black eye.

In 2013 I was asked by the creator and writer of the Channel 4 TV show *Drifters*, Jessica Knappett, to play the part of her dad in the series. It required me to 'act' and to stick to a script. I was extremely nervous but wanted to give it a bash as the scripts were superb. I shouldn't have worried. Jessica, Lydia Rose Bewley and Lauren O'Rourke, the three young stars of the show, were absolutely lovely to me. They never corpsed at my acting and only ever offered me encouragement and support. There was a long speech for me in the show, where I had to finally stand up to Jessica and tell her to sort her life out. I had been dreading it for days. At the end of the scene, Jessica told me that I had done really well. I hadn't been so chuffed for many a year. *Drifters* was also a chance for me to renew my friendship with Arabella Weir from *The Fast Show* and *Two Doors Down*. We were the two oldies on the set and we gossiped together during the long hours when we weren't filming. Arabella is very rude, very forthright and very entertaining. A superb and generous lady. She, in return, considers me to be a 'useless c**t'.

In 1998 Jim and I presented a BBC One prime-time, Saturday-night gameshow called *Families at War*. The basic format was that two ordinary families, all of whom possessed a special skill, were pitted against each other. We would design little games that would test their skills in an unusual way. So, for example, in one of the families the son was an amateur boxer. We devised a game where he had to use his boxing skills to demolish a garden shed so that, when it was destroyed, all of its pieces were lower than a nearby, upright, stuffed Alsatian. One family's father was a marathon runner, so we devised a game where he had to run on a treadmill while giving Leo Sayer a piggyback, and to win the game he had to keep Leo on his back throughout an entire rendition of 'When I Need You', sung by Leo from over his shoulder. In another family the mother reckoned she was a superb ironer of clothes. We devised a game where she had to iron a small basket of clothes on a motorised ironing board that travelled around the studio floor at irregular speeds.

It always gives me and Jim a warm feeling when we think that we managed to get the go-ahead to present these images to a mainstream teatime BBC One audience. In many ways, it was the realisation of a long-held dream.

There are so many other shows, but I think it's time we got back to the Leeds Arena and my heart-challenging dilemma.

PART FOUR

In which I find a spring in my step and a new beginning down by the river.

23

Upwards and Onwards

We're back in January 2016, and I'm about to go on stage at the O2 Arena in Leeds. Seven and a half thousand people are cheering for our arrival, and I'm staring at my heart monitor, which is now reading 150bpm. Which is well over the 143bpm limit that my consultant had advised me to stick to. I open the slit in the backdrop curtain and see Jim run out onto the stage. I have to join him.

Thirty years ago, when I first saw him bound onto a stage, I was transfixed and in awe. I was a spectator then, but now I am his partner. He changed my life and dragged me out of obscurity and into the spotlight. I take a deep breath and run to join him. The audience (genuinely) go wild. The backing track to 'Hello, We're a Couple of Girls' strikes up and I begin to sing and rush around the stage making shapes and attempting to tell stories with my stances and angles. The crowd are loving it, laughing like drains at our entertainment technique. The song finishes and we stand centre stage. I interrupt the flow by telling Jim and the audience that I have to check my heart rate. The monitor is reading 160bpm. I am completely out of breath but feel fine. Jim asks me what the reading is and I tell him and the audience that it is 300bpm. Jim asks me what the maximum I can safely go to is. '600 beats per minute,' I reply. 'Well at least that's what you told me.' The audience laugh and we are on our way. I owe a big thank you to that audience for being so enthusiastic and generous. They helped me throw off the shackles of my heart disease. I had broken through the psychological barrier of heart fear and could now fully release myself from the cage of self-pity in which I had been trapped. It was time to start enjoying life again.

The tour was a sell-out success. It was a 'best of' celebration of the whole thirty years of our career. It was great to be performing the likes of Man with the Stick, Mulligan and O'Hare, and Judge Nutmeg after all these years. We both felt like thirty-year-olds again. The show got longer and longer every night, a reflection of our enjoyment at being on the stage together again. During the day we would meander around the country taking numerous diversions so that Jim could visit bridges, viaducts, beaches and museums. After the shows, we no longer got blind drunk but just had a quick pint at the hotel bar and then went to bed. This was pensioner touring, and it suited us fine.

During the tour we discussed what we should do next in terms of a TV show. Shane Allen, the boss of comedy at the BBC, had indicated that he would commission a series from us and that we could do more or less whatever we fancied. Every night of the tour we had seen the affection that the audience had for our old characters and also how much they enjoyed us just bickering and doing our double act thing. We decided it was time to go back to our roots and make some more shows in a tiny studio with a small audience, recorded 'as live'. *Vic and Bob's Big Night Out* would be its name.

Meanwhile, my heart scare had left me wanting to do more projects and take on more challenges before I popped my clogs. I had always wanted to do something football-related. Jim has no interest whatsoever in football; I'm not sure he even understands the basic rules of the game. I once took him to see Middlesbrough playing in the League Cup final at Wembley. We were interviewed together after the match on national radio, where Jim announced that he was very pleased that Middlesbrough had won. The match was in fact a 1-all draw. Jim seemed to think we had won 3-nil; he had seen goals scored that existed only in his innocent mind.

In 2015, I had met a lad from Sunderland called Andy Dawson. I knew him from Twitter and had invited him to come along to a recording of one of our TV shows in Manchester. He was a fellow North Easterner and a big fan of Sunderland. He suggested that we do a football podcast. I noted his suggestion but packed it away in my brain's trash folder. Now, though, with my new outlook of getting things done, it seemed a decent idea. I wanted to call the podcast Athletico Parsnips; Andy preferred Athletico Mince. Andy won. For the first few episodes we actually tried to analyse and opinionate about football matters. It didn't feel right. What was the point of adding more trash to the already swollen pile of football bullshit? We did, however, know what is was like to be foot-ball obsessives and what sort of chit-chat such people got up to in the pub or on their travels to a match. After about ten weeks, we had abandoned completely any football analysis and instead inhabited the podcast with parodies of people within the game: Mark Lawrenson as a pest controller, Peter Beardsley as a henpecked depressive, Roy Hodgson as a Warhammer obsessive, Steve McClaren as a snake-worshipping faintheart. Although exaggerated and cartoonish, there is a germ of truth to them that genuine football fans are able to recognise. The podcast started to catch on and soon the characters involved didn't even have any connection to football. There is a perverted Alderman, Martin from *Homes Under the Hammer*, Neil Hunt the angry nonsense potter, and many others.

It may seem a strange little project, but it has been of real significance to me, in that it is the first project I have done without the interference of any broadcaster or production company. As such, we have been free to choose our content without critique or interference. It's very liberating and has allowed us to really push the boundaries of football 'humour'. I reckon many others will follow through the door that we have opened. Also, although I have written lots of stuff for other performers (most successfully for *Tittybangbang*, *The Fast Show*, *Monkey Trousers* and Matt Berry's *Shorts*), this was the first time that I had written material for myself to perform. It was very satisfying to be working in a different way after all these years. It also made it possible for me to discover a 'voice' outside of my Vic and Bob bubble. To be honest, I didn't think I had an identifiable persona until I did the podcast. The other revelation for me was that my performances started to sound authentic. When I listened to the podcasts, it actually felt like I was listening to myself sat at home on the sofa or in the pub.

This was something I had never achieved before, and was what had caused me so much anguish when filming *Randall and Hopkirk* and *House of Fools*. All that I had needed was a safe environment free from the critical eye and about forty hours of podcasting to get me there. It feels sweet to learn a new skill when you are nearly sixty years old.

Armed with this new ability, I started to enjoy doing the occasional solo appearance on podcasts like those of Richard Herring and Adam Buxton, and radio interviews such as an episode of *Desert Island Discs* with the lovely Lauren Laverne. I found that I no longer felt the need to just be the funny guy. I was actually better at just being myself. I realised I was able to talk about life in general and tell stories from my past and still seem to entertain an audience. Perhaps most enjoyable were my appearances on *Would I Lie to You?* and *Taskmaster*. I was beginning to feel comfortable in myself as a performer, which made it all the more enjoyable. I once did an interview for a magazine many, many years ago and the interviewer ended his piece by saying: 'As I left the room, I noticed Bob staring out of the window rubbing at his eyes with his thumb and fore-finger ... it looked like he was trying to rub himself out and escape from this story.' He might have had a point at the time, but not anymore.

Meanwhile, Paul Whitehouse and I were going on our reg-ular fishing trips to the River Test in Hampshire. We would arrive on the riverbank around lunchtime and fish together until sunset. It was just the two of us with the occasional kingfisher or swan family for company. I had forgotten how achingly beautiful the British countryside can be, the peace and quiet, and the rhythms of the water, lulling us into a refreshing sense of intimacy with nature and each other.

By this time in my life, I had become jaded and bored with the maintenance of friendships. I had my family and Jim and that was enough for me. I had no friends in Tunbridge Wells, where I lived, and, apart from the rare trip to London to have a gossip with Matt and Reece, I had largely abandoned my circle of friends. As I reflect on this now, I find it interesting that as a young man I yearned to have friends, their absence often making my life feel like a curse. Yet somehow I had reached a point where they no longer mattered to me so much. Maybe it was just my age, but I also think it has something to do with being a 'celebrity'. Once I became a known face, the world became a very different place. In work meetings and working environments, I got obsessed with coming over as a decent bloke. In social situations, I felt constantly under the microscope. I like going to pubs; I'm not one of those people who enjoys going to friends' houses for dinner parties. In fact I can proudly say that I have only ever been to one dinner party in my life. Unfortunately, pubs take on a different flavour when you are a bloke off the TV. There is a constant stream of requests for selfies and it is never long before a stranger invites themselves to join you at your table and then insists that you telephone their mate who is 'your biggest fan'. I never have the balls to refuse and am always ultra polite and friendly but, before you know it, the evening has become a bucket of Todd (perhaps Van Morrison was right to just tell all and sundry to fuck off).

In stark contrast, sitting for hours on the banks of the Test with Paul was a revelation. No beer to be drunk, no strangers to be indulged, no competition to be the funny guy, nothing uncomfortable in silence and an unspoken agreement that no topic was off the menu. I think it was talking about our heart problems that provided a doorway to a more open and support-ive vibe. For whatever reason, my friendships over the years had been based purely on the quest for laughter. This was different. Nature and silence had tricked me into talking with Paul about everything under the sun. The banks of the River Test had become my therapy couch – two men talking and helping each other out. It's very refreshing if you have been starved of it.

On one trip, as we walked along the river at the end of the day, Paul mentioned to me that our little fishing adventures might work as a TV show. Something akin to *Great Canal Journeys* with Timothy West and Prunella Scales or an unscripted version of *The Trip* with Steve Coogan and Rob Brydon. In the bar that night we discussed it further, and the truth of it is we won-dered if we could actually be bothered and if it would ruin our enjoyment of these special carefree days. We ate our food and drank our wine and beer. We always treated these trips as 'cheat days', where we would eat whatever we wanted regardless of its heart-healthiness, and this invariably meant that we ate pie. Pie holds a particularly special place in our hearts. As soon as I bite into that buttery inviting crust, my mind is transported back to happy childhood days around the orange kitchen table with my mum dishing out the mash, peas and gravy. It also, of course, instantly reminds me of the time before all the heart nonsense, when I hadn't truly appreciated the majesty of the pie. Absence makes the heart grow fonder, I suppose. Paul sometimes has pasta just to make me feel bad.

The idea of a fishing show kept nagging at our minds, however, and after some telephone chats together we decided to go
straight to the controller of BBC Two, Patrick Holland, and
ask if he had any interest. We didn't have anything in writing;
we just hoped our enthusiasm might win him over. On the day
of our meeting, Paul and I had a quick pre-meeting chat in a
coffee shop just round the corner from Television Centre. A
man in a monkey suit walked past carrying a mini fridge and
I thought that was a good omen. Paul suggested that we pitch
the show as a factual commission and not comedy. It would not
be scripted, so the chances of it satisfying a comedy audience
would be slim. He also reckoned that the key to the show was
our respective heart problems and the jeopardy that one of us
might keel over on the riverbank. I had no idea what the show
would be, other than a general feeling that people might enjoy
our company for half an hour while we showcased the beauty
of the British countryside.

My memory of that meeting is that both Patrick and I were
transfixed and bedazzled by Paul and his words. His knowledge
of angling and the countryside runs very deep, and his love for
the river and its ecology rings very true. He is also supremely
funny and entertaining. It's a whirlwind of ideas and laughter.
I can remember long ago that a TV commissioner told me that,
when listening to a pitch, what he was really looking for was
an unflappable passion for the project. Well, if that is true, then
Paul delivered it by the bucketload. I mostly ate biscuits and
laughed along with Patrick. I think what sealed the deal is that
Patrick could see that the project came from real life and not
from around the 'ideas table' at a production company office in

Soho. Also, he could see that Paul and I were obviously close friends with an easy and genuine rapport. He liked what he had heard and told us to write it up and send it in.

To make a TV show, you need a TV producer. Ever since Jim and I made the show *Families at War*, in 1999, every show we have made has been produced by Lisa Clark. She is without a shadow of a doubt the UK's top comedy and entertainment producer. From the *Big Breakfast* through all my and Jim's stuff to *Top Gear*, she has done the lot. She is very much the third wheel on my and Jim's clown car. Paul and I asked her on board and when she agreed we knew we had as good a chance as is possible of the show being a success. About four weeks later, Patrick commissioned a series of six half-hour shows. It was undoubtedly a very risky and brave commission. From that point onwards, Lisa dealt with the development of the show. It was decided that a nice way to give it some shape would be if I chose the accommodation for the trips behind Paul's back as well as looking after the catering. I would try as best as I could to cook heart-healthy food for the two of us. Largely due to the hours I spent next to my mum helping her prepare meals for the family, I am a half-decent cook. Paul would choose the fishing locations and try to teach me how to fish. We would target a different species of fish for each show. That was it. We still didn't really have a clue what we would be talking about or what kind of show it would be. Maybe it would be funny; maybe it wouldn't. Maybe it would be an instructional show; maybe it wouldn't. Maybe my cooking would make the final cut, but probably not.

And so, a few months later, Paul and I, along with a very small team, led by Lisa with producers Nicky and Stephanie, director

Leo and crew Toby, Ali, Andy and Sean, pitched up on the banks of the Derbyshire Wye at Monsal Dale. In a word, Paul and I were shitting ourselves. There was no script and just a general promise that we would recreate the fishing trips that Paul and I had shared together. The cameras were set up to film us stood on a little footbridge spanning the river. Lisa provided us with a list of topics that we might want to discuss, such as healthy eating, our childhoods, growing old, regrets and failings. The director shouted Action! and Paul and I looked desperately into each other's eyes, knowing that we were fucked. Neither of us had any experience as presenters. As I remember, our first attempt to introduce the show went something like this:

BOB: So what river is this, Paul?

PAUL: This is the Derbyshire Wye, a classic limestone river in the Peak District.

BOB: And what fish might we catch here?

PAUL: We have a good chance of catching a brown trout or even a native rainbow trout. This is one of the few rivers in the UK that actually has an indigenous stock of rainbow trout.

BOB: And what method of fishing will we be using?

PAUL: We will be fly-fishing using both a dry fly and a sinking nymph.

BOB: Paul, this is shit. We sound like we're presenting *Homes Under the Hammer*.

PAUL: I know. I reckon we're fucked.

We asked for the filming to stop and requested that we just start fishing and see where that led. The atmosphere among the crew was very quiet and downbeat. There is a certain unspoken dread that infects a crew when it looks like they have attached themselves to a turkey. Paul and I could feel it in our bones. Paul set up his fishing rod and started to fish, and after about twenty minutes we were once again seduced by the environment and the silence. We began to be our real fishing selves. We started to chat as mates and not as presenters, something that I had never achieved in front of the cameras before. Paul got a bite and told me to fetch the landing net. As I brought the fish onto the bank in the net I fell over and in doing so knocked Paul over into the mud. The crew didn't know whether to come over and help us or keep the cameras running. It was farcical. Paul tells me that at the time we were both laid on our arses in the mud, he thought to himself, *What the fuck will the angling community make of this shambles?*

We retuned the rainbow trout to the river and the cameras cut. We apologised to Lisa but she would have none of it. 'That's the show! That's what we need to be filming.' In that short, thirty-minute session of chatting and falling, *Gone Fishing* was born. We are now about to embark on our fifth series. In many ways the show is the culmination of my journey back from side-kick Bob to stand-alone Robert. I could never have got there without my heart nonsense. It has made me a more rounded, more enthusiastic person who has regained some ambition and verve. I humbly thank my cloudy arteries for this unexpected development.

Making television is usually quite a stressful business involv-ing hours and hours of meetings and long, difficult days of writing. *Gone Fishing* is a wonderful exception. Lisa Clark and her team do hours and hours of graft, and all I have to do is spend a few hours on the internet searching for accommodation and some heart-healthy recipes. After that, I just turn up at the location on the first day of filming. We introduce the location then just slip into friendship mode. We focus on our fishing and try to have the best time we can possibly have. We have three wonderful days together on the riverbank and then Doug, our genius editor, spends three weeks with Lisa editing it down to length.

The show has proved very popular with the British public and I think has changed their perception of me as a performer. It is not just played for laughs and we often talk about serious matters such as men's health, the challenges of getting older, and how to best live our lives. There is a certain wisdom that comes with age and I suppose Paul and I are just trying to pass some of it on. I am perfectly happy to see myself on the screen being serious these days, which is something I avoided like the plague for some thirty-odd years. It's quite refreshing really and has allowed me to develop as a performer and as a person. Paul and I often reflect on the fact that with all our previous shows, members of the public would approach us and tell us how much they enjoyed the show and how funny they found us. With this show, they generally just thank us for making something that has both moved and entertained them. It's a big difference and one we have learned to be proud of.

Paul is the best company you could wish for: hilarious at all times and caring and tolerant when need be. He has taught me so much about the skills of fishing and has kept his temper even in the face of my intolerable witterings and pratfalls. I'm not sure why I fall over so often. I only seem to do it when I am out fishing with Paul. Given that I spend most of my life sat on the sofa, maybe it is because I am out of practice at negotiating nature's terrain. Another reason may be that when we go fishing I borrow all my kit from Paul. His wading boots are about three sizes too big for me and sometimes it feels like I'm walking along with boots full of mice.

One of the big strengths of the show is Paul's determination to catch a fish. Once he has cast his line, his concentration is hard to break. For the purposes of making a TV show, I do occasionally have to interrupt him so that we get some dialogue. Paul hates this, and you can see the frustration written on his face. It's like a teacher dealing with his cheekiest pupil or a father dealing with his noisiest son. It's a great dynamic and I exploit it to the max. Paul has impeccable manners and a very forgiving nature but I do suspect that one day he will turn around and punch my lights out. That will be my final victory.

PART FIVE

*In which I acknowledge those who have meant
the most to me.*

24

Mrs Lisa Mortimer

I met Lisa in 1991 in the Grove pub in Camberwell. She was with a group of her friends who had come to south London to have a drink with Dorian 'The Toff' Crook. She was tall, beautiful and well out of my league. I remember that she called the singer Cher by the name Chair and the singer Sting by the name String. This drew me in big-time.

By now of course my 'celebrity' status had ridded me of my social ineptitude and I was able to chat to her. She tells me now that I was actually on the cocky side of forwardness.

We bought our first house together, in Camberwell, around 1993 and moved to the countryside in Kent about two years later. Harry and Tom were born at home in 1997 and 1998, and unlike their father both boys have grown up to be handsome, athletic and intelligent.

By around 2005, I had myself given up on any kind of social scene. I was living in Kent with Lisa and my two young sons and, like many people before me, my family unit became my only priority. On the few occasions I did venture out, I began to find it a bit tiresome. Maybe it was lack of practice; maybe it was just my age. Once you're out of the loop, these evenings out can be little more than a catching-up exercise and you do start to hear yourself repeating things you have said many times before. Worthwhile friendships have to be nurtured and worked on. I had let myself down in that respect and couldn't find the motivation to carry out the necessary repairs. The only friend I was seeing was Jim, and I saw him nearly every day. Lisa and I would go out for an evening maybe two or three times a year. Maybe to see Lloyd Cole or Rufus Wainwright or the band Squeeze. Even then it always felt a bit of a palaver. We are never happier than just enjoying each other's company watching the TV, gazing at the alliums and agapanthus in the garden, observing the birds larking about on the bird feeder and chatting to our cats, Goodmonson and Mavis. Nice.

25

Vic, Jim, Jimbo

I've known Jim now for over thirty years. We've shared many ups and downs in our careers and many hours in each other's company, but never has a cross word been exchanged between us. We talk about nothing and everything. We make each other laugh like drains and we always leave each other's company refreshed and alert. People often ask me, 'What is Jim really like?' I always say, 'He is just an ordinary bloke who also happens to be a genius.' Jim has a slight shyness and reticence with strangers, but once he is comfortable in your presence he will amaze you with his mind and his thoughts. He is very solid in his friendships and an extremely proud and active dad. We have had some good times. I would write them all here, but there's enough to fill several other books.

In the early days of Big Night Out, we took a chance one week and agreed to appear at the notorious Tunnel Club in north Greenwich – at that time the graveyard gig for any aspiring comedian. If you got through one minute without being shouted at to 'fuck off' you would consider it a success.

This would take us out of our comfort zone and away from our crowd of regulars. It was something we rarely did as we didn't have a fifteen-minute set that we could perform in isolation. The Tunnel Club was a genuinely scary bear pit. As such, it was something of a rite of passage for comedians on the London comedy circuit.

We decided that we would do an abridged version of 'Vic's Big Quiz', with a member of the audience as our contestant. I was shitting myself; Jim wasn't – he has nerves of steel and an unshakeable belief in any material we present. We rushed through the quiz and finished to a huge round of applause. Backstage, we could hear the audience stamping their feet and banging their tables, requesting that we do an encore. We strolled back onto the stage waving to the audience and thanking them for their support. Then, as if triggered by a predetermined signal, the whole audience started screaming at us to fuck off and began pelting us with plastic pint glasses, some still half-full of beer. We ran off the stage. You had to give them credit; they had stitched us up like a Turkish slipper.

Our first trip abroad together was in 1990, when we were invited by Channel 4 to appear at the 'Just for Laughs' comedy festival in Montreal. We flew out together in business class. It was all paid for by Channel 4, and we felt like rock stars. On the same flight were Harry Enfield and Paul Whitehouse, who had been upgraded to first class and were separated from our seating by a large curtain. Every half hour or so they would appear through the curtain smoking cigars and drinking champagne. Harry would berate everyone in our section by declaring that he had 'loadsamoney' and Paul would announce that each and every one of us was 'an absolute shower' and not even worthy of a 'ding dong'.

Our first night in Montreal we had to perform at a small comedy club so that the producers of the televised show could get a handle on our act. The centrepiece of our ten-minute turn was to present to the audience a 15ft roll of beige carpet that we believed to be a lucky charm. The 'joke' was, of course, that a huge roll of carpet was in its very essence too cumbersome to carry around as a lucky charm. As we paraded the carpet roll around the stage, we would sing an inform-ative song.

> *It's my Lucky Carpet*
> *Let me tell you how it started*
> *Where did you find it?*
> *I bought it down the market*
> *Who from?*
> *From a bloke that sells carpets*
> *It's my lucky charm*
> *And it's a lot more lucky than my lucky barn*
> *And if we were ever parted*
> *I would be broken-hearted . . .*

Backstage we were sharing a dressing room with an American comedy magician. I remember he filled the topless hat he was wearing with water from a jug and then took off his hat and crumpled it up, revealing that the water had disappeared. He asked us what our angle was.

COMEDY MAGICIAN: So what do you guys do? Tell stories and shit?

ME: Yeah, something like that. We've got a lucky carpet as well.

COMEDY MAGICIAN: What, like a prop for an illusion?

JIM: No, it's for real.

COMEDY MAGICIAN: Geez, I'd love to see it.

We take him out into the corridor and show him the roll of beige carpet laid sadly on the dirty floor.

COMEDY MAGICIAN: You mind if I have a look at it?

ME: No, not at all. Be our guest.

He picks up one end and stares down its opening and along its length.

COMEDY MAGICIAN: It's just a carpet, as far as I can see.

JIM: Yeah, but it brings us good luck. It's very powerful.

COMEDY MAGICIAN: But what do you do with it on stage?

ME: We just show it to the audience and explain its powers to them.

COMEDY MAGICIAN: What powers?

JIM: Well, ever since we got it, I've continued to look nothing like Dr Ruth.

ME: Yeah, and I haven't got my foot stuck down the toilet, which used to happen all the time.

COMEDY MAGICIAN: It's too big to carry around as a lucky charm. The audience are never going to buy it.

ME: Well, all we can do is give it a go.

COMEDY MAGICIAN: Sorry, guys, but I think you are going to bomb.

Before we went on stage, Harry and Paul did a turn as Smashy and Nicey, the 'Charity' disc jockeys. Apart from the small

English contingent in the audience, they went down like a turd in a washing machine. The Canadian audience seemed to take them at face value, as perfectly normal radio hosts. They were bemused and unable to understand the nuance or irony of the performances. Our lucky-carpet piece fared only slightly better, mainly because of the raucous musical accompaniment and the fact that we were clearly drunk.

The following night we performed at the main, televised show in front of our largest-ever live audience. Paul and Harry had spent the day working on their Smashy and Nicey piece to make it more Canadian-friendly. Jim and I had spent the day at an amusement park. Paul and Harry went down very well. We, just like the comedy magician had predicted, totally and absolutely bombed. Our ten-minute slot was received with total silence – not even a single sympathetic giggle. When we walked off stage into the green room, the first two people we met were Eddie Izzard and Jack Dee. Both were very sympathetic but I could sense a hint of relief in their faces. They realised that whatever happened to them on stage could never be as bad as what we had experienced. They were guaranteed not to be the evening's fall guys. By the time it was broadcast, the producers had added canned laughter to help cover our failure. I suppose it was a lesson learned, and we have never been quite so badly prepared ever again.

In the summer of 1991, Jim and I went on a motorcycling holiday to the South of France. Jonathan Ross had invited us to stay with him at Christian Dior's mansion near Grasse, and it was one of the best trips of my life. We set off from London early in the morning and arrived at our first destination, Chartres, early evening. As we drove around the town centre, we saw an impressive-looking old-fashioned hotel and booked a couple of rooms. We met up later in the hotel restaurant. It was all very French and very formal. The menu was a thick, leather-bound booklet and largely impenetrable due to our inability to read French. The waiters, likewise, could not or would not register any interest in our English words. As the waiter stood by us impatiently waiting for our order, I spotted the words *boeuf* and *pommes* joined together in a short sentence. I figured this just might be steak and chips, so we pointed at those two nearly adjacent words and requested 'deux, sil vous plat'. The waiter muttered something towards us then disappeared.

About twenty minutes later, two waiters appeared either side of us holding large, silver, dome-lidded plates. On a hidden signal, they lifted the lids in unison and placed them in front of us on the table. Both plates contained a small circular lump of savoury jelly with a couple of crusty shrimps on top. We tried to explain that this was not what we had ordered, but they would have none of it and walked away smiling. I think we assumed it must be a freebie, or perhaps we had ordered it by mistake. We ate it and it was delicious. No sooner had it been cleared away, however, than another two silver-domed platters arrived. This time it was some pâté served on a hardened celery square. We realised that something was afoot and so grabbed a menu from the mahogany podium at the restaurant entrance. As we examined the page from which we had ordered, we realised that at the top were printed the words *Menu Gastronomique*. We had ordered some sort of banquet that stretched to fourteen courses with three different wines. The dishes kept coming and each one was served with a flourish and a bow. We felt like Henry VIII celebrating the launch of a new, sharper range of axes. We have never eaten or drunk so much in one sitting in our lives. At one point we began laughing at the actual pain we were suffering in our stomachs and chests. The final offering, as I remember, was a glass of thick syrupy pudding wine. It tipped us over the edge and we had to help each other upstairs to our rooms. As I lay on my bed, my head was spinning and my stomach felt like it was about to explode.

The next day as we were riding through the French country-side, Jim suddenly pulled over and ran into some woods without explanation. I followed him into the woods a few minutes later and found him sat next to a tree looking exhausted. 'What's up?' I asked him. He raised his hand and pointed towards a spot on the forest floor about ten feet away. It was the largest and tallest pile of human todd I had ever seen. It seemed to pulsate and breathe. I half expected it to start walking away or, worse still, explode. I helped Jim up and as I let go of him he immediately fell to the ground. 'Are you sure you're OK?' I asked.

'Yeah, it's just I felt about ten pounds lighter and it confused my balance.'

In 1995, we starred in the launch advert for a new Cadbury chocolate treat called the Boost bar. Jim came up with the tag-line: 'It's slightly rippled with a flat underside.' We played a couple of cowboys riding in a stagecoach being pursued across the desert by a posse of Native Americans. We discovered that by eating a Boost, we somehow garnered the enthusiasm to put the horses in the coach and pull it ourselves at great speed. It was not a true story.

It was filmed in the deserts of Andalucía in southern Spain

and was a big-budget affair. We even had catering tents erected in the middle of nowhere serving fresh lobster and seafood platters to fill the time between shots. Jim and I became fascinated by the idea of a scorpion hunt and set off into the sandy rocks and hills to try to capture one. The production insisted that we take off our costumes before we went. We had only our underpants for protection, and once we were out of sight we removed them as well to use as sunshields for our heads. It must have been well over 100 degrees out there.

We armed ourselves with sticks and began turning over rocks in search of our prey. We instructed each other using caveman language. On lifting one rock, three or four large brown scorpions ran out. We shat ourselves, but were freshly motivated to achieve a capture. Approaching a largish rock, we realised that it would be too heavy for us to lift. Instead, I poked my stick into a small gap between the rock and the sand. Suddenly the head of a snake thrust out through the gap, swaying and barking like a fucking idiot. We just stood stock-still, underpants on our heads, staring at its angry eyes and its flicking tongue. We were frozen to the spot and our testicles shrunk to the size of Maltesers. The rest of the snake emerged. It was about five feet long with brown, green and black scales. We each instinctively lowered a hand to protect our privates. Jim flicked at the snake's face with his stick and it immediately started to make a noise like a power-washer hose. It looked angry, and seemed to be preparing for attack. I threw my stick at it but missed by several feet. Jim slipped his underpants off his head and threw them at the snake. It dodged them easily. I let out a roar similar to that which a magnificent lion might deliver. The snake turned up its hosepipe noise a ratchet or two. Jim told it to 'Fuck off!' It didn't. Then, suddenly, we heard a voice behind us speaking in Spanish. We both turned around to see the 'leader' of the Native American troupe. We pointed at the snake – 'Snake! Snako! Serpento!' But the snake was gone. We were hopping around naked, and all we were pointing at was a seemingly discarded pair of underpants laid sadly against a rock. The man smiled and raised his hands apologetically before walking away. We followed in the same direction. Later that day, when we were filming with the Native American troupe, we noticed lots of them pointing at us and giving us what seemed like very special smiles.

During the same shoot, we had to do a scene where I bit greedily into a Boost bar and chewed it with enthusiasm and delight. On the set was a lady whose job it was to provide me with perfect 'hero' Boost bars in pristine wrappers for each new take. She also had a bucket with her so that I could spit out the half-chewed bars at the end of the take. I told her I wouldn't need the bucket because I was quite hungry and enjoyed eating them. After about take fifteen I was struggling and asked for the bucket to be placed next to me on the floor. Five takes later and the very thought of having another bite began to make me feel sick. It was all I could do to keep the lump of gunge in my mouth long enough for them to film the scene. From take twenty-five onwards, I was literally spewing into the bucket after every take. The lady with the bucket was completely matter-of-fact about it and waved away my apologies as if it was something she was very familiar with. It always struck me how glorious it would be if someone sneaked out a video of various actors spewing out the chocolate bars that they were earnestly selling to the public.

In 1998, Jim and I were chosen to appear in the finale of the 'Papa/Nicole' adverts for the Renault Clio. These adverts were very popular at the time and followed the exploits of a young woman and her long-suffering father. This advert would provide the answer to whom Nicole was to marry. It was to be me, with Nicole rejecting Jim at the altar. The advertising agency wanted to keep the casting top secret so we were flown separately and ahead of the production team to a remote chateau in rural Provence. It was a beautiful place, apparently owned by the Norwegian royal family. It stood alone, surrounded by acres and acres of lavender fields and olive groves, and while we were there we were under strict instructions never to leave the chateau and to refrain from walking in the grounds. A black people-carrier with two suited security men was constantly watching the chateau from a vantage point at the entrance to its long, impressive drive. These security men were ex-military and ex-humorous. No worries, though; it was a nice place to be imprisoned. After a couple of days, however, we began to get a bit of cabin fever. There was no TV, and Jim and I do like a bit of TV in our day-to-day lives. The nearest village was about three miles away, so we decided to make an escape and see if we could find a bar to pass some time in. We just had to get to the road and make sure we emerged onto it beyond the sight of the security blokes.

Inside the gardener's shed, we found a couple of French blue denim workman's jackets. We put them on and made our way through the olive grove to the side of the house. Darting from tree to tree and utilising a low stance, we felt like bona fide French resistance fighters. From time to time we were able to glance over to the people-carrier parked about 400 metres away to check that the blokes had not spotted us. Eventually we emerged beside the road, well out of our oppressors' sight. It was quite exhilarating and we enjoyed a wonderful sunny mid-morning walk into the village. It was typically Provençal, with a small cobbled town square and a cosy-looking bar with outdoor seating adjacent to a pretty water fountain. We sat at a table and ordered some ham sandwiches and two glasses of beer. The waiter was a short, older man with a wonky eye and a pleasant smile, and just as we were about to take our first hard-earned sip, the black people-carrier rolled into the square and parked up just opposite. It began flashing its lights. We ignored it and started to drink our beer. The lights began to flash at us more vigorously but still the security lads had not got out of the van.

After a few minutes our consciences got the better of us and we walked over to the van to explain ourselves and apologise for giving them the run-around. As we stood by the van, the driver pulled down his window and spoke to us: '*Où sont les bouteilles?*'

It was not our security detail, but a French bloke who was apparently expecting some bottles. He was short and squat and very French, with thick, side-parted brown hair and a slug of a moustache. '*Où sont les bouteilles?*' he repeated angrily.

'*Ne parlez Francais!*' we declared with surprising passion. At this, the driver jumped out of the vehicle and marched over to the café where he started remonstrating with the waiter that had served us. Their conversation suddenly took a turn and the

Moustache Man grabbed the waiter by his collar and started to slap him around the face. Not with extreme violence, but in the style of a 1950s comedian chastising his partner. We marched over and Jim grabbed the van man around his midriff and pulled him off the waiter. Moustache Man shouted at us in French and then marched back to his van shouting and pointing at things. He drove off with a flourish.

The waiter thanked us profusely. We didn't understand a word of what he was saying but it was clear that he felt it best if we left. He fetched us another couple of bottles of beer and gave us some napkins to put our sandwiches in. We thanked him and headed back to the chateau. The sun was shining, the lavender was in bloom, and we felt blessed. After we had walked a couple of miles, we became aware that a vehicle was behind us. We instinctively stepped over to the side of the lane to let it pass, and as we did so it stopped dead and Moustache Man jumped out of the van, this time accompanied by a tall skinny bloke in the Peter Crouch mould. Without saying a word, we ran as fast as we could. I turned round after a couple of hundred yards to see that we were a decent distance ahead. However, they did look very determined to catch us. No matter how fast we ran, we couldn't seem to shake them off. I was getting tired and was falling back slightly from Jim. We knew the chateau wasn't far, but these French lads clearly weren't going to give up. Then we saw it: the security detail's van still parked up opposite the entrance to the chateau. Our saviours. This put a spring in our step. As we got nearer, we started to wave and shout, 'HELP! FUCKING HELP!'

The two bulkies stepped out of the van and started to jog

towards us. I looked behind and could see the Frenchmen slowing down slightly. As the security guys passed us, one of them shouted at us, 'Get back in the fucking house!' We did as we were told. We walked down the long drive and turned to see the Frenchies walking at great speed back towards their van. We collapsed on the verge of the driveway, exhausted and relieved. I had never been rescued before. It was a strange and exhilarating experience.

When the advert came out, it was premiered during an advertising break in *Coronation Street*. It was watched by twenty-three million people, so represents the highest viewing figure Jim and I have ever achieved.

In the spring of 1994, Jim and I decided to fulfil a dream and motorcycle across America from Los Angeles to Chicago on Route 66. We had been asked to go to LA to audition for the voices of a couple of animals in the animated version of *The Lion King*, so we tagged three weeks onto this trip for our motorcycling adventure. The day after we arrived in LA, we picked up our hired Japanese motorcycles and slept the night in a friend's empty home in Laurel Canyon up in the Hollywood Hills. Our neighbours were the Duran Duran guitarist Andy Taylor, and Tarzan, the jungle survivalist.

Our first business was to attend some studio lot to meet the *Lion King* producers, who were very American and very corporate. I remember the main one had a ponytail that he wore over the front of his shoulder. They spoke at a hundred miles an hour and largely in riddles. We had never heard entertainment described in such a detached, business-speak manner. They wanted us to play a couple of cheeky chipmunks and gave us a sheet of script to read. We read it in the voices of Donald and Davy Stott, and they seemed to like it. Ponytail eventually asked us if we would like to be on board, and Jim asked if we could just have a few minutes to think about it. Ponytail agreed and we left the room and went into the adjacent corridor. As soon as we were alone, Jim said to me, 'Come on, shall we fuck off out of here? This is just bullshit.' It took me by surprise, but I was instantly on his side. We walked out of the building and rode off into LA. As far as I can recall, we never heard from them again.

That evening the heavens opened and LA suffered the worst flooding it had experienced in decades. Sunset Strip was under teen feet of floodwater and there were mudslides all over town. We ventured out to assess the situation and as soon as we hit the main road into town were stopped by police and told to return home. For the next ten days we were trapped together in our mate's house. Luckily, it had an excellent TV and we spent hours and hours watching episodes of *MacGyver* and the Three Stooges. In one sense the floods were a blessing. Inspired by the anarchy and violence of the Three Stooges, we wrote a huge chunk of our new BBC series, *The Smell of Reeves and Mortimer*. This is the week that we decided that at every possible juncture we would attack each other with frying pans and other household objects. We are still striking each other with pans to this very day.

By the time the roads had opened again, we had abandoned our plans for a road trip and just spent the last five days fannying about in LA. We went whale-watching, did some people-spotting on Muscle Beach and went drinking on Sunset Avenue.

We had some daytime drinks with Lemmy in the Whisky a Go Go and went disco dancing with Björk.

When we returned our motorbikes to the hire shop, we had done a total of twenty-two miles each. Trip of a lifetime.

When I think of Jim, I'm always reminded of the hours and hours we have spent together out on the road touring. We started touring in 1990, travelling in a people-carrier. We later moved up to a fancy coach and then a double-decker tour bus with all the bells-and-whistles devices. These days it's just the two of us in the back of a car. Some things always remain the same. We listen to the album *Chill Out* by the KLF nearly every day. We stop for our lunch at any pub or restaurant that is offering either mashed potato or syrup pudding and custard on its menu. We are often touring in November and in our younger days would always ask the tour manager to equip the bus with a good amount of sky-rocket fireworks. After eating either our mashed potato or syrup pudding (or both), we would retire to the car park and let off between one and five sky-rockets, depending on how we rated the food.

There is always a good selection of sweets by our side. Jim is a Wine Gum man, while I favour Liquorice Allsorts and Jelly Babies. Jim will always insist that we go and visit some local beauty spot or museum, as he has a great thirst for knowledge and collecting snow globes. Mainly, though, we just talk and talk and talk. Thirty years on and we still enjoy nothing more than making each other laugh. It's the best game you can play. We usually do our sound check at about 5 p.m. and then sit together in our dressing room until show time. We never have separate dressing rooms. Whenever I do a gig or appear on a show without Jim, it is this strange period between sound check and show when I really miss him. We are experts at taking each other's minds off things and passing time together so that it just feels like the blink of an eye. I often wonder what it must be like for a solo comedian, not having a soulmate to share the burden. It must be mind-altering to be the absolute centre of attention of everybody involved in the show. I wonder if this is why some performers become like little Baby Kings when they are on tour or filming. Jim and I always have each other to keep ourselves in check.

On the final journey home at the end of every tour, we get drunk and sing along to all our favourite albums by the band Free. We both know every breath and every note of their music, and it's one of those strange coincidences that when we were only thirteen years old we both attended a concert by Free at Middlesbrough Town Hall. We both fell in love with their music that evening and now, almost fifty years later, we sing it out loud together in the back of vans.

We have grown up and flourished together as a team. We have laughed and cried together and we will never be defeated.

25

MUM

The most important and influential person in a bloke's life will usually be his mum, and that was certainly the case for me.

As well as giving birth to me, and nurturing and caring for me, she taught me so many things that I carry with me to this day. I hope I will pass some of them on to my own sons. They include:

How to boil, scramble, poach and omelette an egg
How to clean the windows
How to wire a plug
How to change a lightbulb
How to hoover a carpet
How to iron my clothes
How to tell if a melon is ripe
How to tell if a potato will have any taste
How to cook offal
How to use a mop
That if soup boils, soup spoils

The nearer the bone, the sweeter the meat

To never mix business with pleasure

That to relieve an upset stomach, you eat partially burnt toast

To not eat while walking in the street

That manners maketh a man

That a blanket beneath you is worth two above

How to polish metals

How to handwash your delicates

That littering is a sin

That infections can be drawn out using a bread poultice

To always walk kerbside of the pavement when you are with a lady

How to fillet a fish

How to tie a fancy knot in your tie

How important gardening is for the soul

That birds must be fed

That cats are essential to a happy home

That tripe is inedible (despite her best efforts to persuade me otherwise)

How to sew a button on

That a home should be full of books

That unusual haircuts are more than acceptable

That if you've got an egg you've got a meal

How to ice a Christmas cake

How to carve a shoulder of lamb

That external paintwork requires regular maintenance

How to play gin rummy

That trapped wind is better shifted by rubbing the back rather than the tummy

Apart from my decision to decline a place at Cambridge University in the '80s, my mum always supported me in my life choices. When I packed in my career as a solicitor in 1990 to film *Big Night Out*, she seemed genuinely excited for me. After the shows had been broadcast, however, she seemed a lot more cautious. I don't think mine and Jim's humour was her cup of tea. I would phone her every Sunday and there wasn't a phone call that passed by without her asking when I would be going back to work as a solicitor. I don't think she stopped asking me this until around 1994, when I starred in a huge advertising campaign for First Direct bank. I guess she reckoned that if a bank had faith in me to promote their products then I probably did have a future in showbiz.

I would go up to Middlesbrough three or four times a year to see Mum and hang out with Cagsy and some of my old mates. I always avoided talking about my life on the TV. It was such a pleasant relief to spend some time as Robert Mortimer. Whenever the whole family was together, I noticed that my mum in particular would avoid talking about my goings-on and always direct conversation towards the achievements of the rest of the family. She was very proud of all her boys and took immense joy from the achievements of her grandchildren. It was particularly joyous for her when her two oldest grandchildren, Sarah and Charles, both secured places at Oxbridge to study for their degrees. This of course lifted my guilt a bit from letting her down all those years ago.

My relationship with Mum was always slightly tainted by the events of 1967, when she lost her husband, her father and her house was burnt down (by me). As a young boy I was scared she might disappear just like Dad had. I knew how sad she was and dedicated myself to trying to prevent her feeling down. If I heard her crying in her bedroom or sobbing in the living room, I would immediately start hoovering the carpets, cleaning the kitchen or washing the windows. In my infant mind, I thought this might somehow cheer her up. I still reach for the hoover to this very day if my wife has got a strop on with me. As I got older, I continued with the helping but began to resent it slightly as it restricted the enjoyment of my early teenage years. My friends would stay out late but I always got myself back home by 10 p.m so that I could sit by the fire with Mum as she ate her bread and tomatoes. My friends went travelling around Europe one summer on Interrail cards. I declined because I didn't want to leave Mum alone for a month. She never asked me to do these things; it was just my insecurity and guilt guiding me with their invisible fingers.

To be honest, my visits back home were always bittersweet. Mum was leading quite a lonely, solitary life. She had never wanted to meet anyone else after Dad died, and she continued to teach home economics at St Michael's Comprehensive School until her early sixties. It was a pretty rough school and she finally packed it in and retired after one of the pupils pulled a knife out on her. She filled her days with little shopping expeditions to buy tomatoes and tins of sardines, and once a week she would meet up with a little group of retired teacher friends. Every Sunday she would go to my brother Rick's house for lunch. Apart from this, though, she would spend hours and hours on her own, reading her books and chatting to her cats, Billy and Toppy (the Tinker Bell Team). Towards the end of her life she would often say to me that she wished she could go to bed one night and never wake up. I think she truly believed that after her death she would meet up again with her beloved husband. When I received a phone call in 2002 informing me that she had passed away peacefully in her sleep in her orange and pink home, my first reaction was to have a little smile to myself. I knew that she had got what she wanted.

Although we spoke often over the phone and she would occasionally come to our live shows, I very much regret that I didn't see more of her during her lonely years. It has also always bothered me that I have no memory of ever telling her that I loved her. In the course of writing this book, I contacted my brothers to pick their brains. My brother Rick had kept my mum's little box of important papers, and in it was a letter I had sent to her in the late '90s, of which I had no memory.

Dear Mum

Thank you for a lovely New Year. It really was very special for me to sing 'Auld Lang Syne' with you and I shall never forget it. I'm so glad we stayed that extra half hour as Johnny had requested.

It was sad to see you not feeling your usual self (and I know you felt more ill than you let on). I hope your recovery is swift.

If you don't feel better soon please please please ring me. It is always a pleasure to come and see you and I would be terribly hurt to find out that you were suffering in silence.

Like all those who know you I love you very much and can't wait for you to come and visit me in my new house when you feel up to it.

Again many thanks and a Happy New Year to you and the Tinker Bell Team.
   Robert

I wrote her many letters over the years, but this is the one she had chosen to keep. I'm glad I wrote it.

THE END

So, that's my story to date. What have I learned from writing it? Not much. But, reading it back, it feels like the big victory of my life is that I've more or less overcome my shyness, which for a big chunk of my life was a debilitating affliction.

I feel a great debt to those people who helped me along the way. My first friend, Keith 'Cagsy' Bridgewood; my two mates in Manchester, Paddy Gaul and Steven Jones; Alan 'Kingy' King, whose kindness introduced me to Jim; my wife Lisa; and of course Paul, who has become my friendly rock.

All I can say in this respect is that if you know a 'quiet one' at work, at home or wherever, try to make an effort to bring them in on things; try to give them a chance to flourish. They might just surprise you and end up enhancing your life. Believe me, it's next to impossible for them to do it on their own.

If you yourself are a shy one, then please try not to settle for living in your isolation cage. Take every opportunity a stranger or colleague or associate may offer and run with it to the moon. There is no need to be scared of people or believe that what you have to contribute is worthless. People are generally nice and most of them are extremely boring most of the time. Take a chance, get involved and slowly the cage will open.

Other than that, I would simply say the following:

Always be on time and always be quiet when others are sleeping.

Always say thank you at a drive-through ordering machine.

Keep the filters clean in all your appliances. Don't forget that your hoover may have a second or third filter hidden within its casing.

Never mix business with pleasure.

Have a hot dog on every visit to the cinema.

Avoid mirrors, especially fleeting glimpses.

Walk at a brisk pace in crowded areas.

Always keep some pocket meat or cheese about your person.

Have a sit-down meal on a train whenever the opportunity arises.

Plant allium and agapanthus seeds every year until your garden is a sea of white, blue and purple.

If you have previously rejected the Caramac bar, why not give it another chance?

Make Middlesbrough FC your football team of choice. You know you want to.

A daft laugh with a mate is worth two in a book or on the TV.

As you age, do not fear the elasticated waistband; it can be a good friend.

Do not try to understand electricity. Best to just fear it.

If you are ill, go to the doctor.

Eat pie as often as you can. Tired of pie, tired of life.

THE END

Have a campachoochoo on me.
Ciao and bella fragmento.

A

  N

    D ...

      AWAY ...

309

ACKNOWLEDGEMENTS

I would like to thank my publisher Holly Harris for her exper-
tise and advice and for encouraging her lovely cat to attend our
Zoom meetings. A final thank you to all the people mentioned
in the book is also due. Some people of great importance to
me didn't make it into these pages due largely to its structure. I
shall mention some here in the hope they all realise what a huge
contribution they have made to my life.

Dan McGrath and Josh Phillips. They are the producer and
musician that have provided us with all the songs and musical
numbers that we have performed on our studio shows over the
years. Jim and I sit at our table and write the words to a song,
we then record the vocals on Jim's telephone to a vague tune we
have worked out in our head. We send this half-baked voicemail
to Dan with a good luck message. When we turn up at Dan's
studio, the songs are all ready and ninety-nine per cent as good
as we could have dreamed. We are very lucky to have them.

Charlie Chuck. Charlie starred alongside Jim and me in *The
Smell of Reeves and Mortimer*. We chanced across him when he
was doing his one-man show at the Edinburgh Festival in 1991.

He strode onto stage, wild-haired and seemingly confused, brandishing a length of 2 x 2 timber, which he proceeded to use to destroy a drum kit while shouting: 'Get out of my shop, you cakey pig!' We were instantly smitten. Lovely, talented man.

Vaun Earl Norman starred alongside us in *Vic and Bob's Big Night Out*. I first came across Vaun when he phoned in to an Iain Lee radio show to respond to a spoof phone call I had previously made to the same show. He was a Middlesbrough lad and very funny. I got in touch and the rest is history.

Shane Allen has been the Controller of Comedy at the BBC since 2012. He has supported Jim and myself throughout our careers. Without him, shows such as *House of Fools* and *Vic and Bob's Big Night Out* would never have been made. He is a very funny bloke himself and I have no doubt he would have made it as a stand-up comedian if he had chosen that path.

Tony Way, Rhys Thomas and Steve Burge: a little gang of daft lads who have always been there when we needed them, whether as writers, performers or supporters.

Lucy Montgomery starred in three series of the sketch show *Tittybangbang*, which I wrote with the superb Jill Parker. Lucy is, without a shadow of a doubt, the most talented comedy actress of her generation.

Directors can make or break a show, and we have been lucky enough to work with some gems. John Birkin, Mark Mylod, Metin Hüseyin, Matt Lipsey, Dave Walker, Ben Wheatley, Mat Whitecross ... take an effin' bow.

Jane Tomblin and Jason Scott, our set and prop design team for many years, who always let me sit and chat with them in their sanctuary when I needed a break from all the stuff and nonsense.

Steve Webster, our special effects guy throughout our career who built all our unusual props from the Paul and Debbie Daniels fun bins to the staircase to heaven, which Griff Rhys Jones climbed while collecting hip replacements in his mouth.

Jack Dee, Johnny Vegas and Will Self, who helped us successfully revive *Shooting Stars* and achieved the impossible by making it as good as it ever was.

June Nevin and Lynsey Moore, our costume designers, and Lisa Cavalli-Green and Nicola Coleman, our make-up designers.

Rachel Ablett and Peter Holmes for inviting me onto *Would I Lie to You?* and sticking with me.

David Brindley, the original commissioning editor of *Gone Fishing*, who taught us so much about making factual TV. Stephanie Fyfe and the whole of the *Gone Fishing* crew (Toby, Ali, Andy, Russell, Sam, Louise, Poppy, Rob Gill and John Bailey).

Roma Koisar for being such a lovely godparent to Harry and Tom. Much loved members of the Mortimer family: Johnny, Brenda, Richard, Angela, Sam, Ann, Sarah, David, Charles, Coleen, Helen, Jane, Ben and Simon. Also Lisa's mum and dad, John and Winsome.

Peter Bennett-Jones, Daisy Skepelhorn, Alex Moody, Simon Day, Mark Swan, Peter Salmon, Stuart Murphy, Aitor Karanka, the late Mr Billy my beloved Dalmatian, and last but not least all the cats I have loved and lost: Billy, Toppy, Billy 2, Chester, Tina, Noodles and Percy.

INDEX

315